OFF CAMERA

OFF CAMERA

Leveling about themselves

· AL PACINO · PAUL NEWMAN · DIANA RIGG
· GEORGE C. SCOTT · DUSTIN HOFFMAN · MIKE NICHOLS
· ELAINE MAY · BARBARA WALTERS · EDWIN NEWMAN
· LYNN REDGRAVE · DICK CAVETT · MARLO THOMAS
· ZERO MOSTEL · SHIRLEY MacLAINE · ANGELA LANSBURY
· GWEN VERDON · WOODY ALLEN

by LEONARD PROBST

Photographs by ARLENE AVRIL

STEIN AND DAY/ *Publishers*/ New York

First published in 1975
Copyright © 1975 by Leonard Probst
All rights reserved
Designed by David Miller
Printed in the United States of America
Stein and Day/*Publishers*/Scarborough House,
Briarcliff Manor, N. Y. 10510

Library of Congress Cataloging in Publication Data

Main entry under title:

Off camera: leveling about themselves. . . .

    Interviews with Al Pacino, Paul Newman, Diana Rigg, George C. Scott,
Dustin Hoffman, Mike Nichols, Elaine May, Barbara Walters, Edwin Newman,
Lynn Redgrave, Dick Cavett, Marlo Thomas, Zero Mostel, Shirley MacLaine,
Angela Lansbury, Gwen Verdon, Woody Allen.
    1. Actors—Interviews.   I. Probst, Leonard.
PN2205.034   791′.092′2   75-15237
ISBN 0-8128-1842-3

Photographs © 1975 by Arlene Avril
For use of photographs please address
Stein and Day, Publishers, Scarborough House
Briarcliff Manor, N. Y. 10510

For my wife Bethami,
and son and daughter
Kenneth and Katherine

Acknowledgments

Without Jeannette Hopkins, who edited this book, there would be no book. Her literary talents are spectacular, her sense of fairness, especially for women, never failing, and her willingness to work far into the day, night, or week, remarkable.

I also wish to thank Allen Austill, dean of the New School, for his support, friendship, and willingness to alter the life of the school to fit my needs.

Lauren Gibbs was invaluable in checking the manuscript and helping to prepare it for publication.

Time and again I relied on the knowledge of Judy Friedman and Vera Mayer of the NBC library. Also, I want to thank NBC News, on whose time I gathered some of the material on which this book is based.

Finally, I wish to thank David Levine for giving up time on the tennis court to caricature me, a drawing he sees as kind and lovable, which he is.

Contents

Author's Note

The majority of these conversations with public artists of theater, film, and television were conducted at the New School in New York City over three semesters, from April, 1974, through June, 1975. The other interviews were conducted backstage, at the home of the person interviewed, or at his or her business agent's office in Manhattan.

The interviews in this book were recorded on tape in sessions running two to five hours. The audience at the New School asked questions in each session, and some have been used here. Many of the conversations continued long into the night after the taping. In some instances this was a second or third interview. There were no participants other than myself in interviews held outside the school, except for Martin Bregman, Al Pacino's business manager, who joined briefly in that conversation.

I prepared for each interview by checking scores of items from newspaper files, magazines, books, and biographical collections. Occasionally, I sought out in advance persons who had been colleagues of the artists. As NBC drama critic, starting in 1960, I had seen most of the films and plays of the actors and directors and had worked with or followed the careers of those in television as part of my professional work.

For each interview I prepared as many as seventy-five questions, but discarded many as new questions emerged in the course of the conversations. The depth and range of questions varied, depending on the personal territory that person was willing to traverse. We had no agreements beforehand on questions to be asked, no prior warning or rehearsal. No question was answered with a "no comment" and none was ignored, although some deft defense mechanisms can be seen at work in some replies.

My intent in the interviews was to challenge each on his or her own ground, not to impose anyone else's criteria, but to push each farther in the direction each had set. Also, I like to ask questions.

No interview here is part of the promotion of a movie, play, book, television show, or of any product or outside project. Mike Nichols said when he saw the list of people in this book: "I see you've got the gang all here." Each was selected because of excellence as an artist and because of the contribution each could make toward understanding the nature of the public artist.

No interview was postponed, no agreement for an interview, once made, verbally, was broken, no one was late for a meeting. Mike Nichols, whose tardiness is legendary, was on time. Marlo Thomas had been in bed with intestinal influenza for a week, but she came out into a black rainstorm and talked with vitality for more than two hours.

A footnote to history of enological if not cultural significance: I suggested drinking wine during each conversation to introduce a relaxed and informal atmosphere. Also, I like wine. For the record, Al Pacino and Dustin Hoffman each decided on red Italian wine, Paul Newman brought two six-packs of beer. Elaine May sipped red French Bordeaux during the taping, but Sangria later, Shirley MacLaine chose ginger ale, Marlo Thomas—recovering from influenza—drank hot tea, Dick Cavett supplied large coffees, George C. Scott took cognac as an apertif, Lynn Redgrave served tea in her minuscule kitchen, Mike Nichols had coffee served by a maid in his penthouse overlooking Central Park, Diana Rigg helped dispose of a bottle of red French Bordeaux, and Angela Lansbury, after rejecting a French Pouilly-Fuissé as "sour," supplied her favorite California Chablis, chilled. Zero Mostel, Barbara Walters, Edwin Newman, Gwen Verdon, and Woody Allen settled for water or abstained.

LEONARD PROBST
New York City, July 10, 1975

THE SUPERSTAR:

Introduction

What is the nature of the superstar? They tend to be people who were out of step and decided—or felt compelled—to march alone, ahead of the crowd rather than with it. When the lights go on or the camera rolls they become someone else and that someone else is often bigger, more exciting, more beautiful, more powerful than life. The superior public artists, as they emerge in these interviews, share an insatiable desire to fulfill the demands of their art. Fulfillment of their art is fulfillment of the self—"you become interchangeable," said Al Pacino. This is true whatever the medium—film, stage, television—even television news. The creativity of these performing artists is not like that of a Michelangelo or Beethoven, whose work can be isolated from the person and can live after them. If we reject the art of the public performing artist, we reject the person.

There is an intense fascination with themselves, with their origins, experiences, anxieties, in each thing that happens to them. This is not narcissistic, self-loving, but pragmatic. The more clearly they know themselves, the better they function. Commitment to work is total.

These conversations, I believe, are more candid and self-knowing than they might have been, say, in the 1940s. A number of those interviewed have been in psychoanalysis, although some mentioned this outside the interview. The public recordholder of the group is Woody Allen, who has logged twenty years on the couch. He told of feeding coins into a pay telephone while people lined up outside the booth on a hot San Francisco street as Woody insisted on his full fifty-minute long-distance conversation with his analyst in New York.

An almost total sacrifice is made to their obsession, but it is not seen as sacrifice. What else would they rather do than do their own work? Dustin Hoffman, suffering excruciating pain from severe burns on his arms and legs, nevertheless played a role and was upset only that his awkwardness led to his losing the role. He is concerned with losing the role, not with the pain. They consume themselves in their passion. I did not hear the words "task" or "labor" applied to what they do. When they speak of the importance of work, it is like speaking of serving a faith.

Indeed, they talk of their job and their art, but seldom of religion. It may be there is no need for an outside force to govern their lives. Woody Allen reads deeply in philosophy, an exercise in understanding of the self and the universe, which may be why he has a distaste for religion and its rituals. Even sex seems peripheral to many—the central passion is for a job well done. They serve some internal drive that behaves like a demanding god, demanding sacrifices and study, providing exaltation and transcendence. Others may be attracted by the fame and the fuss. But to these artists, the applause seems secondary. They are often driven by demons, too busy to wonder why.

Superstars seem to get sick less often, tired less often, need less sleep, less food, less entertainment than the rest of us. They do not drain off their energies except in work. They seem to need less outside nourishment than most. They tend to function almost completely within themselves. They do not see themselves as a part of a mass, a committee, a team, or a corporate structure. Even when they work within such structure, they protect their own individuality. In a sense, the successful public person creates his own skyscraper and is president of his or her own corporation which is himself or herself.

A number of performing artists have given up part of themselves to fulfill their art, sacrificing normal family life—whatever that may be—or even the luxury of having a family at all, feeling that there is little room for a stable home routine. George C. Scott speaks of the destructiveness of the theater on family. Both Scott and Paul Newman say they have tried to keep their children from becoming actors, although they have not wholly succeeded. But two of the women expressed the conviction that their children should be part of their stage lives. Angela Lansbury believes she made a mistake trying to shield her children from seeing her in the role of a star. She now sees that they should "muck in," join in a shared experience so they will better understand. Gwen Verdon has insisted from the start that her daughter be with her wherever she goes, but she respects her daughter's individuality. Both women divide their lives into periods, for the stage and for the family —Gwen Verdon works two years in a part, then takes five years off to travel, garden, enjoy her daughter.

Several say they have failed in marriage or do not wish to commit themselves to it, although Diana Rigg speaks with some feeling about the person who does have a secure home, a "cell," a nucleus, and Al Pacino refers to a growing, if belated, desire for a center to his own private life. That does not mean these are selfish people. They tend to be generous with their money, their time, their energy. The central commitment for most of those interviewed is the job, the art.

One of our interview sessions was delayed while Al Pacino discussed by phone a request from Vanessa Redgrave to give $34,000 to a political group. He made no decision that day—he wanted to be sure what the money was for—but he told me, "Sure, I give money, I give money all the time to good causes." Gwen Verdon has given up some of her valued privacy to pass out leaflets on street corners. Woody Allen, who said, "I would never say no to a good cause," tapes programs for the blind as a volunteer and made a satirical television political documentary potentially so offensive of the Nixon administration that it was kept off the air. Paul Newman has maintained an almost unblemished record supporting unsuccessful liberal political candidates.

Not many years ago, a public artist risked dismissal from a film studio if he showed up at a liberal political rally. I recall as a young Hollywood correspondent spotting Ava Gardner attending a rally in disguise lest her studio bosses fire her. Today, few big political rallies are held without a performer onstage. Several decades ago, the expression of social responsibility reflected in these interviews would have been muted. The movie star of the past was utterly dependent on a big, scared Hollywood studio. Now they are economically more independent, financially and artistically. With their economic base they stand stronger and wider, their allegiance is more to themselves and their own vision than to the studio or bank.

Increasingly, the public artist is more than one-dimensional. Among the seventeen interviewed here, at least eight—Woody Allen, Barbara Walters, Edwin Newman, Shirley MacLaine, Marlo Thomas, Zero Mostel, Elaine May, and Dick Cavett—are also authors, painters, or playwrights.

The increased flexibility, mobility, choice of options, freedom to experiment and to dissent have led, perhaps, to greater integration of purpose for the public artist. It is as though the philosophical concept of the idealist, with mind and body divorced, has been replaced by a gestalt view in which the public performing artist functions as an organic whole, his social concerns and his professional life more interrelated, functioning more closely, not at odds. Still, for the artist, the work is the thing, and when detachment is part of the work—as it is particularly for the television reporters interviewed here—the personal bias is suppressed. As Edwin Newman put it, he does not believe he should impose his views on his audience; he as a person should be irrelevant to the audience.

The criticism that would be regarded as most damning would be that their work is superficial. There is pride in perfection. Each works hard to achieve it—Diana Rigg spending six months studying *Phaedre;* Dustin Hoffman doing research on Lenny Bruce almost a year, interviewing fifty people who had known Bruce; Al Pacino hanging out with Frank Serpico; Gwen Verdon spending months living on the Upper West Side of New York to get a particular accent for *Damn Yankees;* Barbara Walters studying each new project so that she is among the best briefed of reporters on a story.

A number feel guilty because work is not a chore to them. "Life," Elaine May said, "is working at Florsheim's. Every once in a while you think, Gee, I'm getting away with not working at Florsheim's." It's like a hobby," Woody Allen said. "People pay me to do what I would anyhow." Those interviewed speak of feelings of sham and fraud because despite their investment of energy in work, they enjoy themselves, they are rewarded for being allowed to do that which pleases them most. They speak of "getting away with something."

The work is central to the being. In an important sense, work—art—is the person. They speak of wearing blinkers, running their own race, of savoring their loneliness.

Somerset Maugham, in *Summing Up,* wrote that "The artist's egoism is outrageous: it must be; he is by nature a solipsist and the world exists for him to exercise upon it his powers of creation."

These artists may respect, even admire others, but they do not speak of rivals. In a sense they see no rivals. They are competitive, but you sense they compete with their own ideal self, not with others. The superior public artist does not compete with others because there is no one like them. Each is an original. The women especially rejected the stereotype of female jealousy. Barbara Walters told how she and her short-lived television adversary, Sally Quinn, maintained their friendship while others were planting stories of a feud. Gwen Verdon said that Chita Rivera and she had waited for many years to work together again in *Chicago*: "When people are really good you don't envy them, you're not jealous of them, you admire them, especially dancers because there's no easy way to dance. You can't fake it." Lynn Redgrave did not mind getting parts rejected by her sister Vanessa. Her primary concern, as she expresses it here, is how well she did the part once she got it. Al Pacino talked for three hours without mentioning another actor. They have little awe or hero worship of either a person or a principle. Edwin Newman says: "I can think of no one I am in awe of." There is concern with well-being and staying in touch with their essence. Dustin Hoffman says: "As we grow older, we get less in touch with ourselves." Paul Newman's fantasy of the perfect movie is "four incredible weeks of rehearsal and then you shut it down. You never crank a foot of film and you never have an audience come in and see it."

Tolerant and understanding when criticizing others, they are brutal in criticizing themselves. Woody Allen who had made five films mourned, "I've failed in every one of them." For twenty-two months while Gwen Verdon performed eight times a week in the musical *Redhead,* after each show she marked down whether she was fully satisfied with her work onstage. At the end of the run including the road tour, after seven hundred twenty performances, she totaled up only six performances which pleased her, a ratio of one out of one hundred twenty-seven.

These artists work with blowtorch intensity. Each is a star in more than one meaning of the word—not a distant, cool star in the sky as it seems from earth, but a star that is in truth its own sun, luminous with energy, yet controlled, disciplined. In astronomy the star nearest the earth is the sun.

A vein of feeling fraudulent runs through some of the interviews. Al Pacino said, "It is very common to feel like a fraud." There are two chief reasons for that, as Pacino said, "I'm not showing the real me," and because of the anxiety that the creative inspiration will disappear. Creativity is not something you can rest your elbow on. It is not tangible. It is not a substance, has no weight or visibility. Inspiration is elusive. Since the creative person is not sure where his inspiration comes from, he is not sure it will not leave him.

Traditionally, the nature of the artist has been, however, slightly or subtly, to bring enlightenment, a flash of understanding; and in the process to subvert society, to look at life from a slant, on the bias, askew; to shake the world so it reads "tilt." These interviews are with artists, thus public instructors, in the Greek sense, who invite us to share their vision of the world, their view of the people in it. That is why we watch them. They are the enemies of boredom and darkness. When I asked Elaine May whether comedy is the opposite of boredom, she replied: "Interesting is the opposite of boredom." We watch the players to see ourselves differently, through their prism.

The performing artist is not the off-camera, off-screen self. On screen, on camera, the artist takes on another self, a self that is more interesting, more powerful—even, simply, *more.* To transport the audience the artist has to become fully—not simply pretend to become—another. It is not that the self is swallowed up. But rather that the self and the role are, in some sense, one. It is—in its finest moments—magic, a trick the audience sees occur but whose alchemy it does not understand. It is more than accidental that a number of these performers have been in analysis, to better understand their self in order to play someone else's self.

The actors interviewed have an enormous well of emotional response and intellectual vision, and that is what the audience hungers after. Feeling and meaning. The dry, dull life is enriched when our emotions become involved and we laugh, sympathize, think, love, understand, even learn.

These are not terrified people. They are anxious, but not fearful. Nor are they particularly beautiful. Some have learned the art of illusion with uncanny artistry. They can create the illusion of beauty or other illusions—off camera, offstage, a star may not seem beautiful; onstage, the audience sees beauty.

What is their identity, then—which self are they? Are *they* onstage, or are Lenny Bruce, Richard III, Hud, Patton, Auntie Mame, Roxie Hart, the Godfather, Ulysses, or the Happy Hooker there? Obviously, the person we see is not the character but the actor. When I asked if it was Lenny Bruce or Dustin Hoffman on screen in *Lenny,* Dustin Hoffman said: "Well, it's me. It looks like me up there. I think it's me." When Al Pacino was playing Richard III he told a director that if he wanted the part played the way Richard III would play it, "Get Richard. There is no Richard, I'm Richard." Actors, in these interviews, tend paradoxically to be shy people with a strong ego who can feed their ego—their hungry I—in the roles they play. Woody Allen has said elsewhere: "My one regret in life is that I am not someone else." By playing parts, they become someone else. Listen to Angela Lansbury: "I'm never satisfied with myself.... I really like being someone else very much, but when the curtain comes down, I want to turn off." What does she think about Angela Lansbury? "She's dull as ditch water."

The self bereft of the part, offstage or off camera, in the interviews often was quiet, tame, low-key. Al Pacino, who has played mostly violent parts, and George C. Scott, who is known for great power when performing, were almost retiring in person. Pacino says, "I've been very reserved in my living." George C. Scott has a backstage nickname: "Pussycat." And it fits. Pacino and Scott and Elaine May are shy and were reluctant to be interviewed. Woody Allen for years had to be shoved onstage, and to this day he hyperventilates before even answering questions in public. "Actors are mostly shy," Lynn Redgrave said. "They stand up *because* they are shy and then they don't have to be."

These are stars, but they often had to overcome handicaps that would have incapacitated an ordinary person. Zero Mostel said: "You have a bellyache, you use it." Gwen Verdon at age two was knock-kneed, wore corrective boots, and was cross-eyed. She calls these "limitations," not disabilities. Misfortune is the other side of fortune. Gwen Verdon went on to become a beautiful woman and a remarkable dancer, and then an actress and a singer. It did not come easy for any of these people, even though they often describe their success as the result of luck. Al Pacino for a time as a child of three was reared by an aunt who was a deaf mute, and he learned how to act without words; he was not allowed out of the house until seven, and acted out movies for his mother. When he did use words they had a special music to them, and he uses that music now, listening to Stravinsky to help him through *Godfather II*.

None of these individuals came from the landed aristocracy or idle wealth. Only Marlo Thomas and Lynn Redgrave among them were born into famous theatrical families. And both of these speak of the burden more than the opportunity of inheriting a famous name. Lynn Redgrave left England in part to escape the heavy responsibility of being a Redgrave. Marlo Thomas rejected the course laid out for her. Both want to be respected for what they are, not for what their surnames are. The others here were born into families of the economic middle class. Some, such as Al Pacino, George C. Scott, and Diana Rigg, at one time might have described their backgrounds as poor, or lower middle class. Whatever the limitations, they were challenges to be overcome, not excuses for failure.

Not once did any of these individuals mention "bad luck," but they often referred to fate and luck as responsible for success. Dustin Hoffman described how severe burns led him to get his first movie role in *The Graduate*. He said, "Fate is a large part of success." Luck consists in taking advantage of opportunities. "In times of difficulty," Edwin Newman said, "in times of chaos, that's when you can prove yourself—if you are going to. It is why you welcome what to most people is bad news." Everyone of the artists interviewed at some point in their career turned bad breaks into good breaks. What other individuals might accept as a defeat, they transformed into victory.

The superior public artist speaks well, is intelligent, complex, charming, aware, sensitive, and curious. A number are closet intellectuals, smarter than one would suspect. I hope this book reveals them as they are. Al Pacino uses more sophisticated language than he would want people to know, Gwen Verdon has a depth of knowledge that is at odds with the roles, often prostitutes, she has played. George C. Scott is a cold-headed intellectual, but he is known for his bellowing, a broken nose from barroom brawls, and a volcanic personality. Mike Nichols, Woody Allen, Elaine May, Edwin Newman, Diana Rigg, Zero Mostel are impressive intellects.

None of these performers had a good word for the Academy Awards, or indeed, for most awards for excellence. Most said they would not accept an Oscar if it were offered. They look for their highest standards not to the audience, not to an awards committee, but to themselves.

Little concern for money is expressed here. There is a steadfast concern for the highest artistic standards. If money is a consequence of that commitment, fine, but money alone is not enough. Mike Nichols said he is asked two questions in Hollywood: How much did it cost? and How much will it make? He is more likely to be asked in New York: Is it any good? which is why he makes his home in Manhattan and Connecticut, although he works in Hollywood. Al Pacino said: "I do moving jobs for money. I was a messenger for money, and I worked as an usher for money, but I never acted for money."

Paul Newman, Dustin Hoffman, George C. Scott, Al Pacino, Mike Nichols, and Woody Allen apparently can pick up a million dollars a movie almost routinely. But money is not central. Woody Allen made the film *Take the Money and Run,* but he does not actually take the money and run. He explained: "I am willing to take a very, very low salary to do my work in return for total freedom on the picture." George C. Scott, who dislikes acting in movies, does the bare film minimum so that he can direct in the theater and act on stage the role of Willy Loman, the salesman in the revival of Arthur Miller's *Death of a Salesman,* before a nightly audience of 648 people. Al Pacino turned down million-dollar movie contracts to travel from New York to Boston to appear nightly in a small experimental theater in Bertolt Brecht's *Resistible Rise of Arturo Ui,* a comic-vulgar vaudeville about the rise of Hitler set against Al Capone's Chicago.

The control is where it always was, with the money centers, with the banks. But most of these personalities are "bankable," that is, if they agree to appear in a film, stage play, or television show, the money will follow. Directors Mike Nichols, Elaine May and Woody Allen have "final cut" written into their contract; they are free of censorship, free of restrictive social pressure. Except in the sense that they must find and keep an audience.

Controversy and experiment are bankable. "I think anything that somebody thinks will make money will be produced," Elaine May said. "It is no longer true that studios are afraid of controversy. They are afraid of not grossing."

The only limitation on freedom, ultimately, comes from the audience. But today the audience is not singular, there are many audiences and therefore room for many artists of differing visions.

The permissiveness of the audience is the basis of the permissiveness of the performer. We see more and hear more now not because the artist has become willing to disclose more, but because we have changed. The license to venture into once forbidden territory is merely the mirror image of what the audience will allow, or respond to. And who better to decide what the audience will accept, than the audience?

Even more critical, is the effect of television on the relation between artist and audience. In stage terms, actors work in an open-ended cage, with three sides formed by scenery or by the back wall and side walls. In traditional concepts, the "fourth wall" in the theater is the imaginary wall formed by the audience. Now, because of TV, for the public artist, there is a "fourth wall" in almost every house in America, and beyond.

A good performance is self-validating. Yet for the public artist on film, stage, and in television, even more than for the writer or painter, an audience is essential. For a painter or a writer recognition may come even after they are dead. But a public artist needs immediate response. Without the presence of a live audience *now*, the public artist has no existence at all. Therefore, the relationship to the audience and to critics is fundamental.

These interviews indicate that critics are an aggressive nuisance, that the public—the fan—is a passive nuisance. The audience, on the other hand, is regarded with more benevolence; unlike the public, it has paid its dues. The audience is necessary to the survival and success of the star, but does not provide standards for the star or determine what is good or bad. The audience is the ultimate patron of the art and the artists in this society, not as in the past the crown, the church, the prince, or the wealthy landowners. It is an increasingly wide and diverse audience, made almost universal through television and movies. The artist owes to his patrons, in response, a good performance. "The show must go on" for the audience, and for others in the production, not for the critics, not for the nonpaying public. The relationship between artist and audience is a rational, dignified one. Each has brought something to the occasion, is in the house honorably, one to give a performance, the other to receive, to respond, to applaud or to withhold applause.

The audience has paid to see the performer—in television the audience has paid with its time—but the performer rarely sees the audience on whom survival depends. Al Pacino said: "Those fucking lights in my eyes, blinding me." After a lifetime in movies and theater, Gwen Verdon, in *Chicago,* for the first time could see some of the audience because of the extremely sharp incline of the stage, which brought the cast close to the front-row seats, and it disturbed Verdon. She saw people "adoring" her, but they looked unhappy. She was compelled to be concerned about them as persons. It made her sad. And that was not her duty to them. Her duty to them was to dance and to sing and to act, and their responsibility, in return, was to respond but to remain invisible. The audience is formless, it exists only in the mass. It is people without a person. Yet it has a personality. As Mike Nichols says, "You can hear an audience think."

These interviews may be seen as part of the artists' response to the audience, a peculiarly modern response. The artist in the past discussed his work and his life in letters to friends, in notes for journals to be released after death, or in published memoirs. Some still do that. The interview form covers some of the same ground; it is, in a sense, the modern memoir, the contemporary oral history, its best modern use in the arts being the collection of *Paris Review* interviews, "Writers at Work." In such interviews the public artists share themselves with the audience in areas about which they feel the audience has a right to know. Each one here talks eagerly about the way each works. It's as though the interview is an extension of the stage, an attempt to deepen understanding of the public artist among those whose interest is serious—an audience one can trust. But an interview is the most vulnerable form for an actor because there is no role to hide behind.

The performer's task is to do the best possible but not to ask the audience what that should be. Edwin Newman, in discussing how he regards the audience, said, "I talk to the camera, which is a way of saying I talk to myself. I am trying to write a news program and deliver a news program that I would be interested in." Speaking about the audience, George C. Scott said: "The people themselves don't know what they want to see and that's the way it should be, I think." Some people, such as Angela Lansbury, saw the audience as customers. She wants to "sell" her characterization to them so they will believe in it. "I care about them very much," she said. "I want to hit them all very hard. My trouble is, I am always trying to get everybody, instead of just trying to hit a small portion of the audience." The audience does not serve the artist in the sense of giving the artist standards, but it is the testing ground, particularly for comedy. Elaine May said, "If an audience doesn't understand it . . . I figure that I've done something wrong."

Woody Allen's experience is that "In comedy it's impossible to please just yourself. In drama you can. With a comedy, if they don't give you the immediate big laugh on the spot, the boat has sailed and you're dead." However, Allen says he is writing "more for friends and for a more select audience." He settles for smaller audiences and a smaller profit in exchange for his freedom and "final cut" in his film contract.

Occasionally, the audience is seen as restrictive. Paul Newman envies the British actor who can play an unpopular or un-stereotyped role without being penalized, either privately or at the box office. Paul Newman is certain that were he to play the part of a homosexual in a movie, he would damage the movie's chance of success; he feels certain an American audience would not accept him in that character. On the other hand, the two British actors, Diana Rigg and Lynn Redgrave, find greater freedom in America.

But if the audience is usually seen as benevolent, not so the critics or the general public. The critics are an obstacle, and except in hits, tend to discourage the audience, tell it what to think. The public artist continually questions the credentials of the critic; the artist sees the relationship as hostile. Paul Newman said: "Only the actor and the director and the people who are involved know" who is responsible for what is happening on screen or onstage.

Others feel critics' views are uninformed, too low, too personal and petty. Zero Mostel deplores critics for not liking *Ulysses,* which he played on Broadway. He said: "A critic doesn't know how to deal with a work of art. They can deal with cheap TV shows which become Broadway hits but they cannot deal with something which is written by a literary genius [James Joyce]. William Blake said a wonderful thing once. He said, 'They praised Michelangelo for everything for which he had contempt.' " Many public artists feel that way about critics.

The critic and the creative artist do not talk to each other, they are competing for the audience. If the critic were interested only in the artist, the critic could telephone the artist and discuss the work privately. The critic doesn't—I don't—do that because that is not his function as critic. The audience may use the critic for its purposes, and these purposes may be the antithesis of the artist's purpose.

Worst of all, in the eyes of most of the public performing artists, is the fan, the groupie, the autograph hound, the stage-door types waiting hours to be able to tell someone they saw Paul Newman. The fan is the person on the street who wants to make some contact with a celebrity, to bother him, to force him to stop, talk, sign his name.

None of these artists can appear in public without being recognized. Some respond graciously to that public. Edwin Newman often asks the name of the person who wants an autograph and addresses it to that person. After the interview, Angela Lansbury patiently autographed scores of stills, apparently one from each of her forty-eight movies, collected by a fan. Gwen Verdon got down on the floor to sign the cast of a woman dancer's broken leg, but Gwen Verdon says the sole responsibility she owes the public is her performance. Paul Newman refuses to sign autographs. He never agreed to that compact when he became a star, he said. Al Pacino says they grab your glass and say they are going to keep that glass and never drink out of it, or girls call up and offer to go to bed with him. He is not alone. Many public artists report similar experiences.

Several who spoke of being pursued by women say they disassociate themselves from such fans, in part because the role they have created and to which the ardent fan responds is pretense, it is not the private self. Paul Newman, one of the leading romantic heroes in film, said: "I can be almost indifferent to that because [what is created on celluloid] has very little to do with me." Angela Lansbury said: "You are embarrassed when you're with your children and people behave as they do around stars. They lose their dignity . . . and they become driveling idiots sometimes."

To most of the performing artists interviewed, the public in the street can be a monster, an itch, an annoyance, an intrusion, a wholly different concept from the audience. The street pest is irrelevant, brings nothing, gives nothing, but asks the performer's most valuable resources, his time, his privacy, and his identity. Time and again the performing artist expresses a debt to the audience but not to his public. Paul Newman said, "I don't sign autographs. I owe one thing and that is to give the best and most competent performance that I can." Woody Allen spoke for all when he said the public has no right to him, that he is to be judged by his professional performance and his private life is very much his own.

The question of creating an original, a distinct, or as Al Pacino said, a "revolutionary" performance before the camera is not answered by the response from the audience, nor from the critics, and certainly not from the fans. The judge is an inner judge. The three film directors—Mike Nichols, Woody Allen, and Elaine May—need the audience to verify the laugh, but not to tell them how to create it. Mike Nichols says he is working to satisfy something inside himself. Gwen Verdon, when asked "When you are dancing in *Chicago,* who are you dancing for?" replied: "Me. That's the way it should be for everybody, not only dancers. You can't depend on somebody else to know if you are good, they may say you were good on a night when you know you were bad. And then you feel like a fraud."

The performing artists are interested in what their peers think about a performance, they listen to good directors, but they look to themselves for their art. Al Pacino tells how he was almost fired from *The Godfather* because he was not playing Michael Corleone the way Paramount wanted him to. He proved to them and to himself that he was right, finally, he said. No artist here totally commited to his art works to imitate others. Imitation, even if done excellently, is at best second best, second to the originator. These artists are unique. They are the ones who are imitated. They want to set the standards, and these can come only from themselves.

1

AL PACINO:

It's the Lights in My Face, Blinding Me

PROBST: You say it's scary to do *Arturo Ui.*

PACINO: To do anything is scary for me. To do a movie, to do a play. When you take a chance you're as good as the chances you take, so it's a chance to fall. And also it's a little frightening to go into yourself and commit yourself, take the responsibility of it, take hold of the reins and say, I'm somebody and I've got this to say and I've got that to say, here it is. The most exciting thing about it—and I just found this out recently—is that opportunity to change, to go through an experience and come out of it different. I like working in the theater at night because it makes my day. It's a focal point. I read more, I see more people, I have a better time. . . . Of course I die when I have to go there at night, but still and all, in the end . . . I want it to end, I want the run to be over, but every time it is, I miss it, and I go back to it. It makes for a life—change and routine. You know you've someplace to go to, where you're going to take a chance, walk upon the wire.

PROBST: Is that what you call going on stage—a walk upon the wire?

PACINO: I like to call it that. The imaginary wire. But it's just as devastating, a hundred-foot drop there. When you're going for the stakes, when you set those stakes for yourself—you've got to be a little crazy to do it.

PROBST: You're always competing with yourself?

PACINO: You're always going to be compared to the last thing you did. I say you're as good as the best thing you've done. I try to use that philosophy.

BREGMAN *(business manager):* Being an actor and acting are two separate existences really. Being an actor is a passive role. You're waiting for a play to start, film to start. The state of being is a very destructive state because it's living in a vacuum all the time. Existing on stage or on film or in your work is a very positive, almost aggressive thing. You're creating something. But waiting for that work to start is living in a void. Waiting is a very passive and frightening role, and that's why most actors, when they finish a project, become depressed. The depression is normal. There is suddenly the prospect of huge inactivity, even though you're exhausted, it's stopping a force.

PACINO: Especially when you're on the stage. A new kind of thing is going on and then suddenly it's over. Now, how can life, everyday life compare to that? That can make for depression, too.

PROBST: Is theater a separate life?

PACINO: I believe that the goal for everybody is to have work be an integral part of his life. They asked Brecht one time about the actress. Is she happy she's working? And he said, "She's working, she's happy." It is a difficult position to be in when you don't have to work. When you're financially secure there's a tendency to say, Why the fuck should I go out there and open myself up like this and go through all the other pains when I don't need to do it? When you're doing it for money. When you *have* to do it. You get a chance to do parts, maybe, that you wouldn't do normally. And you might find a vehicle of expression that you didn't know was in yourself.

There are parts around that I haven't done that might unleash a part of me. One of the reasons that I want to do *Hamlet*—which I *will* do—is I know that after I've done *Hamlet,* whatever happens with it, whether it succeeds or fails, I will find out something about myself. That's the appeal to me, to learn something about myself and express myself, be creative. That's the excitement for me now. Sometimes you say, Jesus, I don't want to learn about myself, I'm getting along, and you force yourself to work.

PROBST: Are you happier being an actor playing somebody else's life than your own?

PACINO: Yes, of course. Because it's my life. It's a chance to express my life, my views, my way of looking at things. That's where its value is. It's my contribution.

PROBST: Your life is not *Arturo Ui,* your life is not *Hamlet,* is it?

PACINO: There's a desire to be in that world and to go through those experiences artistically. Let me give you an example. If you want to grieve, you have to step outside of yourself and let it out. If you hold on to it, it's there, it's inside you, and that's what it is with acting. You step out of yourself in order to grieve, to be tragic. It's like losing yourself in your objectivity. I don't just mean tragedy—comedy is the same thing.

PROBST: You step out of yourself to become yourself?

PACINO: Yes. What does Michelangelo say . . . God free me of myself so I can please you. That's exactly it. It's confusing. But this again is personal. I like to get caught up in a world and make it imaginative and alive. I need to do it.

When I first realized I wanted to do this and that nothing mattered after that, I was twenty-two and I was doing the Strindberg play [The Creditors]. I knew I had a talent, I knew I was born with it. I was in school plays and I was going around saying I was an actor. It's the only thing I can do, it comes natural. But I never quite understood it. I'm from the South Bronx, you know, I didn't know anything about the Strindberg world. I felt that I had the license to speak and that I was Everyman and that I was timeless and that I was universal. I felt this great sense of saying, I can talk, I can speak, I've got something to say. I knew that I would do nothing else but that. And it didn't matter anymore that I became successful or got a job. This can sustain me.

It sounds very wowie, but I tell you the truth, I became conscious of the fact that I was an artist. And I knew it then, way back then. That's very young, I think. That's why I love to do Shakespeare because I love to talk and say and feel all those things— make things happen.

I don't do much of that in my personal life. I've been very reserved in my living. I'm just beginning to understand that now and trying to live. I've done a lot of living through my work, but that's another story. When you start to make your work your life, too, then it becomes integrated and you're able to be as alive when you're not physically working. You become interchangeable. I sometimes wish that there were no opening nights, that you just rehearsed, and people came, and it just happened.

PROBST: If your work is completely absorbing and challenging, you don't need a personal life. You may need one now.

PACINO: I had a personal life. I wasn't giving myself to that because I kept saying, Well, I'll give myself to the work. And I realize that's foolish. You can give yourself to your life.

PROBST: Can you do both?

PACINO: Sure you can.

PROBST: Why didn't you?

PACINO: I wasn't aware that I *wasn't,* for a lot of reasons. The thing I was afraid of was, well, if I was able to do it in my personal life, I won't want to act anymore and I was going to lose my talent. But you don't. You just understand it more. It took me a long time to realize that. I still have the need, otherwise I wouldn't be doing it. I still have the need. It's my craft. It's what I've spent twenty years doing. I'm not going to give it up yet.

PROBST: You found that by acting somebody else's life you found your own life?

PACINO: There is only one life, that's yours. Once I was doing *Richard III* and the director came up to me and said, "You know, Richard is this and Richard is that and Richard does this and Richard does—" I said, "Wait a minute. I got the answer. Get Richard to play it. And that's it. You know so much about Richard, maybe you should play it. There is no Richard. I'm Richard." There's a real difference between character acting and caricature acting. The character actor says what you're looking for is the who-am-I. In acting terms they talk about it all the time. They say, Who am I? You've seen a lot of my work. There's a difference between Serpico and Michael Corleone, and they're the same . . . it's me, it's me.

I love doing Richard. There's a character. There is a scene in *Richard III* where Richard's mother is haranguing him with all these curses, calling him a toad and stuff. The queen, Queen Elizabeth, is on him toward the end of the play, and Richard is really going into it. He's starting to kill everybody and taking over and getting higher and higher. Charlie Laughton [Pacino's acting teacher] loved the work, but he pointed out that one scene and he said, "Al"—knowing me so well—"Al, if you would just listen to what they're saying to you, something will happen." He knew that I wasn't listening, I didn't want to hear those curses at me, especially coming from my mother and women. And I knew what he said. I came that night and I came to that scene, and I just listened. I heard them and my face changed . . . a twitch came into my face and my whole face changed, the right side of my face, just from listening, having the faith to listen. You have to have the faith to listen. You got to hear it first. It has to happen to you.

PROBST: Who is Alfred Pacino?

PACINO: I'm just beginning to recognize that there is one.

PROBST: That there is an Al Pacino?

PACINO: There has to be.

PROBST: Where did it all begin?

PACINO: When I was very little, about three, I was given to my paternal grandparents—and do you know that two of my aunts are mutes? At three years old, I was brought up by this aunt and my grandmother, my paternal grandmother, Grandma Pacino, who's dead now. This was very traumatic, being taken away from your mother when you're that young.

This is something I've blocked off, I don't remember it. A mute took care of me, so that explains a lot of the mimic kind of thing. You're around deaf-and-dumb people long enough, you begin to express yourself this way. I wasn't allowed out of the house until I was seven because we lived in the back and my maternal grandmother couldn't watch me and my mother worked. The only exposure I got to the outside world was the movies my mother would take me to. The next day I'd enact all the parts alone in my house.

PROBST: Your father now lives in California?

PACINO: I haven't seen much of him in my life. I don't know him well.

PROBST: How much of Al Pacino have we seen?

PACINO: I think there's a whole area of myself that hasn't been seen. A real vehicle for expression for me is comedy—I would love to do that. And I think the time will come when I will do it. It's a strange thing. Here I am at a very high point in my career. I can do most anything. Things come along, and I look at them—they're good films with good directors—and yet I feel that's six months of my life. I can't give myself to something unless it presents some kind of challenge or stimulation. I can read a script and it can be really very good, but I wouldn't want to do it. I've been as discerning as I can be in the picking of films. At this point it seems to be one of the few things I've been consistent at. And as far as violent parts go, I think there's violence in every part.

PROBST: Comedy?

PACINO: Sure. A man slips on a roller skate and falls down and everybody laughs. That's violent.

PROBST: We want something to take us out of ourselves?

PACINO: There's that part of entertainment that takes us out of ourselves, but then there's also something else. Why I get scared sometimes when I go to the theater. Why *The Living Theater* got to me the way it did. I love that theater. They did things that changed my life . . . you know that little fear when you go in and the lights start to go down? What it is is a chance that you're going to come out of the theater different from when you went in.

PROBST: Do you consider yourself a Method actor?

PACINO: I really don't know what that is. I remember doing scenes in The Actors Studio, and then when anybody would talk I would count numbers so I wouldn't hear it. Good actors are made and great actors are born. Either you've got something to say or you don't. And you try to get to the point where you can say something as an artist. I've seen actors who've studied The Method who have become better from it, and I've seen others who've become worse. The Method is based on what great actors did—that's what Stanislavsky based The Method on.

PROBST: Do you take direction?

PACINO: Nobody can tell me how to do it. When Charlie says to me, Listen to what she says [referring to Richard III], that makes sense because it's not saying how to do it. I understand that kind of talk. But what to do, and rules to do it in, no, no, I can't explain to you how I do what I do. I can't explain it.

PROBST: There's a change that comes over you in *Godfather I* and *Godfather II*, you're not the same person. You become more a monster.

PACINO: I'm more alientated.

PROBST: Did those scenes bother you, the restaurant scene in *Godfather I*, where you kill two men?

PACINO: Drove me crazy. Drove me crazy. *Godfather II* put me in the hospital. It was doing this character, the loneliness of him. I couldn't be that guy and have a good time. I wanted to have a good time doing it but I couldn't. And I couldn't go through that stuff inside. We were working twenty weeks on that film. I was living with that weight all the time, and it was suffocating, it was hurting. In film it's much more difficult—especially Michael Corleone. It's a film performance, it's a character done on film. You don't do that on the stage. And in the theater there's a chance to step outside of it, become artistic, objective, and not take it out on your own hide. The more experienced you become, the more aware you become, you start taking less and less out on your own hide. Sometimes I'll take it out on myself. This is my lack of experience, I think. Jimmy Dean did it to a great extent. He was very young and it hurt him.

PROBST: Why was *Godfather II* so oppressive?

PACINO: I became physically exhausted and got bronchial pneumonia. It was frightening. This had to do with a combination of nervous exhaustion and my own need to get away, to pull out. I'm not very fond of doing films—it's wear and tear on me. I have a very strong musical sense in me. In a movie, there's not a chance for that rhythm to build. I really feel that I was meant to compose music—in a different environment I might have done it. It's still my first love, music is, by far. I know more about music than I know about what's happening in the theater. That's why I love Shakespeare, because I can get into a rhythm of the words and the whole rhythm of the thing. That's why I fear doing things in translation, because words are notes to me and I play them. This is an area of myself nobody knows about. Michael Corleone didn't have many words.

If I've got something to say that the poet wrote, it can take me away. Most of the time I don't personalize at all. I don't try to say my own . . . I let them take me. I love words, I love saying them. I don't know why, I don't know. They say I'm a very good looper —you know, in films when you have to go and loop [lip-sync] your voice—they say I'm one of the best. Sometimes I'll just go and ride on the music of words. You have to do a take—and it stops. That's severed somehow, that's aborted.

It's also aborted and difficult when you're doing plays in translation. I found it difficult with Brecht. In a lot of *Godfather II,* believe it or not, because it was hard to get the source, it was hard to get the thing rolling. I'd find myself in my dressing room with my ear to the speaker, listening to Stravinsky or something, so that I'd hear music in my head when I'd be talking, I'd have something to relate to. Because you don't have the rhythm of a play to relate to, you need to draw on things.

PROBST: How do you draw on music? Music is abstract, almost mathematical, it seems to me.

PACINO: It is, of course. But that's when you're composing it, playing it. But when you're listening to it, it has a very emotional effect on me. It can change my state of being. I did a simple scene in the boathouse when I tell Tom Hagen about what's going on and what he has to do. It was a six-minute scene of exposition. Michael is talking about what's going to happen. I mean, impossible stuff. How do you make it active? How do you act it? Well, I knew that I was stuck with that. I'm not somebody who just goes up there and mouths things. And I'm not using Shakespeare's dialogue, either, to say it. Something has to be happening inside me to make me say these things. And I found I didn't have that much time to research, to work to find these things—so I used music.

PROBST: I don't know what you mean when you say, I used music.

PACINO: Music would put me in a state. It would work on my subconscious, subliminal state. And I would come in with that state, so that was going on inside me, whatever that was. . . . Then I would talk, and that would be ringing in my ears. Michael had a lot of stuff going on in the back of his head and I didn't know what it was. So I found something commensurate with it. You get it now?

PROBST: I understand it.

PACINO: So I used that when I could.

PROBST: In *Godfather I,* you have said you felt unwanted, that Francis Ford Coppola . . .

PACINO: Yah, he wanted me.

PROBST: . . . but the other people thought you were a mistake, and therefore you felt very alien. Did you get sick in *Godfather I?*

PACINO: I hurt my ankle. They were thinking of firing me the first week, mainly because they wanted me to be very strong in the beginning and I knew the only way that that part would happen, I knew that the excitement of that role, the way it could come off, is in transition—unlike *Godfather II.* In *Godfather I,* suddenly, as an audience, you say, Where did he come from? That's what I wanted to do. And I wanted to create an enigma, somebody you didn't quite know. And I did it. I'm most proud of *Godfather II,* because that's the most difficult character I ever had to do. I had nowhere to go, nothing to grab, except to sustain it for three and a half hours.

When I saw it, afterward, in rough cut—I only see my films once . . . I have no need to see it anymore—there's nothing I can do about it, it's over—I was pleased because I thought that I had done something artistic in this performance. I felt that. I wanted to create that kind of loneliness and that alienation and that abstraction that I felt. It had a meaning. There was an identity there.

PROBST: Did you want the audience to dislike you?

PACINO: I knew that was going to be a problem, but no, I didn't. I don't mean to compare my performance to a Beethoven quartet, I don't mean to, but I think it's the kind of performance that you have to really look at and see. You don't just sit around and listen to a Beethoven quartet and just say, Hey, that was terrific. You have to give yourself to it. That's why sometimes the performance is not quite seen, it's a little unclear, it's not quite understood. People have said to me that they feel in time it will be. People have said that they feel it's a sort of revolutionary performance. I would talk this way if somebody else did it. I hate to be falsely modest. And it's not about me, really. I feel that there was a revolutionary sense in *Godfather II*.

PROBST: In what way was it revolutionary?

PACINO: It sounds presumptuous of me to say it's revolutionary. What I meant is, it was revolutionary for *me*. I was able to get inside a character and let the character take me. I didn't try to opt for any kind of sympathy or understanding that was gratuitous of the character. I didn't impinge on it. I wanted people to like Michael but like him in the sense that I wanted them to see him, to understand him and his dilemma, without asking them to identify with him. That's what I was after. It's a difficult thing to do . . . and I think I did it. I'm most proud of that.

PROBST: What was Michael's dilemma—the losing and winning?

PACINO: Yes, that balance of losing and winning, his struggle to be a person he couldn't be. He became a non-person. When you start that lie, that pretense, no matter how noble your intentions . . . he didn't know who he was anymore. When he was younger, he didn't want to be a part of the gang. This is fiction but I'm talking about a character I created. I mean Mario Puzo created the character and I took it another step.

It's the same guy who was in *Godfather I*. Michael didn't know where he was way back in the '40s when he was going to school and moving away from "the family," in one sense, but also moving away from his destiny. In *Godfather II*, his problems are manifest more and more. There's such a dichotomy in this guy, he's so ambivalent. Strange thing about Michael and Ui. Arturo Ui, who is the Hitler figure, is an unpredictable guy but he's unpredictable because he's not bright, he's mediocre. Michael, on the other hand, is unpredictable but he's very intelligent. This dichotomy finally leads to his madness. He is lost at the end of this film. He's a beaten man. He is a desperately sad person. That's what comes across and it isn't as commercial. I was very proud that people took to it and in time, I hope, will take to it more.

PROBST: *Part II* is your movie. *Part I* you're sharing with a lot of people.

PACINO: That has something to do with it. If you notice at the end of *Part I* there's a kind of bounce to Michael. There's that ever subtle joy of what he's doing, that newness and that kind of taking it on, but when we pick him up in *II,* he's been doing it for five years, and that's gone. And that's what I went for.

PROBST: What do you now feel about *Serpico?*

PACINO: *Serpico* was a launching pad for me. This was the first time I became interested in film as a medium. I was more on the inside. I found out how you cut a scene, what you can do when you write a scene, what it's like to work together with people like Sidney Lumet and Marty Bregman and Dede Allen. I try to apply it now to everything I do. *Godfather II* wasn't that situation at all. But the next movie I did, *Dog Day Afternoon,* did have that collaboration, and it's a very exciting way to work. You don't feel you're just going up in front of a camera and saying your lines with a certain sincerity and naturalness. You're working with the total. . . . Ultimately, it's the director's vision and that I respect.

PROBST: In the collaborative effort, what did you bring to the character?

PACINO: I got to know Frank Serpico very well. I talked to him, went out with him, lived with him. This is a great advantage for any actor. With me, things rub off subliminally and stay. That made the characterization stronger. I had a source to draw from. Sometimes in the theater, your source is the material and that can be great stuff. But in films the material isn't always as strong as it is in great plays. They haven't had the time to work it. It's a different form. So that if you can find a source to go to. . . . Frank Serpico was a source.

PROBST: Of the characters you've done on film, do you have a favorite?

PACINO: I think my favorite characterization has been Michael Corleone. It was the most difficult for me to do. It was the most challenging.

PROBST: What about very intimate scenes?

PACINO: In all of Shakespeare's plays, nobody's taken their clothes off and nobody's even kissing. Romeo and Juliet, they don't kiss.

PROBST: They die together. That's more intimate than just kissing.

PACINO: It's too easy, too easy. Anybody can do it. I don't

moralize on it now. Believe me, I think it's fine. As for nudity, I was doing a shower scene in a prison in *Panic in Needle Park,* with about eight guys. The script girl is sitting there, and I say, "Is she going to stand there while we take our pants off?" Nobody said anything. She didn't have to sit there, but she sat there and we all took our pants down and it was nothing. Absolutely nothing. But, what bothers me sometimes is when it isn't an integral part of the story, when it doesn't lead . . . then I shy away from it. I find it becomes indulgent and unnecessary. I have seen scenes in film that implied sexuality . . . the impending something I always find more exciting than the act itself. I have rarely seen a scene in a film when the act itself really helped the story. I don't know whether I would do it myself or not. I once said I would do a nude scene if everyone on the set, also everybody in the audience, was nude. Then maybe I would understand. And yet, if it's necessary, then it's necessary.

PROBST: If you were persuaded that it was a necessary part of the film, to be in bed, nude, making love, you would do it or not?

PACINO: No. That is something I do privately. If there is a scene, for instance, a dramatic pivotal scene, the pleasure you should have is artistic. But I have not come across anything yet that has not been gratuitous. I saw a film and in the middle, I saw these two people fucking . . . literally . . . I think. I don't know how they got away with it but it was rated R, it wasn't rated X. It was completely unconnected with the story. I am not offended, it is just that it is very boring . . . very boring.

PROBST: Is the pleasure only artistic, don't you also work for money?

PACINO: I do moving jobs for money, I was a messenger for money, and I worked as an usher for money, but I never acted for money. One time I was starving, one time my whole life. . . . I borrowed fifteen dollars to take the bus to Boston because there was a part for me to do—Theater Company of Boston, as a matter of fact—and I was sleeping on a friend's floor. I was eating rice. I had a little paper bag with my belongings in it. I had no place to stay and no money for food and no money for a room. They offered me fifty dollars a week, which was a huge sum of money, to play this small part in *The Caucasian Chalk Circle,* and I wouldn't do it—I made believe I had something waiting for me in New

York. And David Wheeler [the director] looked at me and said, "But there's other things—next plays and stuff like that." I said, "Yah, I got something." I didn't want to say to him, "I don't act small parts." Who are you to say that? But I couldn't do it. I just couldn't. I couldn't stand around and watch other people act. I never could. What was there for me to learn? I don't learn from watching others. I only learn from doing it myself. From the experience and from life. So I asked for the fifteen bucks back and I took the bus back home. My friend said, "Oh, what are you doing back here? Christ." I said, "Well, it didn't work out." That's a true story.

PROBST: You decided you were going to be an actor, an artist and nothing else?

PACINO: I knew that's what I was meant to do.

PROBST: Where did it come from?

PACINO: The source was the Strindberg play and the source was the fact that I found that I was in a world. I had a world there. I was speaking almost like for the first time in my life. I had a voice. I felt that nothing comes close to this, nothing. And I'll tell you, I've rarely felt that again. I had it then. Maybe a couple of times, here and there, I've felt that sense of being able to speak, but not often.

PROBST: But you are absolutely confident that it's inside you?

PACINO: Well, it's God-given, yes. I have a talent. I have the instrument to do it. It's quite evident. I doubt myself the way everybody else does. I have no confidence. The thing I loved about doing Hummel [*The Basic Training of Pavlo Hummel*] was this kid was inept at everything but he had this great hope. He had hope and I loved him for it. I loved to show that desire. I think with me it's different than other people. It wasn't so much a wanting—it was a having to. There's a difference.

PROBST: Having to be an actor?

PACINO: And also having to be successful. Big thing.

PROBST: In your own eyes, how successful are you?

PACINO: You always feel as though you're a fraud. When you're bad you feel like a fraud, and when you're good you feel like a fraud. It's very common.

PROBST: Who are you fraudulent to?

PACINO: I'm not showing the real me.

PROBST: You've never shown the real Pacino?

PACINO: You want to live with me, you'll see him. The thing I love, like when I sit at a piano and I begin to play—and I've never had formal training—after about twenty minutes I lose myself. I only wish that that kind of thing could happen in my work, my acting. Sometimes it does. That's what I go for, that's the freedom I was talking about before.

PROBST: How difficult is success?

PACINO: We are a success-oriented society and I wanted to be successful. But the work itself freed me from success ... even before I became successful, it liberated me, and that was wonderful. And that's when I became successful. Sometimes I feel that I'm the most unlucky person in the world, and I would trade it all in one minute, but sometimes I feel really lucky and very happy. It's like a pendulum.

PROBST: Do you recognize yourself?

PACINO: That's the frightening thing about it. You are a symbol. Somebody was telling me about somebody, recently, who said, "Al Pacino, I would go to bed with him and I'd live with him, I'd do this and this and this." I said, "No, not Al Pacino. No. The symbol. What Al Pacino represents." It alienates you. You start pulling away and you start becoming what they call you, a superstar. A star. Away. Away from everything else, untouchable, unreachable. Who can live that way? You're living in a psychotic state then if you're living that way. You go through that. After a while you break through that stuff. . . . And then, of course, there's the other, where girls wait for me at night.

PROBST: If a woman calls you up and says, I want to go to bed with you, what do you do?

PACINO: I just hang up. It's that simple.

PROBST: Why?

PACINO: Because it is unnatural for someone to want to go to bed with you who's never met you. These people are people with problems. They need help. Sure, I go to bed with women but I have to have a relationship with them first.

PROBST: Is that one of the problems of being a superstar?

PACINO: It's very difficult to understand the position if you're not in it. My closest friends, people I've known for fifteen, twenty years, don't really understand it. Unless you live it, unless you experience it, it's very hard. It's uncomfortable when someone comes up to you and takes your glass and says, I'm gonna keep this glass because you touched it.

PROBST: What does it do to you?

PACINO: There are times when you want to go to a restaurant and sit down or you want to be alone. Lee Strasberg told me—and it's very true—he said, "You simply have to adjust." Can you be any simpler than that? I mean, that's it. So, you adjust. Girls ring the bell, phone calls, I have to change my number a lot. I can sit down and beat my breast about it or I can just say it's part of what's going on. But if I go any place I'm approached, and that can be trying after a while if you don't feel like being approached. I am somewhat of a people-voyeur. I love to sit and watch things happening. I like to step outside and watch. That now becomes increasingly difficult for me to do. I was in the bathroom the other day taking a pee, and the guy next to me says, "Hey man, what's this? Michael Corleone taking a piss?" I said, "No." He said, "You mean to tell me you're not Al Pacino?" I said, "Yes, I am and that's who's taking a piss!" I was walking around thinking I was special, isolated, and unique, and then I found out I indeed am special, and so is everybody else. I realize then that *that* is the basis of communication. It's the code. Our own uniqueness is what we have in common. I can sit here and say that I am not the only one that goes through this, *that* person goes through it too, then suddenly I am not alone.

PROBST: Is it easier for you to deal with failure than with success?

PACINO: No. There's two kinds of failure. One is the real failure, and that's finding out. The other failure is not giving. I don't mean to be so profound, but I believe it.

PROBST: Are there many kinds of success?

PACINO: Yes, of course. There's the monetary success.

PROBST: What do you do with all your money?

PACINO: I have a lot of money. I don't know what to do with it at this point, I don't know. It would be different had I a family, a wife and children to support. Now it provides me with a certain privacy that I need. I'm not in the moneymaking business, so that I don't try to get my money to make money. I try to keep it as simple as possible. I try to find out about my money, what it means, how it's invested. It's all very complicated. It took me years to just begin to take on that responsibility of having money. I give it away, here and there. I'm a poor kid from the South Bronx and there's certain things with money that I just don't understand and I will never understand. I always felt I had money even when I didn't have it. I always had a dollar in my pocket. I knew I could get that Chianti wine if I wanted it, and a knish. Just the other day I looked at a loaf of bread and realized how much money it is. Cigarettes are very expensive. I realized I haven't looked at a pack of cigarettes in a couple of years. I don't know how much a container of milk costs. I don't care. But when you had to know how much it cost because you didn't have the money . . . that was a different story.

PROBST: We were talking about the kind of success that buys privacy.

PACINO: I need privacy as much as anybody else needs it. I like to walk down the street without people coming up to me and talking to me.

PROBST: What do they call you?

PACINO: Al. They call me Al. And they're very respectful, very good, they're very nice. Once in a while it gets out of hand, but most of the time people say hello.

PROBST: What happens when it gets out of hand?

PACINO: Physically pawing and that kind of thing. But most of the time people are very cool, especially in New York. New Yorkers are great that way. They say hello to me, I say hello to them.

PROBST: Did you ever think of moving to Hollywood?

PACINO: No. New York's my home. Hollywood's Hollywood. It's another world. I'm not part of that culture. What I call a subculture.

PROBST: It's important to be in a place where you're a part of the culture?

PACINO: There's a way of life there and there's a rhythm of life there that I don't know about. But I know it's different than the rhythm of life I have. It's not the same. I never had any desire to live there.

PROBST: Rhythm and change go through your conversation. Is that the way you attack a role or your own life?

PACINO: It seems that way. It seems that way. I get into rhythms; I don't make plans. Things happen—spur-of-the-moment things. I'm starting to want to plan more. I say, Well I go to the Y Tuesdays and Thursdays, I'll go see so-and-so on Friday. And of course, to me, going to the theater to work at night is everything. It really gives me freedom. It gives chaos to all this freedom. Organized freedom.

PROBST: It's almost planned anarchy.

PACINO: Planned anarchy, I like that. Eugene O'Neill said that he was a philosophical anarchist. I am, too. I have seen nothing else work.

PROBST: You're almost thirty-five now. You want more landing spots than before, more places that are a safe harbor to come into?

PROBST: I would imagine it changes as you get a little older. And there was a time when I used to drink, and let that take me wherever I went. You know, I'd give myself to *that*. Of course, it never really got in the way of the work. When I was working, that was okay. Then when I wasn't working—it was starting to affect the work. And then I stopped.

PROBST: How'd you stop?

PACINO: I said, What's more important to me?

PROBST: Can you really be that intellectual about it and say, What's more important to me? and stop drinking?

PACINO: No. But you can try. I was suddenly conscious that I was drinking. I still drink like anybody does but I watch it. There was a time there when I found I didn't want to work. I'd rather do *that*.

PROBST: After *Godfather I* or before?

PACINO: Before, after. I never drank when I worked. That's another good thing about the theater. I don't work and drink.

PROBST: You're a workaholic.

PACINO: Work keeps me straight. It keeps me involved. It keeps me alive. But more and more now, I'm becoming interested in other things.

PROBST: Such as what?

PACINO: Music's a great part of my life. Other people.

PROBST: You talked earlier about getting married. Is that what you're talking about?

PACINO: In the real sense, this is the first time I'm really a bachelor, this last year and a half. Most of my adult life I've lived with another woman. I shared apartments with women. So it was sort of like being married. And I was usually just with one woman, that's how I liked it. It's different now. And I like it. For now, I like being alone.

PROBST: Isn't it lonely?

PACINO: It gets lonely. Sometimes it doesn't, but it's a novelty to me and I like it. The loneliness is something that I have to deal with. It's very deep. My loneliness has to do with other things. Not just being alone. The fact that I get lonely has to do with something I'm holding on ti. The other day I was saying to someone, I would give it all up, as long as they didn't take my work from me. I would give up fame and most of my fortune. Not *all*.

PROBST: Why would you give it up?

PACINO: Because one grows tired of certain inconsistencies, certain alienations, isolations. You want to feel a part of something. I do have friends I am close to . . . but, just a few. If I had a home, a family I felt a part of . . . that would supply me, I guess, with enough whatever it is that makes one go on, and it would make it easier for me to balance the success. Let me tell you something about power that I feel—the power one feels when one is with love, when one loves oneself and somebody else and is loved, the power of being loved. Loving is a power. If you have that you really don't need much else in worldly powers. The fact that somebody would give their life for you and that you would give your life for them . . . that is incredible. I don't want to get too comfortable in success, but I am getting a bit used to it. *The Indian Wants the Bronx* was the most jolting success I ever had, because I came out from complete obscurity. People would hear, there's a guy downtown doing this thing, we don't know what his name is ... we don't know where he came from. I sort of popped up in New York. That adjustment was an extraordinary one. And I was with Jill [Clayburgh] at the time, I was with her for five years. She had a strength, and we worked it out together. She was there for me, before this even started. My close friend, Charlie Laughton, has been with me right down the line and has helped me.

PROBST: What is it like to be Al Pacino?

PACINO: Annoying.

PROBST: Why is it annoying?

PACINO: Well, for one thing I'm doing this interview.... It's annoying. What's it like? Sometimes it's a lot of fun. Like anything else, sometimes it's joyful. One of the reasons I've steered clear of interviews in past years is that I always felt that when the light is shining in your face sometimes, everybody's paying attention to you, everything's about you, life is about you, there's a tendency to lose sight of what's there. You can't see with that flashness, so that when you turn it around sometimes and you take a look around you ... there's life and there's you. I think what annoys me sometimes is that it's fucking lights in my face, blinding me, and that's what annoys me. But, when it's not there, it can be fun.

2

PAUL NEWMAN:

There's a Little Mustard Left in the Old Fox Yet

PROBST: The first play you did was *Picnic* by William Inge. And the first movie you did was no picnic, it was *Silver Chalice*.

NEWMAN: No, I refuse to deprecate that! To have the honor of being in the worst picture made in the 1950s, and to have survived! That is no mean feat, I think. I don't make any apologies for that *anymore*.

PROBST: You took out an advertisement in Los Angeles apologizing for it at one point. Why do you not apologize now for what you apologized then?

NEWMAN: I'm a little more mellow and I'm not quite as feisty as I used to be. The first time it was shown on television, I guess, was fifteen years ago. I took a two-column ad in the Los Angeles *Times* with a kind of funeral wreath around it, saying that I apologize.

PROBST: *The Towering Inferno* came out this year. It was a junk movie, but I thought it was a *good* junk movie. Also, *The Sting* stung America to the tune of sixty-eight million dollars.

NEWMAN: Worse.

PROBST: Worse? How much worse?

NEWMAN: Oh, probably a hundred twenty-five million when it's through.

PROBST: Another thing happened this year that may possibly be the most significant of all—you had a party called "The Big 5-0."

NEWMAN: Oh!

PROBST: That's the sound of pain—human pain! They were celebrating the fact that you had been born on January 25, 1925, in Cleveland, Ohio, the son of Arthur Newman. . . . What did you get for your birthday?

NEWMAN: Well, Redford gave me a Porsche. The Porsche had hit a telephone pole sideways at ninety miles an hour. It had neither transmission or engine in it; it was an antique version of an antique version. The cockpit was absolutely empty, it had no seats in it. It was sitting in my driveway with a ribbon on it. So, I merely had the whole thing compacted and put in a crate about that big, and to the best of my knowledge it's in his vestibule right now. I don't see how he could move it. It took five guys to get it up there.

PROBST: At the party, didn't he give you a token gift?

NEWMAN: Just diamonds.

PROBST: You also got a case of Coors beer?

NEWMAN: Four and a half cases I collected—one way or the other.

PROBST: You gave a speech?

NEWMAN: Not of any consequence. I pointed out the fact that I was very happy that there were no media people there, and that I was also very happy with the media in general because they kept assuring the public that in the last twenty years I'd only shacked up with two people—Joanne and Redford. One article that appeared aferward in a newspaper said Mr. Newman confessed he had only shacked up with two people!

PROBST: I would like to enter a mild complaint. I don't like the word *media*. It's a Nixon word for newsman.

NEWMAN: That's why I'm using it here, Leonard.

PROBST: Who did you invite to the party?

NEWMAN: My friends haven't really changed that much in twenty years. For the most part, they are screenwriters, actors, and people in the theater.

PROBST: George Roy Hill was there, wasn't he? He directed you in *The Sting*, of course.

NEWMAN: He also directed Joanne in one of her first television plays, for which she will never forgive him. She had a marvelous death scene at the end of act two, and she slid quietly to the floor and went into the throes of the agony of dying, but George Roy kept the camera on the radio, which was doing an aria from *Carmen.* He thought that was much more interesting than what was going on on the floor. So it's been nip and tuck with them ever since.

PROBST: Do you get favorite directors?

NEWMAN: George and I have quite a marvelous relationship. He is, I think, an extraordinarily gifted man, he really has a concept of what a movie should be like. He has a great musical sense. He is loyal, affectionate, gifted, and the cheapest son of a bitch that I've ever met in my life. That's why it's marvelous to play practical jokes on him. You know, he can never afford, emotionally, to retaliate. I sawed his desk in half in his office because he wouldn't pay his bill for liquor which he had borrowed from my office. That was kind of the beginning of everything.

When I took over the direction of *Sometimes a Great Notion* and was really in bad shape because I did it involuntarily, he was the first guy to call up and say, "How are you?" I said, "I'm terrible." He said, "I'll be up." He got in his airplane and flew up to Portland and said, "What do you want me to do." I said, "I've got fifteen thousand feet of silent footage and I don't even have time to look at it." So he sat in the cutting room up there for three days, put the sequence together, and I said, "What do I need?" He said, "You need twenty setups, you need a point of view of the kid, you need his walking shot away, and so forth." And then he got in his airplane and left.

PROBST: I understand the reason for your red and very ruddy color is not a sunlamp, but a Caribbean cruise with him for two weeks. There was only one woman on board and that was the cook. And my question is, What did she cook?

NEWMAN: George Roy and me, as far as I know. That's why the media is not really correct—it's Joanne and Redford and George Roy now!

PROBST: How long can you continue to play a romantic hero?

NEWMAN: I don't know, there's a little mustard left in the old fox yet! I think it's all a combination of emotional attitude and genetics. I don't think I've ever felt better. I run a couple or three miles every day and jump in the river out in back. And the reason I run a couple of miles every day is that Joanne puts me on a rope at the end of a car. She's very interested in insurance. She will probably outlive me by twelve or fifteen years—and she would like all of it as quickly as possible. So she cracks the ice down there in the river every morning and makes sure I jump in, on the theory it will start my heart or stop it one way or the other. I've found a little oval that's not near people. I run with this big Irish wolfhound, anyway, and nobody messes around with that dog. That dog outweighs me by thirty pounds.

PROBST: Is it time to become a director?

NEWMAN: Motion pictures being what they are today, I might very easily go into marine biology. There are two things working against the actor. One, if you've been in the business as long as I have, the audience will simply not accept you in certain parts. You can literally ruin a movie by being in it. People simply will not accept me with a black wig and a putty nose. That's not what they want to see. Now this is peculiarly American, it's not European—they allow their people in films and on the stage to assume other characters, Guinness and Olivier, I suppose, are the best examples of all that. They allow their characters a lot more leeway. But once you establish an antihero kind of image—which has nothing to do with me as a person but simply the kind of parts screenwriters were writing—the audience simply will not go and see you. And I think that's too bad.

There's also an escapist kind of film which is very fashionable now. *The Towering Inferno* is a perfect example. I knew that the quicker I got off the screen and the stunt man got on, the quicker the picture would start rolling. I knew it was going to achieve what it wanted to achieve—and that is to really frighten people. It dealt with two rather original things, I thought—height, which is very fearful, and fire. The combination in creating a danger movie is irresistible. You call it a junk movie, and I say, yes, it probably is that, but it is a very *distinguished* junk movie.

PROBST: Distinguished escapist movies are preferable to pretentious movies?

NEWMAN: I really don't know what's happened in the theater, in television, in motion pictures. The writers are exhausted or the times aren't right. If the playwrights do not really originate anything, they are only reflective of the culture. Then, what you've got is the need for escapist films. The writers exhausted themselves in the social upheaval films of the thirties and the forties, and in the kitchen drama, which was Bill Inge, which in a way was Tennessee Williams, the psychological drama of Mommy-never-kissed-me-which-is-why-I-am-the-way-I-am. Television exhausted that very early, much before the cycle would normally have if it had just been theater. We're stuck now with no new vision of life that seems to be dramatizable. Until the playwrights discover that, actors will be left in a vacuum. The actors can only be as healthy as the playwrights. We are, after all, merely interpreters, we don't create anything. It's an interpretive science.

PROBST: Is it that when times are good economically, as they were a few years ago, people like to see serious things?

NEWMAN: They don't like to see serious things, necessarily, but because they feel good they can go to pictures that make them feel guilty about feeling good. But when they're really feeling rotten, then there's no reason to go through all that two thousand years of Christo-Judeo guilt. They really don't want to suffer. They suffer enough in real life.

PROBST: Are you serious about another profession?

NEWMAN: I find I duplicate myself in performances, and that gets to be a drag. If one starts to do that, then I think I should just take a job in a filling station because there should be something much more exhilarating about the arts than a kind of nine-to-five routine which you can do on any television series where you play the same character five days a week fourteen hours a day. That's a rough grind. But no, the playwrights are exhausted.

PROBST: They are? From what?

NEWMAN: Very much as the institutions in this country are exhausted. There's not a single institution in this country which isn't under attack. Congress, the presidency, the church, marriage, feminism, masculinism, the labor unions, corporations, all of them. There is nothing to replace religion and marriage, there is nothing right now to replace the kitchen drama, which, in terms of serious drama and serious theater, replaced the social-upheaval films of Odets and plays of Odets and Kingsley. The writers don't really know what to write about.

PROBST: You recently made a movie, *The Drowning Pool.* How did you respond to that?

NEWMAN: *The Drowning Pool* is really a continuation of the Harper character. I simply adore that character because it will accommodate any kind of actor's invention. He can do the most outrageous things. He can put people on, he's got a great sense of humor, so I can horse around. It's just lovely to get up in the morning, it's great to go to work, because you know you're going to have a lot of fun that day.

PROBST: Is that character close to you personally?

NEWMAN: I think it is because he's funny, but my wife says he isn't.

PROBST: Do you see yourself as funny?

NEWMAN: No. There are very successful mannerisms from certain parts that stick to your own personality. It may be a walk, it may be a way of listening to people, it may be a story, it may be a way of sizing a person up. You finally wind up as being half what you are yourself and half fragmentations of the characters that you play, not the unsuccessful characters but the successful characters. And I don't know where I am in that right now.

PROBST: Neil Simon said he sees himself as a three-and-a-half-sewer stickball hitter in Washington Heights at the age of thirteen. Do you have a view of yourself as a thirteen-year-old in Cleveland?

NEWMAN: No, but I feel like a thirty-three-year-old New Yorker.

PROBST: You are known for preparing very carefully for roles —for *The Sting* you watched William Powell play *The Thin Man.*

NEWMAN: Well, I watched about fifteen of his movies.

PROBST: To observe how a con man plays a con man?

NEWMAN: No, what I did with that, particularly, was just to watch the movies with no idea of creating that character or anything anywhere near it but to just start out with how much rubbed off on me. I think once you conscientiously work for . . . you get to the point of trying to create a dress rehearsal or something, which never works. I think there are certain things that happen by osmosis and that's what I depended on, for that part at any rate.

PROBST: What did you depend on for *The Towering Inferno?*

NEWMAN: I just went back to Shaker Heights—well, nothing. When you create a role that you think is fairly close to your own upbringing, which mine was basically—Shaker Heights, Ohio, Kenyon College, Yale—and you get a part like the architect, there's nothing you need really draw upon except yourself. When you get a part like Rocky Graziano or Hud or Hombre or the Battler, then you have to draw upon your own observations of other people or your own fantasy. The thing that I'm concerned about right now is that I'm running out of original things and I'm falling back on successful things that you can get away with. I duplicate things now. I don't work as compactly as I used to work, simply because the demands aren't asked of me anymore.

PROBST: You compact old Porsches. . . . You said there was nothing left in the way of movies, no place for them to go. Horace Judson in *Harper's* magazine says explicit sex is the only significant, real emotion left for moviemaking to exploit. Is there a future for Paul Newman in pornographic movies?

NEWMAN: Well, I don't think so. Mostly because those films have never really turned me on. I rather think of ladies as more mysterious and much more feminine when it isn't thrown at you like a sack full of cement. No, I'm not interested in pornographic films, not because I have any modesty about them but I'm not really turned on by them. You may have seen me going into *Deep Throat* in a red beard . . . and a big hat.

PROBST: You once said you were not as interested in concepts or messages as in creating emotions. Is that still true?

NEWMAN: Yes.

PROBST: Why, because emotions have reality and concepts do not?

NEWMAN: Because I think there's so little genuine emotion. I think it's manufactured—pornographic films, I think, probably being the best example.

PROBST: Of not genuine emotions?

NEWMAN: Yes, of manufactured emotion which really has . . . well, it's the rehearsals that kill you. You know, it's very funny. A friend told me that some friends of his had come down to his place in New Jersey and had said, Here's five thousand dollars—you know where all the action is, make us a pornographic film. So he got four young ladies from Swarthmore—which I thought was rather interesting—and three or four volunteer truck drivers, and they made a pornographic film for five thousand dollars and brought it back into New York. The distributors, to a man, turned the film down. They said, There is simply no reason for us to do the film because the people were having too much fun, it was done for their benefit and not for the benefit of an audience. And they simply could not distribute the film. Well, now, that would probably be fairly honest.

My fantasy of making the perfect movie is very, very simple. You have an idea for a film, you work with a screenwriter or a playwright—it can be either a film or a play—you get a marvelously inventive director, and you cast it the way it ought to be cast, not because you have to cast it a certain way. You get together and you have four incredible weeks of rehearsal and then you shut it down. And no one ever sees it. That would be a marvelous movie. You never crank a foot of film and you never have an audience to come in and see it.

PROBST: Don't you need public acceptance for what you do?

NEWMAN: No. I don't need it anymore. There may have been a time when I did, but I don't need it anymore.

PROBST: Don't you want to know what the reaction is? Don't you want to test it in public? Isn't that the validity of what one does?

NEWMAN: Probably, but it's a nice idea, anyway. The trouble is we simply can't afford it.

PROBST: What do you see as your work? Is it to act?

NEWMAN: I'm not sure that I know anymore. There are severe limitations. A script came to me about nine months ago, about Robin Hood. He had just come back from the Crusades and he was over the hill and he was having trouble getting up over those walls. Maid Marian was forty-three, just out of a monastery. Incidentally, under certain circumstances I can do a film if I can bring in a piece of material that will cost less than three million dollars. I get no salary, but if they can do that without my salary, without any salary at all—I participate much later, once the budget is in—and if it's under three million dollars, they can't stop me from making the picture.

PROBST: Great contract.

NEWMAN: So, with this picture, they said, How do you plan to play it? And I said, I'm not sure. I said, I would really want to look older and I will probably want to put on some weight, I will probably have a beard. And they said, Yes, we suspected as much. And they simply said the picture would cost about three and a half million dollars without me getting anything, because it is not a small production. They said, We can't stop you from doing the film if you can bring it in under three million, but we know you can't do that, because we simply don't want you to make the film. They don't want to see me play a part like that because they figure they're going to lose three and a half million.

PROBST: You can only play parts in which you are recognizable, in which the image continues. But you've got to run three miles every day?

NEWMAN: Oh, I don't mind that.

PROBST: You have six children?

NEWMAN: More or less.

PROBST: How many of them have become actors or actresses?

NEWMAN: Well, my daughter Susan has been in her first Broadway play. They've all taken the jump rather late. I don't think they wanted to be connected with the old man's shirttails. And my son Scott was in a guest-star role on "Marcus Welby," his first part.

PROBST: He was in *Towering Inferno?*

NEWMAN: Yes.

PROBST: Last year your son had given trouble to some sheriffs in California—I remember reading a book by Lawrence J. Quirk, *The Films of Paul Newman,* and it had a picture of you in Mineola, Long Island, being handled unpleasantly by two cops. It said that you passed a traffic light and had given the officers a hard time. What did you say then when your son called up from California and said, Hey, Dad, I'm charged with resisting arrest?

NEWMAN: The incident with him was blown all out of proportion. And I think that's deliberate. The accusation is always on the first page and the retraction is always on page nineteen. So what you're left with is the memory of the accusation without ever knowing really how the whole thing came out.

PROBST: What do you do when you get that telephone call?

NEWMAN: You go in the kitchen and you get about three ice cubes and you chill a beer mug and you sit there and think awhile. Listen, there's not much you can do except offer what support you feel is required.

The funny thing about it is I got into acting because I got thrown into jail. I was on the football team at Kenyon College. We always used to have brawls between the town's guys and the college kids. We used to swipe their girl friends at the local gin mill. Those brawls, I thought, were great fun. You wind up with a black eye or a bloody nose, but no one had a chain and nobody had a knife and nobody had a gun and you knew it was on a one-to-one basis and there was a great sense of humor because you'd see these guys on Monday and you'd try to knock out a couple of teeth the next Saturday night. It was part of the culture in those days. There was a big brawl out there and the quarterback and the first-line guard and tackle were thrown in the clink, and as they were taken out by the local gestapo, one of the guys threw me his keys and said, "Drive my car in," and so I drove his car in about a half an hour later and went into the sergeant's office and I said, "Burt asked me to give you his keys." He said, "Let me take a look at your knuckles." So the door closed in back of me. Four were thrown out of school and two of us were placed on probation. And it was simply because I couldn't play football anymore and I didn't want to study that I went into the theater. About ten days later I got my first part in a play there—this was my junior year—I was in ten subsequent plays as a result of that. I have the funny feeling if I had never been thrown in the clink I would have become an economics major or something else and would have been in a sporting goods business in Cleveland, Ohio.

PROBST: It's a new method school of acting that Lee Strasberg does not know about.

NEWMAN: Right. Gonna hit them hard.

Q *(question from audience)*: Since you are so bankable, wouldn't you have the power to do what you want to do in the movies?

NEWMAN: The Robin Hood thing is a perfect example. Not entirely.

Q: Your bankability doesn't mean anything then? Must mean something.

NEWMAN: I get the best scripts, under the most prestigious auspices. And they are uniformly bad. I have not read a serious film that's any good. I've read films that purport to be about serious things, and they're simply no good. The big problem, of course, is, if you decide to do a serious film, whether it be about the United Nations or about the Indians or about homosexuality, if it's about a serious subject, then you better make certain that the material is impeccable. It doesn't make any difference if you do a bad Western, it doesn't make any difference if you do a bad disaster film, but if you do a bad film about a serious subject, then you've done the subject a disservice. You've got to be three times as careful, and the writer must be four times as good, if you're going to do a serious film.

PROBST: Did you do those risky things we saw you do in *The Towering Inferno*?

NEWMAN: I tried to stay away from that. My theory about all of that stunt stuff is you do what you can do well. If you can't do it well, you don't blow the movie just to glorify your own ego. You get someone who will do the thing as best as it can be done.

PROBST: Did you get burned?

NEWMAN: In what way? That was the most carefully orchestrated film I've ever seen. One of the things that impressed me more than anything was, I went into Irwin Allen's office, and six weeks before we started filming I could practically see all of the action sequences of every single individual cut. In situations where there was real danger, it showed not only the frame of the camera which it would encompass ... let's say, not only the opening of the elevator but the paramedics standing on top with equipment. For instance, some of those fire stunts, people were encompassed in racing driver underwear, two suits of it, and a fireproof suit and a helmet with a face on it and with hair that wouldn't catch on fire. They put that helmet on and screwed the guy into it. He had a tiny little oxygen tank that would last two minutes and twenty-seven seconds, so they had to get him in, screw him in, put the liquid-fire additives on his suit, set him on fire, roll the cameras, he would do his bit, they would cut the cameras, and they would have to get that mask off him in the required time. It's pretty spooky.

Q: What role did you find most challenging and what did you like best?

NEWMAN: There's a lot of difference. The thing that the critics don't understand and sometimes the public does not understand is you may start off with a script which you have great hopes for. It may or may not come off. Do you give yourself more points for making something almost good out of something that's mediocre? Or do you give yourself more points for doing a picture like *The Hustler* where the character was always there, was always accessible, was always available, in which it was just a matter of digging? I give myself more points for a picture like *WUSA,* let's say, than I do for *The Hustler* simply because that part demanded a lot more. The most successful part is not always the most pleasing, simply because it was there when you went into it. And what you contributed really was just nothing but a certain amount of technique and work.

PROBST: How can anyone sitting in an audience know who is responsible?

NEWMAN: Only the actor and the director and the people who are involved in it know.

Q: Are you more creative as an actor or as a director?

NEWMAN: I like directing a lot better than acting. I don't know. That varies, also, depending upon the part.

Q: What do you think of the Academy Award structure?

NEWMAN: Well, it's been a matter of common knowledge that the Academy Awards do not represent what the actor would call any great critical acclaim. I think it's very, very important for, let's say, a small film. I think it was very, very important that *Rachel* was nominated. Not because it meant more money in the coffers, but because it made people go to the film. That's something you can't escape. The perfect film is never rehearsed and never shot. When I did that film, I had something to prove, since the film had been turned down by every major studio—plus the fact that I wanted people to see it, I wanted people to see the material, I wanted them to see the performances. From that standpoint, the Academy is very, very important. *The Towering Inferno* winning the best special effects award is not going to make any difference. I don't think it makes any difference for a big film, I think it's very, very important for a small film.

I think some things the Academy does are really outrageous; for instance, I think Dede Allen is the best cutter in the business, but she works in New York and she has never been nominated for an Academy Award although she cut *Rachel,* she cut Arthur Penn's film, she cut all of Kazan's films, she cut *The Hustler,* yet she's never been nominated because she's a New York cutter, and the film editors are nominated by Los Angeles film editors. The Academy Awards have no justice, so one is not really interested in that standpoint. But financially and from a spectator standpoint it is very important.

PROBST: Would you take an award if they gave it to you?

NEWMAN: I would have to weigh that very seriously. I don't know. At one point in my life, I suppose, an Oscar would have been very important, but I don't need the medals anymore. I think I've gone beyond that. I'd probably be very indifferent unless it was for a not necessarily commercial reason but very specific reason in terms of penetration.

PROBST: What do you mean, penetration?

NEWMAN: Being able to make a film be seen.

Q: What is your reaction to the New York critics?

NEWMAN: I think the critics have got too much power. I'm not always certain that their credentials are always better than ours in terms of judging something. But it works both ways. It has worked both ways with me. Without the notices *Rachel* got, it would have gone right straight into the sewer. By the same token, I thought they were rather harsh with, let's say, *Gamma Rays.* It's very simple, you know, when things are good the critics are great, and when they're not good they're terrible.

Q: Why do you prefer living in the New York area to Hollywood?

NEWMAN: I can be much more private in Connecticut. People simply can't catch up with you there as easily, and I've never really liked the California scene. No, I can't say that. What I think I like really is mobility. I love California for about a year. I like Connecticut for about two and a half years. The fact that I can move back and forth is a great luxury. We have a lot of options and that's very pleasant. I've stayed here really, I think, because New York was always exciting for me and I suppose even the memory of that odor still lingers although the activity is long gone. And I like the seasons.

When Joanne and I used to come back in the middle fifties and sixties, I remember one time we came back over the Fifty-ninth Street bridge and it was as though someone had dropped the flag or something. We both were quietly weeping into our beer, at just the joy of coming back to where the action was. Those were the days of live television, Chayefsky, Tad Mosel, Tennessee, and Arthur Miller, Bill Inge—and Off-Broadway was just getting started. And to leave that rather sterile pad out in California and come back here was really a high point of the year. It isn't anymore, and I don't know whether I've become less susceptible to stimuli like that or whether it's deader. I suspect it's deader.

Q: What was it like working with Tennessee Williams and Kazan in *Sweet Bird of Youth?*

NEWMAN: It was really interesting. I was getting successful and very confident and that's exactly the quality that Elia Kazan didn't want. And the thing that I give him points for in terms of the play is the way he handled me. I learned a great deal from that. Whenever he would give me a piece of direction or whenever I would come over with an idea, he would always say, "Paul, try this." And I'd say, "Okay." Or he'd come over to Geraldine Page and she'd say, "What if I try this?" and he'd say, "Try it." Or he'd go over and say, "Geraldine, why don't you try this?" And so we would play the scene, and then we would separate, and I would hear him go over to Geraldine and say, "Ah, right on!" I'd say, "God, I thought she was really off a little bit, that's not what I expected her to do." Then he would always walk over to me and say, "Ah, try it again." He was chopping me down. By opening night, it was marvelous. I really didn't have any security in the part at all. And that's precisely what he wanted. Tennessee was going through bad times then, really bad times, and I didn't see as much of him, really, as I should have.

Q: Do you feel acting studios help a young person who wants to be an actor?

NEWMAN: The Actors Studio, whether they like it or not, has either credit or blame for what I've become as an actor. I certainly came out of a very academic background, which was not very helpful, and I learned everything I've really learned about acting at The Actors Studio. But in those days it was known what was required of you. So the people that taught could teach you that. It was naturalism, it was the school of Inge, Miller, and Tennessee, and very realistic and emotional things on television, "Robert Montgomery Presents" and "The Philco Playhouse." As the playwright flounders, then the actor flounders, the acting schools flounder because they don't know what's fashionable or what works. And so I don't know about those schools, how valuable they are now. It isn't institutionalized enough for them to have a beat on it any more than it is institutionalized enough for the actor to know what he should learn. Rough times.

Q: Do you think a director makes a film?

NEWMAN: No. I don't think the director makes the film if the characters are interesting. The characters can carry a film, too. If the story is good enough, the story can carry a film. I think there are probably only two really genuinely original filmmakers in this country. Kubrick is one and the other is Cassavetes. That doesn't necessarily mean that they're good, but they're original. I've turned down a lot of films because there's been a lot of violence in them—but it's reflective of our times. I'm bored by it, that's why I'm not interested in working with Peckinpah.

PROBST: Does it bother you if an actor runs for political office? Like Ronald Reagan? Would you run for political office?

NEWMAN: Well, I don't like Ronald Reagan, but I think an

actor shouldn't be denied the privilege of running for public office because he's an actor, any more than I think an actor should be denied the privilege of campaigning for a candidate because he's an actor.

PROBST: Have you become less political in the last year? I know you supported Ramsey Clark.

NEWMAN: The whole country has become less political. I'm getting tired. I'm going to leave it up to you people now.

Q: How did you find screen-testing with James Dean for *East of Eden?*

NEWMAN: The screen test with Jimmy was not very impressive, I didn't think, but I think he would have surpassed both Marlon and me. I think he really would have gone into the classics.

Q: The gay world sees your films as having a pervasive theme—and Joanne's also—of a same-sex friendship. What about gay civil rights?

NEWMAN: Well, the main thing is, I'm with you. People hurt each other in so many different ways, and if people can find serenity and peace and comfort among each other, I'm certainly not interested in what their sexual proclivities are or their sexual interests are. In England they'll do *Sunday, Bloody Sunday,* they are not concerned about whether they're playing homosexuals, or lesbians, or anarchists, or Fascists. They merely go out and play the characters. If that's what's being written, and it's interesting, then they'll do it. But I have a sneaking feeling that if I were to play a homosexual, it simply would not be accepted by the audience, that they'd go away saying, Well, there's something fake about that. So, I am in a dilemma.

Q *(woman in audience)*: Women adore you. How do you feel about it?

NEWMAN: I'm faintly embarrassed. That comes from something that I have very, very little to do with, since I don't think we've ever met . . . that obviously must come from what you've seen on celluloid. But what is created on celluloid has about half to do with me and half to do with what the playwright gives me to do, so I can only assume that your perceptions are not very realistic. I can be almost indifferent to that because it has very little to do with me.

Q: Do you feel you owe anything to your fans, such as autographs?

NEWMAN: It's a matter of public knowledge that I don't sign autographs. Mostly because you say, What do you owe—well, I think I owe *one* thing, and that is to give the best and most competent performance that I can. To say that I am required by some kind of mystic law to be stopped every fifty feet on Fifth Avenue and be required to put my signature on a piece of paper, or if I'm having dinner with my children in a restaurant, to be bothered, I say, No, I'm sorry, those rules were made thirty or forty years ago, and I was not allowed to vote, I wasn't even around to vote on it.

3

DIANA RIGG:

I Believe in Going in the Face of Success

PROBST: You were very successful in "The Avengers," yet you no longer wanted to be Emma Peel or the star of any television series.

RIGG: I have a theory about television series—why they become successful. People switch on to the familiar. They like to see a familiar person in unfamiliar situations. So you can't expand, you're left with this character everybody knows and loves. You can't deviate from this character because they feel betrayed if you do. I felt I would atrophy. For a start, purely technically, when you're working in front of a camera, you don't use your voice very much. You keep it on the conversational level. My vocal powers went. I believe in going in the face of success, I really do. I believe in cutting across it. I think life is a series of starts, stops, and starts. If you're ahead, much like gambling, stop and start again in another direction. Also, categorizations are one of the curses of this business. It's so much easier to say, Here is a television actress who's been successful in a television series—I understand her, I can encompass her, I know her. If throughout your life, you keep on saying, Ah, but I can also do Lady Macbeth, I can also do a horror movie with Vincent Price, I can also do a James Bond movie, confusion arises. But I enjoy that confusion. All you can expect of a part is that it exercise your talents—that's what acting is all about.

PROBST: Do you read the reviews you get?

RIGG: Not immediately. I read them afterwards. A long time afterwards. I certainly don't go out and get them the next day—that colors your performance for the next three or four days. I'm talking about the lousy ones, of course. The good ones are neither here nor there. It's the bad ones which really hurt and which really tell and can affect your performance. I prefer not to be manipulated in this way. I think it's bad taste to be defensive about reviews with no knowledge. If they think you're lousy, fine, okay. But I also think it's bad taste to be a lousy reviewer with no knowledge, because you have an enormous amount of power and you are manipulating it wrongly, you're manipulating it from ignorance. I personally detest being manipulated anyway, but by an ignorant person, then I think it's wrong.

PROBST: *Time* magazine said, "Diana Rigg is a temptress of dazzling physical allure, a coquette of sportive guile, and her voice has the ring of Baccarat crystal. She is a true daughter of Eros." How do you feel about that?

RIGG: It's nice. It's better than being called lumpish and boring and dull.

PROBST: Have you ever learned anything about yourself from a review?

RIGG: No, I haven't. I've always learned more about the failures of the production. Remember, I come from an ensemble background. Unless it gives the play as a whole a good review, it means we all sink together. This is what theater is about. It's not about having a private trip of your own, it's about a total piece. If you fail, then it's as a group, as an ensemble, that you fail, even though one name may have been picked out for praise.

PROBST: Isn't everybody tied to the mast, which is led by you in this case? In the playbill your name comes first.

RIGG: Not always. Agents say it's very necessary to come first on the bill. So, in *The Misanthrope,* Alec McGowen is an actor of enormous stature and Diana Rigg is an actress who's well known on television, and maybe she sells more tickets in the theater than Alec McGowen. I'm just speaking purely practically now, I'm not having an ego trip. But his agents say, "Alec must go first." My agent says, "Diana must go first." Alec and I look at each other and say, "What the hell is all this fuss about? Why don't we alternate, just to keep our agents happy?" So, if you regard the playbills, *The New York Times,* you'll find from time to time it's Alec comes first, and then it's me comes first. And it's very droll, indeed, and doesn't mean a thing.

PROBST: It seems to me the total production rises or falls—let's say *A Doll's House* rises or falls on Liv Ullmann.

RIGG: No, it doesn't, it shouldn't. It certainly shouldn't. These days the star is the draw. We all know that, but on the other hand, that doesn't mean that the production as a whole shouldn't be entered into by everybody concerned, everybody giving their share. In *In Praise of Love,* which I saw in New York, Rex Harrison was doing a Rex Harrison which is miraculous and saves the play. But not for twenty thousand dollars guaranteed per week would I step on stage with Rex Harrison, because he is a star performer and not generous in the areas I consider necessary.

PROBST: He's not an ensemble player?

RIGG: No.

PROBST: Have you ever worked with him?

RIGG: No, I met him afterwards and I told him that I wouldn't.

PROBST: What did he tell you?

RIGG: He said, "But, I'd turn my back to the audience on the stage for you." And I said, "Yes, that would be the most manifest gesture of generosity."

Q *(question from audience)*: What do you think of the director John Dexter?

RIGG: He's no respector of people or persons. He gives me notes in front of the entire cast that could destroy me—*could,* and by the assumption that it *won't* destroy me, I grow greater. Most directors, when they're treating stars or working with stars, will draw them aside and tell them gently what they think of them. Kind of nudge them into a performance. John believes that if he has something to say to you as a leading player, then everybody else has a right to hear it as well. And I believe that. I embrace it, I receive it. I think it is for the good of the piece.

PROBST: Was "The Avengers" a challenge?

RIGG: Yes. I did enjoy doing it, very much indeed. The man I worked with, Patrick MacNee, is a delight and a dear, dear man and funny and clever and incredibly generous. I entered that series when it was a television tape success in England and then subsequently it went into film. I entered when the girl who was doing it with Patrick left. Now here was a classic situation of an actor, successful in an already acknowledged series, having to cope with somebody new. I will never forget the generosity that he showed toward me. It was wonderful.

I even enjoyed my own stunts. I did them for about the first sixteen episodes, then we got behind schedule because it began to be shown in America and we were doing two or three episodes at once. So I'd have a double for the long shots and I would come in for the close-ups. But for those first fourteen episodes, partly because I'm sort of quite physically intrepid and I really don't mind and I'll have a go at anything, I found myself doing a lot of extraordinary things which were really quite dangerous. It wasn't till afterwards that I thought, Hey, I could have broken something.

PROBST: You've said that you do not want to be categorized. Does that apply to your private life as well as to your acting life?

RIGG: Well, private is something else. I suppose I'm slightly defensive about the private-life aspect of it.

PROBST: Is the important thing not to be labeled professionally, not to be made permanent, to change, and when things are going well, it's time to leave? Is it also important privately to keep going in the face of what is successful? Must you do both?

RIGG: I don't think you have to do both, but I think you can have a perfectly good, consistent private life. There's no reason why you should constantly change. Absolutely none. I think a consistent private life benefits a professional life.

PROBST: In what way?

RIGG: It's a cell. It's a totality from which you emerge from time to time to do your work, and from which you can withdraw from time to time.

PROBST: Home base?

RIGG: Yes.

PROBST: You've been to the Royal Shakespeare Company,

you've been to the National Theatre, you've been to the Royal Academy of Dramatic Arts. But you said that that's not where you learned acting.

RIGG: I learned to act on the stage, doing it. I was lucky at the Royal Shakespeare Company, because I was a walk-on. Not only do you have the nightly discipline of walking on in a number of productions—and in my case they were star-studded productions, Charles Laughton was playing Lear, Paul Robeson was playing Othello, Laurence Olivier was playing Coriolanus—you see demonstrated nightly in front of you the real actors and actresses. During the day we had lessons in voice, movement, singing, verse speaking. This to me is the perfect combination, the perfect school. Most schools are very rarefied. You get a group of students and it's theoretical, talking about doing, instead of doing. Ultimately it has to be practiced, it's like everything else—it has to be absorbed. You're very young when you go to drama school and you tend to treat everything as gospel. You have to learn to discriminate for yourself. You can discriminate by watching performances. It's fascinating. Certain nights, Sir Laurence would be doing things certain ways and they would work, and certain nights he would be doing them certain ways and they wouldn't work. You'd be able to see for yourself the constant attempt that a very great actor made each night to make a part work. Experiments before your eyes. You realize nothing in this life is set, nothing in acting is absolutely set. Your performance is set for the critics on the first night, but you have to keep striving, and to see the greatest striving was a monumental lesson.

PROBST: What's the difference between American and English actors?

RIGG: In the history of English theater, we have a lot of classical writers. The word became extremely important. And because of the word, the voice became extremely important. American actors have had a much thinner text to work with. What has emerged is a capacity for subtext. We English don't have it. At its best, it is perfection. We English actors simply can't compete.

Q: Who would you consider some of the American great actors?

RIGG: I think the greatest is Brando. Absolutely the greatest. He can turn a piece of crap into magic just by whatever he has inside himself, whatever parallel lines he's running inside himself. He's incredible. Absolutely incredible. If you regard the British actors and actresses, we have absolutely no person who compares with him, nobody.

Q: Do American actors evoke the actual emotion, while English actors tend to simulate?

RIGG: How many of us, Oedipus, have made love to our mothers? How can you possibly apply that to an American actor playing Oedipus? It doesn't make sense, it really doesn't. Every great actor lives in emotion. But he has his own way of doing it. The Stanislavsky Method has been, I think, abused to a large extent. Never for an instant did he suggest that everybody has to follow the same course to achieve the same end, not for an instant. It is the personal method which is the essential part of this. You cannot apply The Method to a group of people. We don't have enough in common. We don't share so much. Each of us has to reach that emotion in our own personal way.

PROBST: What do you look for as an actress?

RIGG: I seek for the appetite. Somebody once told me, You must listen to your body. In order to listen to your body, you have to have a certain amount of silence around you. I have to be alone for a part of the day. Paintings mean a great deal to me, and I go towards those. I need the appetite of paintings when I'm here in New York, for the paintings which I can't see in London. Films, cinema—music not quite as much, I'm pretty ignorant of music. Walking, exercise, air. I don't have a sense of going towards the evening performance, but I do have a sense of anticipation about what is to come in the evening. I don't necessarily reserve my energies. I think that's rather questionable—definitely, for the older actors and actresses, but when you're my age, approaching middle, to give an interesting performance, my day has to be filled with something interesting apart from just the theater. You wake up, you get your coffee, and you say, Now, sniff the air. What do I want to do today? What do I need to do today? Whether it's to read, whether it's to talk to people, whether it's to see paintings, I mean, it is an indulgent life I am describing, you realize. One is very lucky to be able to do this. One can go towards absolutely anything. You must be free to go towards anything.

PROBST: Celimine in *The Misanthrope* is a twenty-year-old widow and Héloise was seventeen. At that time I believe you were thirty-two and you were playing a seventeen-year-old. How much leeway does an actress have?

RIGG: Infinite, really, if you wish. Dame Edith played Rosalind, I think, when she was fifty odd. It relies a lot, of course, upon the indulgence of the audience and a lot of good lighting and the right kind of costumes. One of the traditions in the theater, of course, is that a lot of the famous classic juvenile roles can only be played by women of mature years. This, I think, has been disproven time and time again. For my part I'm very glad that the license is accorded me to play a twenty-one-year-old on stage.

PROBST: Two plays you've been in, *Jumpers* and *Abelard and Héloise*, in both plays you were without clothes at some point. How do you feel about that?

RIGG: My background is workingclass, struggling into middle class in England. My father was more or less self-educated, self-made, and I was brought up to cover my body. I think, deep in the recesses of the mind, I was probably brought up to be slightly ashamed of my body. I don't find it easy to do what I do. People always imagine you take a vicarious pleasure in doing it. On the contrary, it's hard. It's a difficult thing to do. You feel completely naked. And cold. It's not comfortable. And there's a sort of whisper that goes through the house. You always know that there's a blimper or two out front—"blimper" is an English expression for a voyeur, somebody's who's there simply to see. If you really come down to the nitty-gritty of it all, bodies are not that important. We all share characteristics common amongst ourselves, some larger, some smaller, it's as simple as that. I got an anonymous letter written on a London telegraph form from a gentleman who said, "I don't know why you bother. My girl friend's tits are much larger than yours." So this proves my point. I wasn't out there as the perfect female body. I was simply doing what was necessary for the play.

PROBST: As I recall *Abelard and Héloise,* you and Keith Mich-
ell were the first major actors to do this. When you appear nude,
how do you prepare for that each night? Is it just matter of fact or
do you have to get geared up for it?

RIGG: You have to force yourself to do it. I used to make my
body up because otherwise you look like a piece of old cod on the
stage. Putting this body makeup on helped me. It was like another
skin. It was like another cloth. But it was always deep-breath time.
In *Jumpers,* I was always face down on the bed, and sure as hell, as
fast as I could, I used to put that dressing gown on.

PROBST: And *Abelard and Héloise?*

RIGG: That was much worse. You had to walk across the stage.

PROBST: It was a darkened stage, as I recall.

RIGG: It was very darkened. But on one occasion when we
were touring, the lighting went all to hell and we had to walk out
in blazing light.

PROBST: You kept walking?

RIGG: Oh, yes, one had to. I think I was pushed.

Q: Isn't it extremely difficult to confront your partner on the
stage in the nude?

RIGG: It isn't your partner that's the problem. It's everybody
else out there. He's in the same parlous state you're in. Which is
without a stitch on. He's as frightened and as cold as you are. One
has no curiosity about his physiognomy. I mean, I didn't. I didn't
particularly want to look at his penis and say, Wow, let's have a
look at it. For the first time, that's not the point. You're acting,
you're in a scene together, you're in a love scene together. These
are supposedly the overriding things. But back in your mind is,
What would my mother say if she could see me now?

PROBST: Do you have any feelings about women's lib?

RIGG: Yes, of course, being a woman. I think women's lib has
done an enormous amount of good. I also think they talk along the
way an enormous amount of crap. When we get into sexual
liberation, this is when I get a bit testy. Sexual liberation is a
personal, entirely personal journey. There is no dictum handed
down which will allow you, or even encourage you, to take it. You

have to take it by yourself, however hard and however difficult. There's a lot of generalities about what women should do and feel. The multiple orgasm, for example. If you don't have it these days, you're somehow lesser. It's an inversion of a situation of which we were victims before, we were victims of the nonorgasm, suddenly we are victims of not having a multiple orgasm. The sheer irrationality of that has to make you laugh a little.

PROBST: Who gives the dictum?

RIGG: Unfortunately, the women. Your own background is the only truth from which you can start. My mother taught me very little about sex. She taught me very little about sex because, I subsequently discovered, she knew very little about sex. We women are responsible for handing down to children a lot of misconceptions. Having found a certain security, however unrealistic, in a domestic situation, you possibly unconsciously hand it down to your child, without giving your child the license to ask questions, because those questions would disturb you. You haven't asked those questions of yourself, so please God don't let my child ask me these questions, I don't know the answer. I think the real ogre in women's path to liberation is what women have handed down to women. I think men are responsible for keeping women repressed in certain situations, the professions, for example. But I think, domestically, a lot of damage has been done by women themselves.

PROBST: You have spoken out very strongly against marriage. And then, lo and behold, you got married.

RIGG: The wheel turns full circle. Previously people would say, Don't knock it, you haven't tried it. Now I can say I've tried it. It's not brickbats at the man, it's a possible insufficiency in myself. It's a possible insufficiency in the actual state of marriage. I don't know. You think you ought to behave in a certain way now that you're married, and you create acts of bad faith. You begin to despise yourself and you begin to despise the state of marriage. It's a very difficult thing to talk about, obviously, because there's a lot of pain involved. And it's not anything that you'd likely shake off. Again, it's failure. And you say to yourself, I have failed. I've not failed necessarily in marriage—marriage is neither here nor there —but I've failed in a relationship. That's the most important thing.

PROBST: Do you feel that the concept of marriage is a bad idea?

RIGG: I'm not about to—and this is a differentiation between Vanessa Redgrave and myself—I'm not about to tub thump and say you should or should not. All I can say is about myself, it doesn't work.

PROBST: What is your relationship with Vanessa Redgrave now? Do you two get along?

RIGG: Yes, of course we do. We were walk-ons together. You know this business of not speaking to each other—there's a sort of theatrical cliché that if two women are in the same profession, they must necessarily be rivals. This is absolute nonsense.

PROBST: You've said you felt rivalry with her in *Taming of the Shrew*.

RIGG: I did then, of course I did, because it was a part I was dying to play. But on the other hand, I go and see Vanessa playing Rosalind and I say I could never do it that way, ever. She's brilliant. I could never touch her. It's a sense of . . . how can I describe it, common sense. A sense of realism.

Vanessa, I think, is an extraordinarily marvelous actress. She's the best romantic actress I've ever seen. The fact that she cares to, sort of, muck about in politics too much and too extremely is really her business, except that it is also affecting our business in England. It is affecting the actor's profession and the actors' union in England. At a time when we should be a united front, we're divided. This is what I criticize her for. We feel deep in our hearts we're not justified in getting paid for what we're doing, that we should be working at something much more worthwhile. This is why a lot of actors strive for respectability as well as notoriety. The two go hand in hand.

PROBST: Do you feel that the establishment doesn't accept actors?

RIGG: Of course they do, but they accept successful actors. They wouldn't accept unsuccessful actors. The establishment is very success-oriented. Or if your bloodline is extremely blue or you have a lot of money—these are the two things which count in the establishment. We have to face this fact.

PROBST: Do you feel that actors feel they don't earn an honest living just as actors? There's something guilty about it?

RIGG: Often.

PROBST: Are you one of those that feel that way?

RIGG: No, I don't feel at all guilty. I feel extremely lucky. I have my days free, I work in the evening, and I get paid a more than living wage. How lucky can you get?

PROBST: What does one do when one is not acting?

RIGG: Well, it's extremely hard. Extremely hard.

PROBST: Take to drink?

RIGG: No, they don't. Actors are improvisers. In my out-of-work days, which, thank God, are long gone—I hope, in the future, long gone—but I did all sorts of things. I served coffee in a coffee bar. I was a model. I was a telephonist. I worked in a blood bank. I've sold things. You name it, we can do it.

PROBST: You were a waitress in a Greek sailors' bar?

RIGG: They all thought I was a prostitute. This was in a small street in London. I was a student working at the Royal Academy during the day and working for six hours for a pittance at night. It was at a time when the prostitutes were still walking the streets of London. They used to go rest their feet in this particular bar. These girls thought that possibly I was horning in on their trade. They'd kick me under the table if I was serving them coffee.

PROBST: A number of persons refer to you as the thinking man's sex symbol. Are you happy with that or displeased?

RIGG: Well, of course you're happy because it means that people find you attractive and everybody wants to be found attractive. On the other hand, it's not something I promote consciously. The Hollywood line of a great deal of pizzazz with your body siliconed and your face structured and the teeth capped—I can't be bothered to do that, quite honestly. When I go on stage, I try as hard as possible to be as perfect as possible. But in my own life I haven't the patience. I don't think I've got that self-interest, really. They must find me as they find me.

PROBST: Have you ever seen yourself as failing?

RIGG: I consider the series "Diana" was a failure. I was going to accept the plaudits if it was a success, so I stand to accept the rotten tomatoes.

PROBST: Why did you fail?

RIGG: I was ignorant of that kind of television. I don't mean the sheer technicality of it. I can learn sixty pages of dialogue a week. I can hit my marks on the floor. I can get my laugh from the audience. But I discovered something about myself which is a limitation. I'm not a comedienne in the sense that I rise to an occasion and make anything funny. I need a good text and good director. In other words, I need other people. I'm not a solo performer. This was a series built around a solo performer. It was named "Diana." I couldn't carry it.

PROBST: Now that you've learned about the solo system in Hollywood, will you try it again?

RIGG: No. I don't think I could and I don't think I would because I believe in, very much, the ensemble business of acting. The star system in America is unfortunate because you have in America some of the best character actors and actresses in the world. They are the prop and support of any good production. You come on and see a small part played brilliantly and it is a joy. And that small part played brilliantly becomes part of the whole where everybody is perfectly cast. The total evening is the play and the way the people interacted. I'm not interested in pursuing the solo number. I did it. I didn't do it out of a sense of, Let's put Diana Rigg on the map. I did it in a sense of, Let's see how she gets on. Well, I found out. Lousy. So we won't do that again. I couldn't. I need other people very much. My preference is theater, and has always been theater and people.

PROBST: You were part of an ensemble on television in a special, "The House of Brede."

RIGG: I loved doing it. The first school I went to was a convent and then I was at a Quaker school.

PROBST: Do you feel religious?

RIGG: I've fought religion all my life. I find it very hard to accept a Deity, the inconsistencies of the Deity, and the injustice of Deity. But at the same time, man needs something greater than himself to believe in. It's the human spirit I believe in. That is my Deity.

But I nevertheless still go to church. Church and theater are very close. Theater began in church. Possibly as a pilgrimage back to the roots, I keep going back to church. I have a number of friends who are clergymen because they're well informed, they're interesting—they're also wonderfully argumentative people.

I go into churches sometimes because they're architecturally very beautiful. I go into churches sometimes because I know there's a choir practice going on there and it's good to listen to this sound which the church has perfected—voices in unison, I think, is one of the most wonderful sounds in the world.

4

GEORGE C. SCOTT:

I've Never Wanted to Be the Last Guest at the Goddamn Banquet

PROBST: People keep writing about you as the meanest Richard III ever.

SCOTT: I like to think of it as effective.

PROBST: You started out as a star. Would you have accepted a role in *Richard III* as anything other than Richard? Did you decide you had to be a star from the beginning?

SCOTT: No, no. I just wanted the part, that's all.

PROBST: You wanted the star part.

SCOTT: I wanted that particular part. I knew the part was right for me. I can't explain it to you any other way. It's just something you feel. You just feel it. You say, It clicks like a safe lock clicks, and you say, That's right.

PROBST: You came into New York—you had been out in stock—to get the lead role, to get the role in *Richard III*. Seems like a fairy tale when one reads about it. How did you manage it?

SCOTT: I went to read. I read fairly well, I thought. Stuart Vaughn called me back for a second reading. I read very badly. I was very upset and I did something I had never done before or since—I called him on the phone and said, "Could I come and read the third time?" He said, "Why? I think I've seen everything. There's not really any point in it." I said, "Please let me." So he said, "All right." I stayed up that night and I learned two soliloquies by heart and I went in that following day and read, performed rather, and I got the part. It was the biggest break I ever had . . . ever have had, I suppose. But I've always been a rather shy person and never . . . I was never a good office actor. There are a lot of great office actors.

PROBST: What's an office actor?

SCOTT: Guys who come on like gangbusters and flirt with the secretary and snow the producer and so forth. I was never that kind of person and I was never a great reader, particularly. But I felt strongly about it, and as luck would have it, it worked out, because I probably would literally have died off a long time ago.

PROBST: You say you're a shy person, but Richard III is a brutal, horrible fellow with enormous bloodthirstiness. . . . Did you feel all that as Richard III?

SCOTT: No, I don't work like that.

PROBST: How do you work?

SCOTT: I'm an extremely cold actor. I don't feel that there's any necessity to have any kind of affinity for any part that you play except perhaps an intellectual affinity. You must be able to understand why you're trying to do it and you must be able to try to communicate it. But as far as feeling what any character that I've ever played feels, I consider that is a convoluted way to approach a part. Many, many people disagree with me.

PROBST: How do you intellectualize a part? Patton had a high-pitched voice and when he got excited he got even more high-pitched, yet when you played Patton you played gravelly George Scott. Who's up on that screen? Is it Patton or Scott?

SCOTT: I think it's a combination of the two, but the point is to minimize one's own personality as much as possible and maximize the character's personality.

PROBST: But he had a high-pitched voice and you don't have a high-pitched voice.

SCOTT: No. I deliberately didn't. He spoke up here like this [Scott raises voice higher and higher] and he had a kind of an east Virginia accent and the higher he got the madder he got and the madder he got the higher he got. I said to myself, People are going to be so affected by the voice, they're not going to be able to listen to what he's saying or . . . it's going to get in the way, so I said, Drop it, don't do it. Now perhaps a more daring actor would have decided to go that route. It would have been an interesting thing to do, but I was frightened to death about that voice, that vocal quality interfering with the essence of the character, so I didn't do it. It's a matter of choice, you know.

PROBST: Do you feel that you have to go with whatever you think is right, regardless of how risky it is?

SCOTT: I think anything that gets in the way of illumination and communication must necessarily be some kind of hang-up and a handicap. There are so many other handicaps, particularly in film. . . . It's such a mercilessly technological medium, the actor has very little chance, anyway, to start with. He's more or less at the mercy of this enormous machination that's going on all the time around you. So, I try to simplify. Emerson says, Simplify, and I think that's a good way to approach acting. Simplemindedness, I hope not, but simplification, yes.

PROBST: In 1973, in *The New York Times,* you said that within the next year you plan to abandon acting forever and go on to writing and directing film.

SCOTT: I certainly did. I most assuredly did. I still plan to abandon acting—unfortunately I went broke, again, so here I am.

PROBST: Why do you want to abandon acting?

SCOTT: I'm tired of it. I think it's tired of me. You reach a certain point in your life where you'd rather do something else. I think people get tired of you, too. I've never wanted to hang around and be the last guest at the goddamn banquet. So, I thought I'd try to mosey out while I still have a chance. But listen, I'll make it out, one way or the other.

PROBST: Were there complications in directing your wife [Trish Van DeVere] in *All God's Chillun Got Wings?*

SCOTT: Yes. The main problem, of course, is that you can't leave the work at the work place and go home and talk to your wife about the stupid actresses you have to work with during the day. On the other hand, she can't go home and talk about the dummy director, either. It's a problem, but aside from that, if you can maintain some sort of equilibrium on it, it has many benefits.

If you get an idea at three o'clock in the morning, you can wake each other up and talk about it, which is nice, too.

PROBST: Does that set up problems with the other actors?

SCOTT: I hope not. I think that if you approach it in a very honest and open manner and you have the respect for your spouse and she for you, then the other actors ostensibly realize that the respect is due everyone, and it does not get in the way. I've never had that problem, happily.

PROBST: You intellectualize acting and directing, and yet you're known for the rages you get into on camera and off camera and the "terrible fire within you." . . .

SCOTT: It's totally contrived.

PROBST: I don't believe that, you don't either. Awhile back, Zero Mostel said, "If you have a bellyache, use it." Is that what you're saying, in effect, If you're enraged or want to break out —use it?

SCOTT: I think, again, nothing is of any value in this profession unless it is broadcast. In other words, unless it goes from a transmitter to a receiver. If it doesn't get to the receiver, it's pointless, useless, and wasteful. Anything that is transmittable and gets there is valuable. Otherwise you're not doing what you're being paid for. Does that make any sense?

PROBST: Yes. You're saying the message has got to be delivered and received or it's nothing. But the question is, How does one deliver. Do you deliver by exploding?

SCOTT: No. You deliver by thinking a lot about how to make it as explosive as possible and how to make it as legitimately explosive as possible, and the other twenty-seven emotions— tenderness, clarity, compassion. There are all sorts of things that one is called upon to elicit from the audience.

PROBST: Can you be in control about being *out* of control?

SCOTT: You must be in control about being out of control. There's nothing more contemptible than an actor who's out of control. It's like being in a car with a drunk driver and no brakes. It's a frightening experience. I've played with actors who are that way, and I don't want to do it again. I don't consider myself that kind of actor, ever.

PROBST: A lot of people say it's difficult to work with you on stage. Maureen Stapleton, in *Plaza Suite,* said, "I'm so frightened of George, I don't know what to do," to which Mike Nichols replied, "My dear, the whole world is frightened of George C. Scott."

SCOTT: Well, I have to call your attention ... Maureen is frightened of flying, she's frightened of riding in cars, frightened of lawn mowers—it's not particularly me. She's the kind of actress who will come to the theater eight times a week and get in the wings and her heart will palpitate, she'll sweat, she will become faint, she will say, "I can't go on tonight." And you'll say, "It's all right, honey, you'll be all right." Now you expect that she will barely make it, right? She hits the stage and it's gangbusters, like Gibraltar, for two hours and fifteen minutes. She comes off and, "I don't know how I made it." It's just incredible. The same thing over and over and over. That's a personality. It works so magnificently for her, you can't possibly fault it. Of course, everybody *else* is in a panic, but not Maureen.

PROBST: Are you saying she acts out of fear?

SCOTT: I think so. I'm not saying that she contrives this at all. I think it's legitimate suffering. It's just that once she hits the stage, some sort of incredible metamorphosis takes place, and she's off and running. But she suffers dreadfully from it. There's no question about it.

PROBST: You went to the University of Missouri, one of the better journalism schools in the country, and you later said that you didn't continue in journalism because you were too shy to ask difficult questions. You went into acting because you were able to escape from your personality into something else. Would you say you act not out of fear but as a way to get out of yourself?

SCOTT: Yes, it's always been a salvation for me, in a certain way. Of course, it produces other psychological problems, too, which are not as easy to overcome. But acting has served me well. It has allowed me to escape from a personality that I was never particularly fond of at all. But we're all trapped in these capsules, you know. There's not much we can do about it. The only release is death.

PROBST: Are they both the real George Scott? The actor and the nonactor?

SCOTT: I suppose so. In some regard, the representational Scott is probably more real than the supposedly real one, who's more phony . . . I'll go through that again for you.

PROBST: They're both part of a total person. . . . Many of the stories talk about your temper. And yet people who work with you tell me that you're called the big pussycat. Do you know that's a nickname for you around certain places?

SCOTT: Yes. Miss Stapleton coined that. I don't think among my peers I have an ugly reputation at all. I may have had some altercations with a few comrades from time to time, but nothing of any great consequence, I don't think. I certainly bear no grudges toward anyone.

PROBST: One of the things that your biographers don't agree with is how many times your nose has been broken.

SCOTT: Five times.

PROBST: On two occasions or five occasions?

SCOTT: On five separate occasions, and operated on once, to try to correct some of the deviation.

PROBST: But these were all excesses?

SCOTT: It was a long time ago. A long time ago.

PROBST: But it is five separate occasions?

SCOTT: I'm afraid so, yes.

PROBST: Four Academy Award nominations and five . . .

SCOTT: It could go either way.

PROBST: Do you feel compelled to act?

SCOTT: No one puts a gun to your head and says, Act. You do it out of some necessity, some need, some desire, some drive, and you're stuck with it if you don't smarten up and do something else. Some of us can't. Some of us can't make a living doing anything else, we're not fit for anything else. I tried to get out of acting many times, I couldn't do anything else.

PROBST: You're still trying.

SCOTT: I'm going to make it.

PROBST: Brando said that actors are treated as household pets, especially in Hollywood.

SCOTT: I think there's no question about that. They're idolized and patronized and vilified, all in the same breath. People look at you as though you really should go to work and do something respectable. But that's nothing new. Actors . . . I'm very fond of saying that we're just one cut above charlatans and mountebanks. We've always been classified as just a tad above pickpockets, you know. But people love you very much and resent you a great deal at the same time. It's strange. They envy you and despise you at the same time. The desire to have one's autograph or to have a piece of one's clothing ripped off, if necessary, is a frightening thing. Why people do that, I don't know. They do it to other figures, but actors get it an awful lot. We've come to expect it, I suppose.

PROBST: Do you see yourself as a public symbol of anything?

SCOTT: I sincerely hope not.

PROBST: You've become in a sense a symbol against the Oscar statuette. How did that come about?

SCOTT: Symbolism, that's a very good word. You're right.

PROBST: When you were nominated for the Oscar, you told them you didn't want one. You said it was a beauty contest conducted in a slaughterhouse.

SCOTT: I was nominated in '59 or '60 for a picture called *Anatomy of a Murder,* that was the first time. And I would like very much to have won. At any rate, I didn't like what happened to me during that period between the time I was nominated and between the time I didn't win. Some kind of ugly change came over me. I got very aggrandizing and I got very desirous of obtaining that little thing. And it was a very good thing that I didn't win. I didn't like what happened to me. I said, I'm never going to allow myself to go through that again because it was agony, you're sitting around waiting and sweating. I said, If the chance or opportunity ever comes to me again, I'm going to decline it—I'm not going to say to myself, All that bullshit. Which is what I did. I was nominated the following year for *The Hustler,* and declined. They refused to allow me to decline. Ten years later, I was nominated for *Patton,* declined again on exactly the same grounds, and they once again refused to allow me to decline, and then they gave me the award—posthumously, so to speak. And I was again nominated for *The Hospital* and didn't even bother to decline that time. I figured it all had become so absurd by this time that I just decided to not say anything because whatever you say....

PROBST: Where is that Oscar?

SCOTT: I assume it's back in the warehouse at the Academy.

PROBST: You've just completed the role of Louis Nizer for television? How do you approach it?

SCOTT: I've never met Nizer. I decided not to. I don't resemble him at all, physically. So, I thought, well, I'll just approach this almost as though he were no longer with us. I hope he doesn't resent that if he's listening. So I didn't try to imitate his mannerisms or anything. I simply approached him as an obviously extremely intelligent lawyer and a man who knew what he was about and a man who was willing also to risk.

PROBST: How different is it for an actor, films from stage?

SCOTT: I think you take a great deal of help from a director in the theater. Much less so in films. In films, the actor must be left relatively alone. In the theater, there's the luxury of time, the luxury of rehearsal, the luxury of continuity—and, of course, the master luxury of working with a live audience.

PROBST: When you turn around and become a director, do you try to make the actors feel at ease and supported or do you act out a scene for an actor?

SCOTT: I try not to. I'm accused of acting out things for people, and I try not to. Sometimes that's the most efficient way if it works. You try anything, anything in the world you can do to get a point across or to help an actor over a rough spot. Basically, I try to follow the leadership of a man who, I think, is one of the fine stage directors of our time, Mike Nichols, who creates an atmosphere for actors to work that is as comfortable and as fluid as possible. That's the kind of person I would like to emulate.

PROBST: Have you worked with an acting coach?

SCOTT: No, I never have, no. I don't know what they can tell me about acting that I don't know.

PROBST: Where did you learn about acting?

SCOTT: By acting in front of people. When I was a child, I

always went to films. I had no desire to be an actor, though, you see. I never realized I wanted to be an actor till I was twenty-one years old. I realized I wouldn't be a journalist, so I had to find something to do quick. There I was in college on a GI bill, taking the government's money—that ninety dollars a month they gave me—and I had to find something to do, so I just literally went into the theater. I found it extremely attractive and I found that it was a release for me.

PROBST: On your last film, *The Savage Is Loose*, you produced it, you acted in it, you directed it, and then you distributed it.

SCOTT: I financed it and distributed it, yes.

PROBST: Which seems to be bucking the system at every level.

SCOTT: Well, if you care enough about something, that you don't want it spoiled—my experience has been that things do get spoiled, twisted, perverted along the way—you try to see to it that it gets to the public in the manner, in the form, that you want it. There's only one way to do that, and that's maintain total control over the project from start to finish.

PROBST: How did it work out?

SCOTT: That's why I'm back working. We lost a lot of money on it. My investors made eighty-five percent of their money back, and they'll get the rest of it back. I don't think they're going to make a killing off it, let me tell you, but the picture is still mine and it is marketable and it still will be marketable for a number of years to come and I intend to market it.

Q *(question from audience)*: Do you have cutting rights and do you have a movie doctor go over it other than yourself?

SCOTT: If you go to a studio to get financing, they own the picture. Now you can put down as many words as you want to, on as many contract pages, but there's always that one little page somewhere that says, I'm sorry, Charlie, it's ours and not yours, because it's our money and not yours. If you do a picture yourself and finance it yourself and go to a distributor, then they say, "Well I'm sorry, pally, we're doing all the work, we're taking thirty-three percent on the distribution fee, and it's our picture, we'll cut it if we want to. We'll advertise it the way we want to advertise. With *The Savage Is Loose*, I refused to allow that to happen. I still refuse to allow it to happen. For good or bad, it's still my picture and it's going to be my picture for the next twenty years. Nobody's going to see it, maybe, but it's still mine.

PROBST: Your most recent appearance in film is in *The Hindenburg*. Why this series of pictures about enormous disasters?

SCOTT: The motion picture business is ruled by what is marketable and what is not marketable.

PROBST: Is there something about these times that makes that type of picture marketable?

SCOTT: I don't know. I'm not a sociologist. People have said that that's true. *Poseidon* was the beginning of that trend. If you'll recall a few years ago, we had the *Easy Rider* syndrome. Everybody was going to make a five-hundred-thousand-dollar picture and make fifty million dollars off of it. Well, we went through about twenty-five imitation *Easy Rider*'s and they all went in the big swirler because they were all lousy pictures. Now they got out of that because they realized—not any other reason—that they couldn't make five-hundred-thousand-dollar pictures that made five million dollars. That's all. If they could, believe me, they'd still be doing it, with a vengeance. So they had to go to something else. They go in trends. God knows what the next trend will be.

PROBST: You seem to feel that making movies is boring, that they're manipulated for the market, and yet you've made twenty-one movies.

SCOTT: Is it that many? It's very boring for actors. It's not boring for technical people, they're all extremely efficient, earn every dime they're paid, work very hard. It's not boring for directors or producers or producers' girl friends. It's very, very boring for actors. You work seventeen seconds and you wait two hours and you work nineteen seconds and you wait two and a half hours and you go home. You come back the next day and you do the same thing for twelve weeks. No wonder you either become an alcoholic or a great chess player. One or the other.

PROBST: Where do you fit in that?

SCOTT: Right around in there.

PROBST: You also bake your own bread besides playing chess.

SCOTT: Yes, I do.

PROBST: And play baseball.

SCOTT: I used to play baseball. I'm too old for that. I play golf.

Q: Of the twenty-one movies, which is best?

SCOTT: Well, the one I like more than any is *Dr. Strangelove.* It was a beginning, it was an original piece of its time. It set a very high mark to shoot at, I think, in black comedy. And it has rarely been met since that time. It was done by Kubrick, who's a genius, and done very well, and I liked what I did in it, probably more than any other film part I've ever done.

Q: I understand that Kubrick changed the last scene of *Dr. Strangelove.* Were you annoyed by that?

SCOTT: Yes, I thought it was a dreadful mistake and said so. I still think it's a mistake. But there were certain political and social happenings that occurred at that time, for instance, the assassination of John F. Kennedy. We had a pie fight at the end of the picture. We threw a thousand pies a day for a week, and one of the lines I had, when Peter Sellers was struck with a pie, was, "Gentlemen, our beloved President has been struck down in the prime of life by a pie." Well, obviously nobody was going to allow that to stay in. They got to going to work on the whole pie fight, and ultimately Stanley cut the entire sequence out. He has always thought that he did right and I've always thought he did wrong. But, you know, that's what makes baseball.

PROBST: How much effect do critics have on the work you do?

SCOTT: Well, the stage, of course, is difficult. They can hurt a play. A commercial vehicle is more or less dependent upon reasonably good notices, what, as you know, we call a money review. That, again, is the restriction of the economic situation of the Broadway theater. Films can survive—and do survive—willy-nilly of strong critical disapproval. It's what the people want to see. The people themselves don't know what they want to see. And that's the way it should be, I think.

Q: Is there a problem of getting behind the character and finding it embarrassing to present that character?

SCOTT: There are problems that you do face, things that you don't want to be associated with. Perhaps weaknesses in yourself that you would not want to be misconstrued as being reflected to the general public even through the device of a character. Other aberrations or drawbacks or hang-ups or whatever. Again, I think, to approach acting as subjective leads to that kind of thing more and more. If you continue to thrust yourself as the paramount instrument into a role, you're going to be damaged in that way. You're going to be hurt and you're going to have to continually face this crisis of personal evaluation and identification if you are—as I claim to be, at least for my own purposes—more of a technical actor. I already get a wonderful cop-out up front, see, I don't have to deal with that, I delude myself. It's worked rather well for me.

PROBST: Have you ever suffered as a result of playing a role?

SCOTT: I have repeatedly suffered, overall. But one particular thing brings to my mind *The Andersonville Trial,* which I did on Broadway fifteen years ago. I was speaking to my wife about it the other day. We were talking about how damaging playing a character can be. I don't know if any of you remember the play or not. I directed it for television. It won an Emmy, I'm happy to say. The character was one of a man who's extremely righteous, not self-righteous, but on the side of right, a moral man who had to prosecute an immoral man who deserved prosecution and hanging, which is what he got. At the end of the evening the weight of empathy and compassion for the poor man who was being prosecuted was so preponderant that everyone on the side of right was despised literally. When the curtain went up, you could feel waves of hatred coming at you across the footlights. It began to get on my nerves after a while. It was very difficult. I recall suffering badly from it. José Ferrer was the director and he wrote me a wonderful letter one time, because he could see that I was undergoing a considerable amount of strain because of this. He said, You must continue to do what you're doing because you're doing it very well and you must not allow this feeling, this hatred, to stop the kind of work you're doing. I never forgot it and I never conquered it either, never. It was agony every night to go on the stage, literally agony.

Q: How do you decide which roles to work in?

SCOTT: You do some parts because you need the money, or

you think you've had four flops in a row and you'd like to have a hit, or maybe you'd like to work with somebody whom you respect. There are a lot of reasons. I fancy that I have tried to pick roles because I thought they were decent, distinctive, and nonrepetitive. Now I'm not saying that you can always hew to that monastic line, but you try to. Maybe you're successful fifty percent of the time.

Q: Would you do a television series again?

SCOTT: To try to do a weekly television series is madness. Time and money, those are the gods of television.

PROBST: You X out television and you X out movies and you leave the stage as a place for an actor to work best.

SCOTT: Well, sure. The stage is the actor's medium. Television is not and neither is film. It's as simple as that. The actor has a responsibility. The actor is reasonably in control for a specified period of time. His responsibility lies to the character, to the playwright, to the audience, and lastly to the director for whom he's worked. But it is his responsibility to execute at a given time, for a specified length of time, to the utmost of his ability. Now he has that ability going for him, and at the same time it's difficult. He has no other aids. He must rely upon himself and his colleagues. It's much more challenging.

Q: What are your criteria for a successful role?

SCOTT: I honestly believe that if you can pick the role, execute it for a specific period of time, live with it, get into the fiber of it, you can say to yourself afterwards, I did it quite well. I did seventy-five percent of what I wanted to do, forty percent here, fifty percent there, and I'm satisfied, I feel rewarded. Then you've done a great job, there's no question about that. Now maybe you didn't make a lot of money, maybe you'd made a lot of money, it doesn't really matter that much. To me, the paramount criterion is whether it gave you the satisfaction you expected and hoped for in the first place.

Q: Did you have any inkling that *The Day of the Dolphin* would turn out to be a disaster?

SCOTT: I must say I had some inkling, yes.

Q: Is Mike Nichols a better stage director than film director?

SCOTT: I've had better luck with him. I've only made one film—*Day of the Dolphin*—for him and I've done three plays with him, so I would have to say, Yes, I think he's an infinitely better stage director.

Q: How can so many talented people produce a not-very-good play?

SCOTT: It's one of the mysteries and mystiques of the theater. There's no question about it. People have been doing it for hundreds of years. Not to the extent that the economic reaction is so quick as it is today, but you've heard the old saw, "Nobody sets out to make a bad play or a bad movie," and that's certainly true. People believe in what they're doing. They try desperately to make it work. They work very, very hard, and it either fails or it doesn't. If they had the answer to that, somebody would retire along with me.

Q: Is your son going into acting? Would you be upset if he does?

SCOTT: Yes. I've discouraged all my children. I have six children and I've tried to discourage all of them from going into acting. I don't think Matthew has that problem. He's much too fond of traveling around France and living the good life. I don't know what he's going to do. He's an extremely bright young man and a dear young man and I hope will find some way to become gainfully employed in not too long. My youngest daughter, Devin, has—against my strong remonstrations—become an actress on a television series, which I hope sincerely fails. It's a thing called "We'll Get By," on CBS. She loves it very much. She intends to pursue it. I intend to keep her in college as long as I can. And that's the way the battle goes.

Q: Why don't you want your children to go into acting?

SCOTT: I believe it's a ... it can be a very damaging life. Psychologically, it can be a difficult life. I don't think it's a life that's terribly conducive to a strong, constructive home environment. It's not only my personal life but the lives of my colleagues over the years. I don't blame acting for it entirely, but it's the milieu of acting. I would just much rather that they would try to go into some other field. Of course, everything is risky and can be damaging, but this seems to be a little more frenetic, a little more psychologically damaging. I'm sorry I feel that way. I wish I didn't, but I do.

Q: The motion picture industry has been pretty good to you financially.

SCOTT: Certainly has.

Q: And yet you're very antagonistic toward the industry. Isn't that biting the hand that feeds you?

SCOTT: Well, I think that's a very fair question. I've never thought that I belonged to the motion picture industry. I never started out to be a member of the motion picture industry. Had I done so, I would have been an agent or a producer or someone of that nature. I would have worked my way into a studio hierarchy and perhaps, God knows, perhaps someday been the head of a studio. I've always thought what I did was to be an actor and that I was worthy in that regard and that regard only. If you have respect for your profession, then you must have the right to criticize any and all things that you feel are corrupt, immoral, or contemptible about it. That's the way I've approached it. I have said repeatedly, just as you've said, that this has been an extremely good profession to me economically. I've never denied it. It would be a lie to deny it. However, I still reserve the right to call it what I believe it to be and will continue to do so.

5

DUSTIN HOFFMAN:

Go with What Smells Right

PROBST: Why weren't you allowed in The Actors Studio?

HOFFMAN: I took classes with Lee Strasberg but I could never get in the Studio. I used to try out. I tried out five times but I never passed the preliminary audition.

PROBST: What did they say you lacked?

HOFFMAN: They don't tell you. You just got a postcard with a checkmark.

PROBST: If you failed five times auditioning for the Studio, how did you come to take lessons from Lee Strasberg?

HOFFMAN: I was studying with him—he had private classes at Carnegie Hall, where he made his money. The Studio—the beauty of it was that you could study with him, and not pay, and also be one of the elite.

PROBST: The first thing I recall you in was a play called *Eh!* by Henry Livings, which Alan Arkin directed. You were a strange night watchman in a boiler factory. . . .

HOFFMAN: Not strange.

PROBST: Very strange.

HOFFMAN: Yes, very strange.

PROBST: You were unhinged. Everyone who saw you that night knew he had seen something special. . . . What was it like to direct *All Over Town?*

HOFFMAN: This play is the first Broadway or Off-Broadway play I've ever directed. I was with it constantly till it opened. As a director I did everything I could to make it live.

PROBST: Do you act out, do you say what you want people to do?

HOFFMAN: Sometimes. Both. Everything, everything, try everything. The point is if you do see it in your head, the idea is to find a way to get that across. Certain actors like you to act it out. Others are more threatened if you do, so you have to find other ways. When I would act it out, because until I was a director I was an actor, you begin to see the way the actor is performing the role. You begin to act it the way they act, the way you think they're painting it. I hate it when a director starts to act for you the way *they* would act it. It seems to be all right if you just extend them in the direction they're going. It's not any different from being a parent, I guess, in the best sense of the word. There's a way of guiding children so that they develop into themselves.

PROBST: Is there a sequel to any of your movies?

HOFFMAN: I always die in the pictures that I make.

PROBST: Is that you on the screen in *Lenny,* or is that Lenny Bruce?

HOFFMAN: Well, it's me. It looks like me up there. I think it's me.

PROBST: Who is on the screen if that's Dustin Hoffman?

HOFFMAN: It's always me on screen if I do a role. You just can't divorce yourself from it, nor do I want to. What you do is a distortion always, in the sense that art is a distortion. If you say, Is that Truffaut in *Day for Night?*, yes, that's Truffaut, but it's also a distortion, it's a subjective feeling he wants to present as a director. What you see on the screen, let's say, in Lenny Bruce, is simply myself playing this role as I learned to see it over a period of little less than a year, given the material I was given, arguing with certain aspects of it, having to compromise in certain ways. It is a collaborative business, an art form. You give and take with the director, writer, etc. Also, it's a point of view I felt strongly about. It's, I'm sure, a flawed piece of work. It is not a documentary. It is certainly not Lenny Bruce. It is me doing a certain feeling I have about him, as I learned him or studied what I could.

PROBST: Are you satisfied with it as it is now?

HOFFMAN: I never have been satisfied with any work I've

done. I've never done a piece of work of film that has not been somehow disappointing—I wanted it to be more and hoped it would be more. I do like to think that that is not a normal way of feeling. I'm not likening my work to great works of art, certainly, but I do ask myself this question . . . Am I being fair with myself? I do wonder if you were to ask Beethoven—and as I say, I'm not likening myself to these people, but it's a good example to use great geniuses as we know them—what he thinks of his symphonies, or if you ask Tolstoy what he thinks of *War and Peace,* if they were alive and sitting here, I'm sure they would have quite different feelings.

PROBST: Is the version of Lenny Bruce more idealized than what you had found to be the real man?

HOFFMAN: I think perhaps it is. I know there's a lot of controversy about it and I find myself defensive about it. I do not think the film is a dishonest piece of work, nor do I feel it was a whitewash or exploitive. I feel there are flaws in it. One doesn't get to know enough about this man. What is shown, I think, is valid and accurate. I defy anyone to tell me that he was not a lovely man, that there was not a lovely, lovely side to this man. You can hear all you want that he was a prick and that he was mean, that he was this and that. Naturally, if you talk to fifty people, you'll hear different things, as I would about myself or any of us. The common denominator was that this man had, somehow, a very warm effect on his personal friends. I talked to fifty or sixty people that were closely related to him. He had a great effect on people. That's not to say he didn't waste himself in certain ways. The people who were his friends were people I responded to. I liked those people.

However, I do begin to feel it's all irrelevant. If you want the facts, don't go see a movie. You're not ever going to get the facts from art. It's not the purpose of art. Art is to convey a view of life as the artist sees it. It's subjective, it's to convey feelings. This is, to me, the beauty of Fellini. . . . I don't think anyone is saying for one second that *Amarcord* is Fellini's childhood. They are saying, That's Fellini's childhood as he remembers it. And he's saying, I distort it, I remember these great voluminous bosoms. They probably were grapefruits, not watermelons. But he remembers them as this. Yet the thing I feel defensive about *Lenny* is the attack it gets from the pseudohip cult which says, Man, that's not the way it was, baby. I don't think they're being quite honest. I feel they're attacking from behind a screen. I'm reminded of Gertrude Stein's portrait done by Picasso, when her lover, Alice B. Toklas, ran up to Picasso and said, "That doesn't look like Gertrude," and Picasso says, "You're right, but it will." And that's all I can say about *Lenny*. . . . There are many things in it I would change as I would change anything. . . .

PROBST: Give us a couple.

HOFFMAN: I knew that we did many routines that aren't in the film. I would have left the routines Lenny does intact. The important thing is to get forth a certain verve, a certain spontaneity. If you ask Lenny Bruce to repeat his routines verbatim twenty times for the camera over long shot, medium shot, and close shot, you lose something. No comedian can sustain at that kind of thing. If I were to do it again as director, hypothetically speaking, I think it would be best to give the framework of the routine, and within it to riff and not be literal.

PROBST: You have said it was the hardest picture you ever made.

HOFFMAN: Yes, it is, so far, it's the toughest. It had the greatest pressure. I was playing, for the first time, a character who had been a real person, who had been dead only eight years.

PROBST: Did the family, the wife, the mother, the daughter, did they curtail, censor, limit, frame the picture?

HOFFMAN: No, not at all. There was an amusing thing . . . I don't think it's bad taste to say it. . . . Honey, the ex-wife, admitted certain lesbian relationships that she knew might be in the film, and she simply said in her contract, I never went to bed with any dogs. So it's in her contract that the girl that she sleeps with is attractive. I thought that was sweet. That's the only curtailment.

PROBST: How was it working with Valerie Perrine?

HOFFMAN: I like her. She's very much as she comes across on screen. She's just a kind of crazy girl. She's been through a lot. She's about thirty and she started out . . . I think she grew up in a kind of upper-middle-class background with Barry Goldwater's daughter—who visited on the set—and then she went the way of, I think, Haight-Ashbury for a while and to Europe and back, wound up as a stripper in Las Vegas. It was uncanny of Bob Fosse to pick her to play the part. When you meet Honey, you see this wonderful textual similarity between Valerie and Honey.

PROBST: Why did he pick you to play Lenny Bruce?

HOFFMAN: I don't know. He had seen me in the part from the beginning, as he told me. I'd never been a fan because I never had the money to go to nightclubs then.

PROBST: You couldn't go to the Crescendo on the Strip?

HOFFMAN: I never had money, I was working tables myself. The interesting thing is, I've gotten phone calls from actors which made me feel good, but my best reviews came from good friends and the family, as opposed to what someone like Pauline Kael would say ... oh, Christ, she's the authority. It's disturbing, sometimes you meet these people and you wonder why you ever feared them.

PROBST: How was it working with Bob Fosse?

HOFFMAN: Fosse's a very fair man. He's a very hardworking director, and there's some things he doesn't tolerate. He drives himself to death, literally. He doesn't tolerate it when a person doesn't do his job. One guy used to sit there sleeping all day, and it killed Fosse. But this is a fact of life. I remember once talking to a surgeon and saying, "Boy, you don't know what it's like to be in the movies. So many people are incompetent. You work with producers and you work with people on a crew and you work with actors who all don't give a fuck and who just walk through it. You're trying to do good work. You know you have that one day to shoot a scene and people aren't working hard enough." I said, "You don't face that. You're a surgeon. You're in the operating room." He said, "You don't know what it is in the operating room." And you realize ... with Nixon, my God, why wasn't he protected by brighter people? I mean, it's constant. The surgeon says, Don't you think I want my own people? The director winds up casting the same people. The director winds up using this person on makeup, this person on costume, this person as the production manager. The ones that work hard, that's all you want.

Not only someone that's gifted but someone that works hard. A surgeon wants his anesthetist, he wants his head nurse. . . . Patients can be lost because of faulty anesthesia. This guy shows me: "I don't even use the tools at the hospital." He goes into his locker and brings his own scalpel because he doesn't trust the instruments at the hospital.

PROBST: Is it true that you got only twenty thousand dollars for *The Graduate?*

HOFFMAN: Seventeen thousand. It was the best business deal I ever made in my life, because before I screen-tested they had said to my agent that all the actors had agreed to sign contracts to do six pictures. I refused to do this, and my agent said, You're gonna blow it. I said, I don't care, I've been fired in the past from Off-Broadway and I know myself as an actor. If they tell me to make a movie I don't want to make, I'll go crazy. So, I said, Tell them I'll work for nothing, but I want to be free afterwards. No one had any idea what it was going to be. Even after the film was made they had no idea. They did not know until they showed it to a general audience at a preview. We never saw any rushes.

PROBST: You did an interview some years back in which you said you didn't know what to think about a thing until your analyst told you?

HOFFMAN: That was not right. That was the first interview I ever gave in my life. I was Off-Broadway in *Eh!* I'll never forget it because it taught me my first lesson with interviewers, how many interviewers come in preframed. They've already decided what you are. I was your average Off-Broadway, Greenwich Village beatnik, hippie, bohemian, whippy actor. I had just Beacon-waxed my floor and she came in, smelled, and says, "You been smoking pot in here?" And I said, "That's Beacon wax." And she says, "Come on . . . I know what you people do."

PROBST: What about the analyst? Have you finally graduated?

HOFFMAN: You never do. I like analysis. I like my analyst.

PROBST: How do you account to yourself for your own success?

HOFFMAN: I account for my success by a number of ways. One is, yes, I think I'm talented. I think many of us are talented. If the screen test for *The Graduate* had not come about, I most likely would have wound up being a working character actor. At the same time as *The Graduate* I had an offer which I had already accepted. I asked Mel Brooks if I could turn it down. I would have been a character actor, which is what I wanted to be. I wanted to be a working actor. I was hoping just to make a living. If I had never become successful, I'd still be doing theater wherever I could. If you're talking about success, I can tell you stories that would make your head spin to prove that fate is a large part of it. And we are kidding ourselves if we say. . . .

PROBST: I'm assuming fate plays a role. What else?

HOFFMAN: Many people work hard and don't succeed. Many people don't work hard at success but are greatly gifted. Many people aren't greatly gifted but they work hard at success. Not to knock Racquel Welch, but Racquel Welch is an example of someone who, I would say, puts in or did put in at one time in her life a tremendous amount of hours, to be—let's say—a sex symbol. And thought it out. Never to appear naked. Have a little bulge on the crotch. And worked it out and worked at it harder than other ladies who are also, in media terms, sexy or attractive.

To dramatize my point, when I was studying for many years in New York, I was quite unaggressive. Bob Duvall and Gene Hackman and I would put our pictures underneath the door and run rather than have to sit and be interviewed and get rejected. We were not salesmen. We would back into the spotlight rather than walk directly into it. And after many, many years I do this play Off-Broadway and another play Off-Broadway and suddenly what I consider to be my first big break comes along—*The Subject Was Roses.* Frank Gilroy had seen me in this Off-Broadway play in a church. So here's a Pulitzer Prize–winning play, and to me this is my big success, my chance, and I get the role. I learn the lines in about three weeks and I go into rehearsal with the stage manager. After the first rehearsal, I go over to a girl friend's house. A kitchen explosion occurs. I try to save her, and I wind up with flaming oil all over my body. I put it out with my hands, and I wind up very severely burned. . . .

PROBST: Are you still burned?

HOFFMAN: Yes. On my arms and my legs, just missed my

peepee. Leonard, you're getting red. Anyway, I go back to rehearsal for one week. They wanted me to go in the hospital, I refused, and I'm lying to the stage manager that the pain is not too great. "Why do you have your hands over your head?" they said. I said, "I have this little burn, don't worry about it." "Why do you rehearse with your hands like that." "Well, I use my gestures as a crutch." I'd come out of rehearsal and drop my arms, and the pain would be excruciating. I wouldn't take any drugs because I didn't want it to hurt me in rehearsal. And after a week I become terribly infected. The doctor—he is the doctor that lets me photograph his operations now, but I didn't know him at that time—he looks at me and says, "You're very badly infected, it's in your bloodstream, you're gonna die," and puts me in the hospital. They made out a card on me that said "terminal." I was on my way out and it was very, very touch and go and I am operated on that following morning. Anyway, I survived.

Four weeks later, I get out of the hospital and I learn that my understudy has gotten my role. If I want to, when I get out I can become his understudy and the assistant stage manager because it was understudy-slash-assistant-stage-manager. The day I get out of the hospital, all wrapped up with my burns, I go to the theater. I'm crying as I pull the curtain or yell the curtain cue. And there's this guy playing my role, one of three parts of a Pulitzer Prize-winning play. He's under contract for a year. It would have happened to me. But, when one looks back on one's career, had that not occurred, I wouldn't have been in *Eh!,* which brought me to the attention of Mike Nichols. I would have wound up playing *The Subject Was Roses* for a year. There's just a dramatic example of what fate has to do with it.

PROBST: It's too easy for you to account for what you have achieved by fate. I think it's an avoidance.

HOFFMAN: It's an ingredient. . . . Let me also add that in the years I've been in the theater, almost twenty—I'm almost thirty-eight. . . .

PROBST: August sixth?

HOFFMAN: Eighth. Redford was born the eighteenth, he tells me, same year, same neighborhood. We both came to New York in '58 to start.

PROBST: But he has the Woodward role and you have the Bernstein role in *All the President's Men*.

HOFFMAN: They have no guts, those studios. If they'd only made Redford the Jew, it'd be a whole new career for him. At any rate, the only point to make, let's say, in eighteen years of being involved in the theater, I have seen an awful lot of what I feel to be great, wonderful, remarkable talent go by the wayside.

PROBST: How do you attack a role?

HOFFMAN: I do what anybody would do, I guess, I try to find out as much as I can about what I don't know in the time that's allotted to me. I try to build a framework, a certain kind of loose but strict framework, and try to remain open within it. That open spontaneity. It's very hard many times to decide which way to go in this stuff, in terms of film, especially. It's so immediate and so crucial that you must do it that day. You can't come back like a sculptor and take the nose out and put it back in and reshape the eyes. You do it that day and never return to it because there's so much money involved. It's many times very difficult to go with the "moment" even if that precludes a very interesting concept that you had. It's more important to go for that truth of that moment. Brando once said a very interesting thing about film, and it's a very good lesson to actors: Don't make any choices you can't repeat honestly thirty times. I think it's a wonderful statement. If you do something that is real that has to be repeated, you first do it in what they call a master or a big shot, then the cameras come in medium, then they come in close, then they come in single. If you're not matching that original thing, it's unusable. So whatever you're doing, you have to be able to recreate honestly, and many times what you'll see is a wonderful piece of work suddenly pushing. You say, Why is the actor pushing? Well he's pushing because he's trying to get back to that thing that he had that really took place, so it is quite difficult and it's very much in the director's hands.

But what I do as an actor is just to do as much research as I can about what I don't understand and to go with my feelings and to try to be guided by that inner thing which is the toughest thing always to follow, I think, in life as well as one's work. That inner guide, that intuition, to be in touch with that intuition, to go with what smells right. We take avenues we know are not the ones that smell right and yet we go with them. We rationalize ourselves into it. That's the most difficult thing, to say, Why don't I go with my nose? Why don't I go with just that feel, that feel? Why do I say, Oh, I can't do that, that's crazy. What do I see in that person or in life? Simply to go with that feel, that's the most difficult, difficult thing to do. Research, yes, I think, but to go with that feeling and not to judge yourself and not to censor yourself and not to criticize yourself and not to be frightened.

The most difficult thing is to know what you want and to follow that. You go through a lifetime paying a price for not doing that. I'm convinced that a lifetime, unfortunately, is made up of so few decisions. Who you want to be with, what kind of work you want to do, where you want to be. You make the wrong moves, and that can be so costly. And the difficulty in life is the same difficulty that is in one's work. Why didn't I go the way I felt about the character? Why didn't I go that way? There are certain things you have to do—the character has to limp or the character has to have a certain accent or has to learn how to play the piano or the character has to know something about what prison conditions are like, so you do whatever research you can. But finding that you're working off of that thing in you . . . and we all have it and we don't use it, that's the sadness of it. It's that thing children seem to have . . . that children seem to have over us. They don't censor, they're less frightened, they're more in touch with themselves. As we get older, we get less in touch with ourselves.

What you do as an actor is what we are all trying to do as people. And what the artist tries to do is to get back, is to stop all that terrible self-conscious clothing we put on ourselves. Not that one doesn't get older and one doesn't learn more things or one doesn't grow in certain ways, but we leave that most valuable purity behind, that great courage, that great open stuff.

PROBST: Is the actor pure?

HOFFMAN: An actor is not quite the purist he would like to be. He's somewhat parasitic. He's doing what someone else has created. The fantasy to me has always been to be able to wake up in the morning and do what my fantasy is of the writer, or the composer, or the painter, or the pottery maker. You just begin to shape what you feel at that moment. The actor winds up waiting to get the script. If he's not a successful actor, he just wants to work, will just take anything that comes along. If he's a successful actor, then he begins to say, I would also like to do what I am closely feeling at the moment. It's like when you say, What do I really feel like wearing today? I want to wear jeans. I want to be in my underwear. I want to walk around naked. No particular reason, I just feel like it. Role playing is very much like that. Unfortunately, it's not that pure because you don't do and can't do as the painter or the writer. You wake up saying what you want to do, but the day prescribes what you have to do.

Q *(question from audience)*: Is it easier to play a role on location than on a set?

HOFFMAN: Well, it varies, unfortunately. Sometimes the location is quite important because it gives you the ambience and you don't have to work for the ambience and think of it and it's right there in front of you. Yes, it is easier. However, there are many times when you want to control the situation and you wish for a studio and you don't have one. Valerie Perrine and I had to do a number of love scenes in a hotel room, a hundred and five degrees—they had to seal up the room and you can't use the air-conditioning because it hurts the sound. Here we are, baking and sweating and doing these love scenes together, and we can't even see straight. We're saying, I wish we were in a studio that was silently air-conditioned, under controlled circumstances, and then you can have some kind of spontaneity. Here you couldn't think about anything except the terrific weather conditions.

Q: Do you find it difficult to concentrate when the cameras are rolling, and do you stop?

HOFFMAN: I have a tremendous self-consciousness about the camera, but after a few days everything becomes relative and you do forget it. I do, at any rate. It becomes an abstraction. What is more difficult is the stopping. I don't think people realize that you cannot act completely spontaneously. You have to hit a mark, and if you're off an inch, you're out of the frame or it's soft focus, or you do a very good take and they say they have to do it again because they're not in focus and the lighting is off. To shoot two minutes, you're going to spend fourteen hours, usually.

Q: What movie roles were you most satisfied with?

HOFFMAN: Again, that's subjective. I just have a fondness for *Midnight Cowboy*. I came closer in *Midnight Cowboy* to achieving the kind of work that is most personal to me. You color it in such a way that you not only do something that's personal to you but try to define it and make a statement in terms of what you feel. I not only felt there was a large Ratso inside me but also that we are all both—we are *all* the Bowery derelicts and we are *all* the successful movie star, and that it is simply the thin thread that decides where we're going to go. When one can cut through what one feels about life through one's work, you come closest to doing what you want to do.

6

MIKE NICHOLS:

You Can Hear an Audience Think

PROBST: Going back over the body of your films, it seems to me that they've all been very heavily social but not political. Is that possible?

NICHOLS: Yes. I think that's possible and accurate. When I worked with Elaine May, our concerns were with personal behavior, usually between men and women because we were one of each. We tended, as individuals, and together, to be more concerned with behavior than with ideas purely political. That is not to say I don't have strong political feelings, but that my work, it seems to me, is more concerned with things interpersonal than political. Political things tend, in movies and plays, and God knows, in sketches, to be general rather than specific. I've always been interested in specific things between people.

PROBST: In the position you're in, you seem to get heavily involved with the law. *Carnal Knowledge* was up before the Georgia courts.

NICHOLS: The Georgia Supreme Court, yes. And ultimately, the U.S. Supreme Court. Because of its notorious ruling that films and other such things, whatever they are, would have to satisfy community standards. The court didn't then bother to define either community standards or, more seriously, *community*. What is a community? How big is it? *Carnal Knowledge* happened to run into that. We got an almost meaningless Supreme Court decision that *Carnal Knowledge* could be shown in Georgia. That doesn't help anyone else. And it evaded an issue I suspect will come up again, as the pendulum swings. Right now, it's swung towards permissiveness.

PROBST: Is there anything you as a film director can't show because of taste today?

NICHOLS: No. The first and the last time I ran into that was *Who's Afraid of Virginia Woolf?* At that time things were different. I did not yet have final cut on the picture, I didn't have the final say. It was my first picture. Some things were taken out of *Virginia Woolf.* For instance, the famous "Screw you" when the character of Martha is yelling at her husband, just as he is opening the door to guests—that is a chain of softenings. Albee originally wrote "Fuck you." I was forced by Warner Brothers to change it to "Goddamn you," and I regretted that. Out of the crassest motives of comedy, "Fuck you" would have been a bigger laugh—and more like life for these particular people. And there were a few other things like that in *Virginia Woolf* that I regretted, but since then both the United States attitudes and my own control over pictures have changed. I haven't run into anything else I wanted to do and couldn't.

PROBST: Do you have final cut on all movies you do now?

NICHOLS: Yes.

PROBST: That's given to very few people, isn't it?

NICHOLS: Apparently, yes.

PROBST: That means that you're a bankable director?

NICHOLS: Whatever that is.

PROBST: You once auditioned for The Actors Studio.

NICHOLS: I never auditioned for Actors Studio. I was never in Actors Studio until much, much later. Then I was not a member but had access to it, the way certain directors do. In fact, they've now asked me to take over a teaching section, which I would like to do if the time can be found. I never auditioned for anything. I wasn't even sure I wanted to be in the theater, much less an actor. I simply didn't know what I was going to do.

It happened in stages. I joined University Theatre at the University of Chicago—various guys joined in order to meet girls. Some friends and I then started another theater, then something called Playwrights' Theater, and then, ultimately, together with Paul Sills, a cabaret called Compass, which evolved into Second City.

Through all that, I didn't really intend to be in the theater. I'd fallen into it as a way to make a minimal living—I think, thirty-five or twenty-eight dollars a week. After three or four years we were raised to sixty-five dollars. At some point, during Playwrights' Theater, I said to myself, I like what we're doing but something is wrong—we're doing the lines well or badly but we don't appear —to me—to be *people* in the course of their lives, as, for instance, in a Kazan play. I thought I would find out about that, and I went to Strasberg's classes. But I was deeply insecure about the possibility of ever getting a job as an actor, so I didn't audition or anything. I had an interview with Strasberg and he asked me the kind of question he asks, ranging from who is your favorite author to what kind of ice cream do you like. And then I went to his classes. . . .

PROBST: Did you say Chekhov and pistachio?

NICHOLS: Yes, oddly enough. I had just been fired from Howard Johnson's after somebody asked me what the flavor of the week was, and I said, "Chicken." I went for a couple of years and I did learn a great deal. Because of my own makeup I learned more about directing than acting, something I didn't realize until I began to direct and found suddenly that the things I had learned from Strasberg were eminently applicable and useful.

PROBST: I remember seeing you and Elaine May working in *An Evening With* on stage in 1961. It seemed that improvisation did work. As I understood it, for "Monitor," on radio, you would come into the studio telling dirty jokes and she would tell dirty jokes. There was no prepared script.

NICHOLS: Well, there was no prepared script, but I'm not so sure we told dirty jokes. We would start various improvisations, then they would be edited—mostly our hysterical laughter would be taken out.

PROBST: The two of you made improvisational theater work. But it wasn't really improvisational.

NICHOLS: It's as good as the people who are doing it. The people doing improvisational theater didn't claim, I think, that they were improvising all the time, but rather that the material had been evolved through improvisation. It was not written. It's an important distinction, and it happens to be a very good way to develop material. Elaine and I soon realized, when we began to appear as a team, that the audience didn't particularly care whether something was improvised on the spot or last week or last year. The audience cared whether it worked, as did we. We ended up in clubs, on television, and finally on Broadway, with a relatively set number of pieces, each of which had developed as improvisations in front of an audience. They would change somewhat over the weeks and months and years. At the end of each show, we would do an out-and-out improvisation. We would ask the audience for a first line, the last line, and a style. It was a very effective trick, it kept us alive, and every few weeks that miracle would happen that you can't control, that you can only hope for. We were possessed by something, came up with something that was the best thing that evening.

PROBST: You and Elaine have followed similar paths. She is, I suppose it's fair to say, the leading woman film director in America today.

NICHOLS: Yes. I think that's accurate.

PROBST: And you are a leading man film director in America today. When you look back over it all, what do you think?

NICHOLS: Various things. I think that if Elaine and I hadn't found each other and that if we hadn't fallen into Compass, I don't know about Elaine but I would not even be in the theater, much less a film director. It was fortuitous. From Cabaret in Chicago to what our manager called "the hottest team in show business," at no point did either of us ever feel that this was what we were going to do. This was a terrific way to make a living and have a good time. We felt our lives would start at some later point, this didn't count. I never felt any kind of final click, nor really at home, until I began to direct, and then everything I had done seemed unconscious preparation. I was, finally, at home.

Another thing, perhaps less specific and less interesting that maybe has to do with my entering my forties—I feel as if I've been asleep for ten or fifteen years. I don't quite know how all this happened. How I got here. I don't know who made these decisions because I don't think I did. I am surprised to find myself doing the things I'm doing, and ultimately, grateful.

PROBST: People didn't expect *The Graduate* to be the seminal influence it turned out to be.

NICHOLS: If you set out to make a seminal influence or a hit, you're lost, you can't. People set out to solve some specific series of problems and then what happens, happens. But I wouldn't say that whatever I'm doing now is a result of *The Graduate.* I think it's a result of the first play I ever directed, *Barefoot in the Park.* During the rehearsals of that, I thought, This is what I want to do, this is what I'm meant to do, I finally know what my work is.

PROBST: I recall that night. There was some master backstage we couldn't see. It was a small idea that allowed you to make it funny.

NICHOLS: It was a modest idea. I don't know that you can make anything funny. It is the funny *premise.* What's so good about Neil Simon is that his premises are funny.

PROBST: They're tragic, generally.

NICHOLS: Well, Aristotle tells us, etc., etc. . . . Elaine and I found, when we improvised over ten years or so, that there are basically two kinds of improvisation. Those in which we could do nothing wrong—they built and built, and there was great pleasure for the audience and for us. And the other kind, in which we were as good as the last line, and if that was a good, funny line, there was a laugh. What distinguished the two kinds of scenes was premise. If it rested on a strong enough premise, you could ride on it, and you could ornament and elaborate. That's true of a play or a movie, it must rest on a premise. You can't make something funny if the premise isn't very funny.

There are two things that I've learned over and over and over, and I will never understand why one forgets them in between, but it was·true with the scenes with Elaine, it's true in plays, and it's true in movies. The audience asks two questions. One, Why are you telling me this? You must have an answer. I'm telling you this because it's funny is not a bad answer. If you don't have that answer, you better damn well have another, good one. And the other question the audience asks is, Is it real?

PROBST: You sound as though you attack comedy the way a lawyer prepares a legal brief. It's not scatterbrained.

NICHOLS: It's neither scatterbrained nor, if I can venture, is it like a legal brief. Comedy isn't very different from the opposite of comedy, whatever that is. When I started directing comedies, I said to myself and to the actors that I didn't believe that comedy was running around and slamming a lot of doors and talking very fast. It was no different from what one did in a serious play—to connect with what is recognizable and personal and real in the lives of the characters.

To do a play or movie, after all, is to say to the audience, Do you know this? Do you feel like this, too? Do you share this with us? Does this happen to you, too? And in some cases, even saying, Remember when? If you are accurate and specific enough, it can be recognized by others. It's always seemed to me that the specific, the detailed, is the recognizable and the interesting, and that the enemy of work in the theater or movies is the random and the general.

Strasberg made a spectacular analogy when I was in class with him. Some girl had done a scene, and he said, "Tell us what you worked for." I don't remember what she said, something about wanting the feeling of this or that and the springtime outside the window. And he said, "Let me ask you something. Do you know how to make fruit salad?" She said, "Yes." He said, "Tell us." She said, "You want me to tell you how to make fruit salad? Well, you take an apple and peel it and cut it up and you peel an orange and cut it up and you peel a banana and cut it up and you peel a pear and cut it up. And then you mix them all together." And he said, "That's right. That's how you make fruit salad. And it's the only way to make fruit salad. You can stand in front of the fruit for days and scream, Okay, fruit salad, you can run over it with a steamroller, but you'll never have fruit salad until you pick up each individual piece of fruit and quietly and calmly cut it into pieces." I think it's the answer to all work, really—and certainly work in the theater or in film—to be detailed and specific and solve each problem simply and carefully rather than going for large, bold, sweeping, generalized, random things.

PROBST: You remind me of that quote of Mies van der Rohe: "God is in the details." . . . There are rumors that you are stern, dictatorial, strong-willed. When you direct, how much do you communicate through words, how much do you act out the part, and how much do you demand adherence to what you decide is the right thing to do?

NICHOLS: It's entirely different for each situation and for each person. It's a little bit like the blind man and the elephant. One of the things I am learning as I get older is not to come to any final conclusion about anyone. It's a characteristic of the people that I care for most. When you are a director, or for that matter, a movie actor, people tend to come to conclusions too quickly. Conclusions based on their particular experience. We all come to far too many conclusions about one another. When I'm working on a picture, I am very demanding of the crew because it seems to me that the crew is performing a difficult but controllable task, and that the actor is the special person in the situation, more special than anyone, including the director. The actor is the one who must feel right. You can't fake something. If you feel bad, you will look silly faking that you feel good, and vice versa. The actor is to be nourished, and the actor's fears, it has always seemed to me, are very real. He only gets one chance to do any particular scene and then it's over.

There is a kind of quiet terror that comes over everyone—actors, director, crew—when someone says, "Roll!" A little bit of life goes out of everyone and a lot of self-consciousness comes into everyone. I've always been concerned, as much as possible, with feeding the life and finding things for the actors to concentrate on so that the self-consciousness can be overcome or forgotten. Different actors require different things. For Richard Burton, I actually did act out scenes and read them because he responds through his ear. When he hears something, he grasps the idea within the sound, within the reading. It's faster and easier to do that with him than to spend a long time talking about why he is here. With other actors it's important to find other images. Any two people together become something different from what they have been before.

A movie company is, in many cases, more than a hundred people. It's an extremely complicated, involved, and delicate chemistry. It either feeds the actors and causes them to be what an actor can be at his highest, which is more than himself, or the reverse, it can cause an actor to be constrained, to feel that he couldn't function at his highest, at his happiest. A movie is a snowball. It starts rolling, and then there's no stopping it. All you can do is hope it's rolling in the right direction.

PROBST: Richard Burton has paid you a high compliment. He said, "I thought I knew everything anybody had to teach me about comedy. From Mike, I learned." What happens when there's a difference of opinion with an actor or with a playwright?

NICHOLS: The same thing applies to a playwright as to an actor. You can only do what you can do and what you grasp and what you can share. Nobody can sit down and write a scene that he doesn't understand. Nobody can get on the stage and act a scene in a way that is not part of himself. All you can hope to do is to find something that shows him a new way of looking at whatever the thing is. You must get him to share your viewpoint, or it's useless. You can't order someone to do something in this kind of work. If you have a specific personal insight, it is not difficult to inflame someone else with it. I can't think, at the moment, of any example of coming down to anything as simple as: X says it should be *this* way, and I say, No, it should be *that* way. You're, after all, looking for the life in a given situation together.

When I read the novel *The Graduate*, one particular moment in it allowed me to understand it and allowed me to say, Yes, I want to do this. This is why. It had to do with the moment Mrs. Robinson had in bed with Benjamin, the Dustin Hoffman character. He says, We must have a conversation, what should we talk about, and she says, I don't know, why don't you talk about art. He says, You start, and she says, You start, I don't know anything about it. Quite a bit later, he asks, What was your major in college? And she says, Art. He says, Really. You must have kind of drifted away from it. And she says, Kind of. That tiny moment allowed me to see a Mrs. Robinson I knew very well—a woman who had been one kind of person and had very consciously moved away from what she was into something for which she had contempt, a woman who had a very low opinion of herself, who was now almost parodying herself out of anger with herself for having left who she had been.

When we were rehearsing, I told this to Ann Bancroft and she said, "Oh, that's terrific! Oh, yes, thank you, I understand, that's absolutely wonderful." When we got to the scene, I asked, "What happened to that thing I told you?" She said, "Oh, I forgot, I forgot." And then she did it. Once you've found something for yourself, it's not difficult to communicate it to somebody else.

PROBST: You're describing a dialectical relationship: You have A, they have B, and you make a synthesis of C, possibly.

NICHOLS: Yes, you could say that. I think of it more as a . . . I don't know how I think of it, I haven't looked for metaphors for the process. I think the director must lead the way. He must, after all, be the one who explains what the story it is we intend to tell, what the events are and what is happening at any given point. I find that actors are immediately happy when they know why a given thing is taking place and what it is they are trying to accomplish. I once said to Maureen Stapleton, rehearsing a play, "Would you do this and this and this and that?" She did it and I said, "How does it feel, is it comfortable?" And she said, "Who gives a shit if it's comfortable, is it right?"

PROBST: When you're working on a play, what is the test that works for you? Is it what the audience likes, what the actor likes, the director likes—or is there something in your head that tells you you're right?

NICHOLS: There's something in your head that tells you it's right. It is not infallible. It can be changed by your reaction when you are sitting there with the audience. The example I can give you, everyone has experienced—you start to play a new record that you like very much for a friend. You think, Hum, it doesn't sound so good today, wait till we get to the good part, that's really going to be terrific. And you get to the good part, and that's not much either. What's happened is that you are hearing the unexpressed opinion of your friend and it is making you hear the record differently.

I claim that you can hear an audience think. That does guide what one does. The thing that complicates it somewhat is, I don't believe one should cater to it, particularly. If they're uncomfortable at a certain point, that may be what you want. But it is very important to see how you yourself feel when something has an audience, and then make decisions based on that.

PROBST: You have become a public symbol. . . .

NICHOLS: Of what?

PROBST: A successful, independent-minded, original director, whether in films or theater. If you do something, I am curious to see what it is. Do you bear any burdens as Mike Nichols? Do you feel you have any responsibility other than doing a good job, to anybody?

NICHOLS: Absolutely not. To be in any way concerned with public image, for those of us that work in movies, is dangerous and a waste of time. It's not a reality. The person that one is thought to be by people who've heard the name or seen the movies or seen a newspaper, is, to me, a rather uninteresting figment. Any connection with it takes time and energy away from one's actual life, which is more interesting and more fulfilling. I think our obligations are to the people we love and to our families, and the other kind of obligations, for instance, to countries that we have gutted, and to the people that we touch on that we might or might not be able to help in some way. But not to any imaginary, journalistic hook that someone has made up because he's had a deadline.

I remember writing papers in college, it was quite easy to get an A, but was almost impossible to say what one meant. I'm always aware that journalists have the same problem. It's necessary to look for something that works, that has a hook, that hangs together, that makes a point. Nobody can stop and worry about whether it's true or not because there simply isn't time. To write something that's true about any particular person would take months and months, and it still wouldn't be true. It is a nonproductive and ultimately boring thing to get into about yourself and, therefore, best ignored.

PROBST: You were born Michael Igor Peschkowsky.

NICHOLS: My father changed our family name when we came to this country because he was a doctor. His little joke was by the time he'd spell Peschkowsky the patient was in the hospital. His patronymic was Nikolaevich, and he changed it to Nichols.

PROBST: Do you regret not having kept the full name?

NICHOLS: I wouldn't mind having the name, and I don't mind the name I have. I don't attach much importance to it.

PROBST: You came into the country at the age of seven from Berlin?

NICHOLS: Yes. I sometimes think we all begin to see life as a series of strange accidents, that by a difference of six months I would have been either dead or another person. When I have a low moment, I tell myself, look at you, you're worried about reel four when you could have died in the concentration camp. It always reminds me of a sketch I did with Sevren Darden in Chicago. He had broken his leg on his motorcycle and was in a cast and on crutches for a long time. And we did a scene in which I came and said, 'Hi, Sevvy, how do you feel?" and he said, "Oh, I'm very depressed—the doctor says I have the cast for another month and the crutches and then a cane for another month." And I said, "Do you realize how lucky you are? I know a guy who had the exact same kind of motorcycle accident as you, and he lost both legs." And Sevren said, "Really? I feel wonderful!" We can't cheer ourselves with possibilities of things that might have been. But I think that because of coming to this country when I was seven and various other personal experiences, to a larger extent than many people I know, I have the feeling that I am visiting, that I am from somewhere else, that everyone else is living a life I am not quite part of. I think that's a common feeling.

PROBST: You account for the past twenty years by strange, unpredictable accidents. A lot of accidents happen to a lot of people, but there aren't many Mike Nicholses. There's something missing in the equation.

NICHOLS: I don't spend a lot of time trying to account for myself or even grading myself. We all start saying, Am I as good as this guy, is that guy better than me, will I ever be as good as so-and-so? Is it better than the one before, is it worse? But that's a one-way street. God knows, there are so many other people doing that for us that grading yourself and marking yourself and trying to account for yourself are not impulses to be encouraged. They lead neither to any kind of work nor any kind of good feeling.

PROBST: Is it *work* that is most important?

NICHOLS: I really don't know what's most important. I'm aware that a lot I think and say is temporizing. You may be sitting on an airplane depressed, thinking, Ah, who cares, what does it all mean, let it crash—and then there's a little air pocket, and you say, I was kidding, I didn't mean it, everything is okay. I really feel like that. I don't anymore know what's most important. I enjoy my work, but not all the time. A lot of it is difficult and a lot of it is discouraging. By the time a movie comes out, hundreds and hundreds of people have been involved in it. There are dozens of people in the sound studio when you dub it. There are hundreds of people in the lab that make the negative and the print and the negative splices. It is a process literally impossible to control.

All directors have the experience of working for a couple of years on something and the last two months you say, It's too green, it's too red, it's too dark, it's too light, it's too loud, it's too soft. You go to a theater and you can't see it, you can't hear it. It leads you to change. You cannot control everything. You cannot control every projectionist in every theater in the world. Somewhere, right now, movies are cut off three feet from the top, reels are skipped, the sound inaudible, a scratch down the face of the lead actress. Movies are mood, and all these things serve to destroy the mood. But you can't control them, so you finally just go through every day hoping that it's nice and that you get some things done.

PROBST: Would you see yourself as an existentialist?

NICHOLS: I'm not sure what an existentialist is.

PROBST: Do you believe in the irrationality of existence?

NICHOLS: It happens to all of us, we get to be middle-aged and suddenly realize that there's nothing new coming, this is it. This is it—and it's quite nice, I like it okay. As a result, I generalize a great deal less than I used to. I'm a lot less interested in the nature of life or work or love or success. I'm more interested in moments. I'll give you an example. You sit in a restaurant. After ordering, forty-five minutes pass and the waitress comes and says to you, We don't have red snapper. There's a split second in which you can decide whether you're going to say, You dumb bitch, why didn't you tell me that forty-five minutes ago? If you do that, which I sometimes have done, not only don't you have your food but you also dislike yourself for having snapped at a waitress. If you can grab the moment in time and say, All right, tell me what else you have, you at least have the minor pleasure of having dealt with somebody else decently. Those moments are very hard to catch because they come along every half hour. I don't pretend that I can catch all of them. I'm trying to increase the number of them. I don't know about existentialism, but I figure that I can't control what happens but I can attempt to control my reaction to it. And that's what I'm really concerned with. What it all means, I couldn't tell you.

PROBST: Is there a progression as you've grown older, are you limiting yourself? You're responsible for Mike Nichols ordering red snapper.

NICHOLS: I'm responsible for the people I am committed to and the jobs I've taken on and the things that affect me strongly I feel I can have some effect on. But the larger things, the things that have to do with the rest of the world, it now appears to me . . . of course, giving money is easy and giving time is relatively easy, but that kind of quality of concentration and concern and that kind of circle of whatever it is, of thought or harmony that you can send out when you're your best self, is an actual, useful force. You can work at your best when you're in your own groove. Mel Brooks is in his groove and it's beautiful to watch.

PROBST: How do you stay in your own groove? Do you play tennis? Do you run, swim?

NICHOLS: I'm a singularly inactive person. I'll occasionally go ride around on a horse or go for a walk with my little son. I don't do much. I sleep as much as I can, and I like our life in the country.

Sort of puttering around out on the lawn and playing with animals and finding out what's for dinner. When I'm not working I tend to sort of vegetate. And I've been working more than I think I should. I'm a little tired at the moment. I hope to find some time to hang out for a while after the next picture.

PROBST: Do you find that you have to replenish?

NICHOLS: In shooting a movie, very, very often the best things come just as you come into a blank wall. I have literally shut down a movie for three days because I didn't know how to do something. And by God, that time, luckily, at the end of the three days, I came up with what I, at least, considered to be the best thing in that movie. Sometimes you stop and the solution doesn't come. Sometimes you think it's a solution and no one else does. I don't know any way. I do know that what comes after us all the time, things that are chasing us all constantly, the phone calls and the mail . . . I have a fantasy of changing the telephone at home and throwing out all the mail. I can and do simply go home and not answer the phone and disappear. If you don't do that for yourself, nobody is going to help you do it. They're just going to ask you to come to their party or send your underwear for an auction or whatever it is. And nobody can say No except yourself.

PROBST: You know who you are, and when you've reached a stopping point. . . .

NICHOLS: When you just need some time to just live your life, whatever that may be.

PROBST: What's your feeling of living in Los Angeles, Beverly Hills?

NICHOLS: I'm perfectly happy to do it while I'm working. It's very pleasant and it's sunny and so forth. It's not good for me for any length of time, I've never done it and I don't think I ever will. It's not good for me to be in a place in which everyone, of necessity—not because of any decadence in them but because of the necessity of the place—asks constantly, How much did it make, how much will it make? and not, Is it any good? That's a perfectly fair thing for them all to ask because it's a business and the medium we all work in is the money. It's not film, it's money that it takes to make a movie. But it's a generalized concern. You can't make a blockbuster. You can only make a movie. I find that I have to be in a climate where the question, Is it any good, does it work, is it true to what you started out to do? is a rational question.

PROBST: Does one find truth in movies?

NICHOLS: I find truth in some movies that I see. I will say, Yes, yes, I know this, this is true. At their highest, in certain Bergman pictures, or occasionally, for me, a Fellini picture, I will be amazed that someone else should have known my fantasies and my dream and what was in my head. I think that is a truthful movie.

PROBST: Which of your movies do you think are the better ones?

NICHOLS: I like different ones at different times. Some of them I've never seen again. I saw *Carnal Knowledge* recently and I think it may be my favorite, but that changes. I like *Catch-22*, I like *The Graduate*. I really like all of them at different times and different parts. Some of them I would do differently now. Some of them I'm watching, and I think, Why did I do that, I could have done this. But I very rarely see my pictures and I very rarely think about any except the one I'm working on.

PROBST: Why *Carnal Knowledge?*

NICHOLS: It seems to me simple and connected with what it's about. I was happy making it. We were a happy group. It was a happy experience.

PROBST: How was it to work with Jules Feiffer?

NICHOLS: It was a pleasure. We think alike in many ways and we make each other laugh—and that means you're halfway there. Neither of us, and it was the same with the other writers I've worked with—Neil Simon, Buck Henry—neither of us wasted any time. If one of you says, This doesn't work, the other doesn't waste any time saying, Oh, but there's this and there's that. He says, Well, then, let's try this. I very much enjoy working with people who look to themselves first when there's a problem. Simon and I have always said that we were mystified by stories of big blowups on shows out of town because our experience on plays was that there would be a scene and I'd say, Oh, Christ, I've got to restage it, and he'd say, No, no, no, I've got to rewrite it, and the actor would say, You're both crazy, give me another three days, I've got to act it right. This is the proper way to approach such work, rather than saying, You idiot, nobody can act these words. I've been lucky, and to some extent, chosen well. And that's what happened with Feiffer. We didn't waste each other's time and we had some enjoyment out of the process.

PROBST: What do you look for? You've completed *The Fortune*. You're about to start *Bogart Slept Here*. What clicks?

NICHOLS: I've never been sure. I think it's really the feeling that I, specifically, know this. I had that reaction to *Bogart Slept Here*. I know what this is, I hear it, I see it, I want to do it. I've had that feeling every time, with the exception of the *Day of the Dolphin* picture, where I talked myself into thinking I knew the story—but you couldn't say I know it, because nobody knows talking fish. I forgot to wait for a very specific reason, something I'll never do again. I had a commitment and I was looking for something to do—very dangerous, it appears to me. Either I have to generate it myself—something I hope to do very soon now—or wait till something comes and grabs me. If I don't know what it is, I'm completely, you should forgive the expression, at sea.

PROBST: How affected are you by unfavorable critical reviews?

NICHOLS: I believe them implicitly. The good ones you tend to say, Oh, well, I fooled them, and the bad ones you think, Yep, they've got my number. That is a tendency I dislike in myself and in others. By the time I've seen something with an audience a couple of times, I know at least what I think of it. Nobody likes bad reviews. I try not to flagellate myself too much, because there's also something craven, it appears to me, about turning against something you've done just because someone else has.

PROBST: Are you part of any things like Transcendental Meditation or consciousness-raising groups?

NICHOLS: No. I have adequate respect for them, and I wouldn't and don't laugh at or put down any of my friends that are interested by them. But I've known for a long time that no movement is going to be much good to me. Whatever it is, I've got to find it, and I find it and I lose it and I find it and I lose it. Nobody's going to come along with some new method of meditation or manner of breathing or diet that's going to solve the things I'm concerned with.

PROBST: The solution is in each one. Is that what you feel?

NICHOLS: I think so. I think so. I no longer look for large solutions. We all know the feeling of wishing for some radical, sudden gesture to move to somewhere, to change everything. But as we all know, those gestures either don't exist or are not effective day by day. If I've had a good day, I hope for a good evening and a good night and a good day tomorrow. That's already a lot.

PROBST: It seems to me you have a very unassailable position. It reminds me of a very tightly knit, indestructible. . .

NICHOLS: It's not indestructible. . . .

PROBST: What is it that makes something funny? There are identities we don't laugh at.

NICHOLS: I think a laugh is just a very loud Yes.

PROBST: What does the humor come from? Are you laughing when you do it?

NICHOLS: Oh, yes—in the beginning, for weeks. Then you get used to it, and you laugh less, and finally you don't laugh. It starts out with what seems funny to you.

PROBST: You go with it, then, if it's funny only to you?

NICHOLS: Yes. Elaine and I had a rule—you can't go to be funny, you have to be doing something else and funny has to be on the way. You can't be caught trying to be nothing but funny.

PROBST: Was it you that said, If you take a comedy and take away all the humor and the laugh lines, it's supposed to be able to stand up?

NICHOLS: Yes. It has to be about people and has to have the same reality or accuracy that anything else does, or you're just some people trying to make people laugh, a sorry spectacle.

PROBST: It's really a question of specifics. Each moment—to make it funny?

NICHOLS: I don't think I've ever tried to make something funny.

PROBST: When you set out to do a comedy, you want to make us laugh.

NICHOLS: But I want to do something else first. I want to make you say, Yes, that's what it's like.

PROBST: That still could happen with no laugh.

NICHOLS: Yes, it could. Depending on the importance of the event and whether life or death are involved, and all such things.

PROBST: *God's Favorite* is about death, and it's funny. Means to be.

NICHOLS: The more studiously you try to put your finger on what it is, the more of a fool you make of yourself. It is that thing that is most mysterious and gives most pleasure. You see it in kids. What makes them laugh? I don't know. I just love to hear it. Why do some people make you laugh? Maybe it has something to do with not taking everything terribly seriously, with not seeing life as this vale of tragedy. The sadder it is, the funnier it is.

PROBST: Two masks of tragedy and comedy?

NICHOLS: Suffering is something that one likes to discourage in one's self and, God willing, in others. Everybody knows it's around. We don't have to be reminded. It takes care of itself.

7

ELAINE MAY:

Funny Is Closer to Life

PROBST: Richard Burton is quoted as having said, Elaine May is "the most fascinating, maddening girl I ever met. I hope I never see her again." What do you think he meant by all that?

MAY: I think it was my table manners.

PROBST: A lot of people want to know about you and it seems to me you spend a lot of your life hiding. Why do you hide?

MAY: Oh, I don't know.

PROBST: I'd like to find out something about you as a young-ster. At fourteen you left school, is that right?

MAY: No, it isn't. But I did it anyway.

PROBST: Do you recall taking acting lessons?

MAY: Yes.

PROBST: Did you always want to be a director?

MAY: I never wanted to be a director. I happen to be directing movies because I wrote this movie script that I wanted to sell for a lot of money so that I could be richer. I was certain it was abso-lutely commercial. It was an adaptation of a story I read in *The Alfred Hitchcock omnibus.* It had two murders in it so it could be a mystery, and if it wasn't a mystery it could be funny, and if nobody laughed it could be a love story. I didn't see how it could fail. Hilly Elkins, who was my manager at the time, set a $200,000 price on the script and was negotiating for approvals. He came back from the coast—he'd been my manager for two days—and said, "I've got a wonderful deal. I produce, you write and direct, and you get $50,000." I said, "what happened to the other

$150,000?" And he said, "You can't expect to get that much the first time you direct."

PROBST: When you look back over it all, the University of Chicago days and Compass Theatre, and you look at where you are today, do you think that you worked clearly from one step to the other or it just happened?

MAY: It just happened. I certainly didn't work clearly. I was much smarter on my first movie than on my second. I was much smarter, I think, on my first play than on my second. When I saw my first movie budget during *A New Leaf*, I thought, "This is really a crazy industry. You wouldn't be able to open a fruit stand this way. They would laugh you out of town." By the second movie I already took it for granted that, yes, of course, somebody can make a budget even though he doesn't know all the prices, doesn't know what the locations cost, doesn't know what the actors get. He can make it on the basis of what everybody would like it to cost. By the third movie I was sort of a pro. A schmuck pro.

PROBST: What are you a pro *at*?

MAY: I'm a pro at talking about budgets, schedules, meal penalties, gross, net, and distribution.

PROBST: How do you talk to an actor? To Peter Falk or John Cassavetes? Do you tell them what you want them to do? Do you act it for them? Do you walk through it? How do you communicate what you want them to do in a scene?

MAY: Well, you communicate in different ways with different actors. I don't always know what I want an actor to do in a scene, and when I do I don't always know how to communicate it. Actors and directors use each other for sounding boards, or should, I think. I think it's best not to say too much too soon. If the actor is right then you don't have to say anything. If he's wrong he usually knows it, if he's good, then you try to figure out why it isn't working. Sometimes an actor knows before you do why it isn't working. Sometimes, if you know just what you want, you tell an actor what to play. And then you hope that he's comfortable enough in his part not to only do what you've told him. What if you're wrong?

PROBST: When you decide you have to talk to the actor, do you play the scene or do you discuss it or both?

MAY: You do anything. Sometimes you describe the scene. Sometimes you play the scene, not for the actor but with him. Sometimes you cut the scene. It's like life. You do anything that works.

PROBST: You say it's like life. Is there truth in movies? Can we ever believe anything we see in a movie?

MAY: Yes, there is truth in movies. No, movies are not like life. They are constructed in advance. They have a beginning that has probably been rewritten several times, a middle that has been cut and reshaped, and an end that often has music over it. Most movies and plays have a confrontation scene that provides some kind of insight that affects the characters or the audience, or both. In life we have hundreds of such scenes, scenes in which we say the worst thing we can say, in which each person tells what he thinks is the whole truth. Two hours later we have the same scene again. Nothing has really changed. You can't get any insights. You usually just get mad. Movies or plays can sound natural, or seem real, or have truth, but they can never be like life. Afterall, they're not supposed to run over two hours.

PROBST: Is there anything that you want to show in movies as a director that you are not allowed to show? Does anybody prevent you from showing anything?

MAY: No. You have problems with certain subjects because they aren't considered commercial but not because they're considered controversial. Things have changed. I think anything that somebody thinks will make money will be produced. It's no longer true that studios are afraid of controversy. They're afraid of not grossing. The problem is that nobody knows in advance what will make money. It's a gamble. And the stakes are so high that studios try to gamble on ideas or directors or stars that have a record of winning. It's like horse racing, about which I know very little. If you've won a lot of races, you get to lose two or three—three, I think—before people stop betting on you. I am speaking now, of course, as a horse.

PROBST: Your previous races have made money, haven't they?

A New Leaf, which you wrote and directed and acted in, and *Heartbreak Kid,* which you directed?

MAY: Yes, they have.

PROBST: So you're a good horse to bet on?

MAY: It was a clumsy metaphor. I'm not really a horse. I'm a person. And if I had the money I would invest it in me.

PROBST: Do you have a chance to experiment?

MAY: No. If you want to experiment you just take the chance. Mike Nichols once said that if you have a career, your career is diametrically opposed to your work. It's true. Once you succeed you're not supposed to fail. That's a very hard atmosphere to experiment in. But there are places that have workshop conditions. If you want to experiment enough you just take time out and forget about your income and go experiment.

PROBST: You work very long on a movie. Who is it you are working for? Paramount? Yourself? The audience? Who is it that the standards are for? Is it a completely personal thing? Do you want all of us to understand something? Do you have a responsibility to the writer? All of the above? None of the above?

MAY: Well, it's all of it. You have something in your head and you obviously want somebody to understand it because why would you bother to make a movie out of it, otherwise.

PROBST: How do you decide what you keep in and what you leave out?

MAY: If I really like something that I put in a movie a lot—and sometimes there's, say, three and a half minutes that I really like a lot—I keep it anyway. But most of the time, if the audience doesn't understand it, and it's meant to be understood, I figure that I've done something wrong. Audiences are very smart. I have nothing to say that everybody doesn't know already. I just want everybody to see it the way I do. It's like telling a joke that you think is wildly funny. If nobody laughs and you still think the joke is funny, you have to conclude that either you've told it badly or you're the only person in the world with a sense of humor.

PROBST: You're trying to do something the audience will understand, be interested in, not bored by.

MAY: Preferably. I think we're bored in movies much more

than we realize. We're just so used to it that we sit through a lot of dull scenes in the hope that the next one will be interesting. To actually make something that isn't boring is sort of hard to do.

PROBST: Is comedy the opposite of boredom?

MAY: No. Interesting is the opposite of boredom.

PROBST: Some people who make movies, act in movies, direct movies, have said that sometimes because they enjoyed doing it so much they feel they are frauds. Does that ever occur to you?

MAY: No, but it really doesn't seem like life, which to me is working at Florsheim's. It's odd to think that you are going to impose or inflict something you have in your head on a large number of people and get paid for it, too. Every once in a while you think, Gee, I'm getting away with not working at Florsheim's.

PROBST: There's a story in the *Times* that you may go back and start acting again with Mike Nichols in *Who's Afraid of Virginia Woolf?*

MAY: Yes, we might. I do it much faster than directing.

PROBST: Why is that?

MAY: It's much easier.

PROBST: How was it directing your daughter in *The Heartbreak Kid*?

MAY: It was a pleasure.

PROBST: Would you ever be interested in directing a film about a woman? All your films have been about men.

MAY: If it was an interesting film I'd be interested. I wouldn't be interested in directing it because it was about a woman. I don't think anybody would unless it was to exploit some star or some market.

PROBST: At one point you were outside . . . there's a story in *The New Yorker* telling how you brought a new type of comedy to America that was more aware, more social, more psychological, more cultural—not the old style of comedy America had been brought up on such as, I think they mentioned, jokes about Jane Mansfield and Bing Crosby's toupe. And now many years later you are a director Paramount will invest in. Have you come inside the establishment but maintained your credentials outside? Are you both in and outside the system?

MAY: There is no establishment any more. You can become a fad in twenty minutes with a little publicity. I think they have a rock song about the SDS that made a fortune.

PROBST: Would you ever consider directing something on Broadway?

MAY: No. I don't like Broadway. I think it's worse than the movies. And Off-Broadway is exactly like Broadway. But Joe Papp has a terrific theatre and I'm going to work in it.

PROBST: Why is Broadway worse than the movies?

MAY: They can't make as much money and so it costs more to produce. And they can close in one night.

PROBST: I'd like to know your reaction to critics.

MAY: I'm going to be absolutely honest with you. If I get a good review I think they're wonderful.

PROBST: John Simon?

MAY: But everybody knows John Simon's rules. I mean it's sort of fun to read somebody who only liked *The Seven Samurai*.

PROBST: How do you know when something is funny?

MAY: Somebody asked George Bernard Shaw that, and he said, "When I laugh"—this is not a direct quote. I wish I had said that. And now I have.

PROBST: Mike Nichols said you can't be caught trying to be nothing but funny in order to be funny.

MAY: I'll go along with that. You can do something dramatically or you can do it funny. You can kill somebody dramatically or you can kill them funny. Funny is closer to life. If you kill somebody in a drama you get a gun and shoot them and they die, and then you're left to face the consequences of your act. If you kill somebody in a comedy you have to start out by finding a place where you can buy a gun that can't be traced. Or you have to buy a gun and then spend your evenings and weekends filing off the serial number. Then you have to buy cartridges. Then you have to learn how to load the gun and fire it. Then you have to put the gun and cartridges somewhere where they won't be found by the maid or your wife. Then when the right time comes you have to get the guy you're going to kill either to come up to your apartment or make a date to meet him some place where you can fire a gun and no one will notice. Like Central Park. If you can get him to meet you in Central Park without making him nervous, you will have to put the gun in your pocket and try to decide whether to leave the safety off and risk shooting your foot off, or leave the safety on and find someway to take the gun out of your pocket gracefully and release the safety in front of your victim without rousing his suspicion. If you manage to actually kill someone under these circumstances, you then have to get rid of the body and get out of Central Park alive. Getting rid of the body has got to be a hair-raising experience. Especially, if you've decided to kill somebody bigger than you are, which you probably have, because in a comedy almost everybody is bigger than you are. Comedy is almost entirely the doing of something in detail, step by tiny step. Drama sort of sweeps everything away.

PROBST: What about the rhythm of comedy writing?

MAY: What about it?

PROBST: Is there a difference between comedy and humor?

MAY: I suppose so. They're certainly not contradictory but comedy requires effort. You take every line, every moment, and try to get a laugh from the audience without their noticing the effort. Humor sort of happens, sometimes against your will. It's more a way of looking at things. You look at something one way and it's a disaster, you look at it another way and it's humorous. It depends on how you tilt your head.

8

BARBARA WALTERS:

"Today" Has Changed My Life

PROBST: You have said that success is making you lazy. Are you getting lazy?

WALTERS: I think success can do two things to you. . . . Success can either make you greedy and ambitious so that you try to get it all while you can—if you really think it's going to be over the next day, as I did for a very long time, you do try to get it all. First of all, financially, because, yes, you make a lot of money, comparatively speaking. I now have a feeling about myself, that it isn't going to be over tomorrow. Maybe a week from Thursday, but not tomorrow.

And I have a different feeling about my life. I've worked very hard. I have a little child who I find getting very big, and I want to spend more time with her. I care more about my private life. I want to work less, and I don't have to prove myself anymore.

PROBST: There's a quote in *Newsweek* magazine from your father, saying something to the effect that from very early on, Barbara was driven by a fear of failure.

WALTERS: No. I don't think it's a fear of failure. It was a very apt quote of my father's, but I think he was saying that I was always afraid, that there was always a fear of financial insecurity of some kind. . . . My father was in show business, from the generation of the Billy Roses and the Earl Carrolls, and before that of the Ziegfelds. They were very creative men who were essentially gamblers by nature. Mike Todd would be the closest one of our generation. When they had money, they really spent it and lived in penthouses. When they traveled to Europe, they traveled first class, and died broke. I had seen this kind of up-and-down in my own life. I always felt that it was going to go, and therefore I had a great need to work and to know that I could support myself.

When I think about women working, we only hear about the joyous jobs, we don't hear about the drab jobs which men automatically assumed they would take. I always felt very insecure financially. I was always sure that it would be totally over. And this is what my father was talking about when people have said, Why did she work? She came from a family with money. My father, Lou Walters, founded and ran a series of nightclubs called The Latin Quarter. The insecurities of show business permeated my life, so that I knew: A, I had to work. B, I had to be self-supporting. No matter how much money there was, it was always going to finish. The curtain was going to come down. We would not all go to the seashore on Sunday.

PROBST: What do you think of people who've been brought in to match your ratings? Stephanie Edwards and Sally Quinn were pitted against you.

WALTERS: These two specific women? Would you ask that question if you were talking to Frank McGee or Jim Hartz about Bill Beutel?

PROBST: They were not brought in to deal with Frank McGee or Jim Hartz.

WALTERS: They sure were. Why not?

PROBST: The "Today" show is now identifiable as you. First of all, you're the longest surviving member of the "Today" show, right? Hughes Rudd was not the person they talked about. Bill Beutel was not the person they talked about. They talked about a woman.

WALTERS: It made for very good publicity and very bad publicity. I'm very proud of the way Sally and I handled ourselves in these circumstances. We dealt with each other in dignity and we never allowed ourselves to sink to the occasion. And I think we came out of it, both of us, the better for it. What it did for me, in a funny way, was to make me the underdog, and I never had been. For many years on the "Today" show, there was a feeling that if a woman asked direct questions, and maybe asked some tough questions—certainly during the Hugh Downs era, he was very gentle—I used to get upset if I didn't get The Question. Hugh felt much more about the ambience of it—if the time ran out, that was okay as long as we had a charming guest. I never felt they were guests. So I think there was a certain amount of antagonism to me both from men and women. The women might have felt that in a funny way I was putting them down because I was working when they weren't, and the men might have said, Look at her up there, castrating all of these people. . . . And suddenly Sally came in, and Sally was described as the sexpot. I became Jane Wyman, kind of dowdy, and I wasn't living with anybody. The day that Sally came on, I remember we were doing our show outdoors from Rockefeller Center and people would come up to me and say, "It's okay. You've still got your job." People began to look at me as a human being, as someone who also could bleed. What I resented mostly was the image that women had to scrap and tear each other apart and hurt each other. I wanted Sally to be a success—not because I'm such a wonderful person, I have as many jealousies and fears as the next one. But if Sally didn't make it, people would say that there's no place really for women in television. Barbara could make it on the "Today" show, but really nowhere else. I didn't want that to happen. Also, Sally was the first cohost. At the time that she was made cohost, I wasn't. For a lot of reasons, it would have helped me if she had been a success. I didn't feel that I had to die for her to live.

Stephanie Edwards I don't know at all. It seemed to me that she was fresh and warm and very charming. I watched her very keenly and couldn't find anything to criticize, but I think Stephanie had been picked to be the opposite of me. The apple-cheeked girl next door who comes from a farm and milks the cows. There is room for my type. There is room for Stephanie's type. And I was very gratified that people—with rare exceptions—stopped pitting each of us against the other. I hoped the show would not go off the air—and I hoped that it didn't become terribly successful.

PROBST: Do you have an obligation to state the women's point of view? Do you carry a public burden?

WALTERS: If you do, you're tongue-tied. I never feel resentment towards me from younger women, or younger men, ever. If I feel it, it's from the people my age, where still there's a kind of a threat about a woman having a position of authority and stating it. I feel that younger women, and maybe men, too, can identify because I made it through working—against some odds—by being myself, not because I was the boss's daughter and not because I slept with the boss. Although, if I had to do it all over again and he would have asked me, I would have done it, and it wouldn't have taken me twelve years, I think. Too late now. And that pleases me very much.

PROBST: It has been said that at first you were antistudent, antifeminist.

WALTERS: I've never been as militant as the militants. Women's liberation didn't put me where I am. But no woman who works can help but be very grateful to women's liberation for the awareness it's made on executives—I probably would not be cohost if it were not for women's liberation—for the internal awareness it's created. It takes the far-out to draw the crowd with them. On the other hand, I feel that we're the only game in town, that is, we are the only show that does in-depth interviews and reaches a wide audience. It's very important, I feel, for many of the women's issues to be raised there. I try to be objective, though I'm afraid I'm not always when it comes to discussions of the Equal Rights Amendment or abortions and so on, but I try to keep my personal opinions to myself. If you are a strong member of the women's movement, you might feel that I have not been at the head. I have been very pleased to receive citations from NOW, which I wave whenever anybody says, She hasn't done enough.

PROBST: Was it difficult to break through because you are a woman?

WALTERS: It was, is, will be.

PROBST: Let me turn the whole thing around. Assuming everything is the same on "Today," but one thing had been different, would it have ended up where it is today, if you hadn't been a woman?

WALTERS: I wouldn't have been hired in the first place if I

hadn't been a woman. I was hired on a program in which women had been the weather girls. I was the first Today Girl who wasn't a Today Girl—I was the first one who came on and didn't do the weather. But they needed a girl. I was hired by default. I was hired when Maureen O'Sullivan, who was the last Today Girl, said, "There's no place for a woman in this show. Women are bookends."

I had been doing my own stories, I would have been doing much better stories much earlier. I wouldn't have been relegated for so many years—until six months ago—to a very particular kind of story. I wouldn't have had to go out and get my own interviews, the Kissingers or the Dean Rusks or Sadats or even some of the special women. If they came into the studio, the man on the show would do it, but if I did it myself, and I did it on film, it was mine. It got me a reputation for being a very good interviewer and it got me a reputation for being a tough, aggressive, scary woman. I would have been able to avoid all that. It caused me personal pain—did, and still does. I was hired because I'm a woman. Had I not been, I might have been just one more man. There is something when you bear the joy of it and the pain of it in being one of the few women. There will be more. I won't be at all unique in five years. Right now, when it's good it's very, very good, and when it's bad it's painful. I have much publicity, much more attention, much more excitement, much more everything than Jim Hartz. I also have much more criticism, much more pain, many more false stories written about me. But to say what would it have been like if I weren't a girl, a woman, a female. . . .

PROBST: Would you have come as far . . . ?

WALTERS: Who knows, I might have been Walter Cronkite.

PROBST: Do you want to be Walter Cronkite?

WALTERS: No, I don't. But who can say? I might have been Tom Brokaw and the White House correspondent. My next step might have been doing "Nightly News." Had I been a man, given the same circumstances and the same amount of hard work, I might have been Jim Hartz. I might have been Hugh Downs—and not left. I might have made much more money a long time ago than I'm just beginning to make. Everybody hears about my salary—and I'm hardly complaining—but all the men consistently made two or three times more than I did. I probably would have made it as a male reporter because I cared and I liked it and I was good at it. But I don't want to be a man, this is what I am.

PROBST: Do you consider yourself a reporter?

WALTERS: Sometimes I'm a reporter.

PROBST: Do you find acceptance as a journalist?

WALTERS: Now. Now I do. Even today there's a very heavy line between what is supposedly entertainment and what is news. The first blurred line that I could see was in the three-hour special "Of Women and Men"—I automatically want to say "Of Men and Women," and I know that it's the years of brainwashing. There is a feeling in the news departments in television, and newspapers as well, that you have to come from the news departments, you have to have newspaper experience, you have to have AP and UPI experience, you have to be from what we call at NBC "the fifth floor," because that's where the News Department is. I was a child of television. I came out of college and went into television. Many of us now are, we are the younger breed.

Also, the "Today Show" had originally been part of the Entertainment Department, then it changed to News. A lot of people felt, She is a personality, it's a talk show. There was a kind of put-down in that. That's changed. One of the breakthroughs was when NBC sent me to China. I can now go out and cover any story, and the men will not say, What is she doing there? But that's a great deal of internal, really news snobbism. There are none as old-fashioned and jealous of their position as the old-time newsmen. They're still wearing the green shades.

PROBST: The three-hour documentary you did with Tom Snyder—"Of Women and Men"—in the first two hours you wore a red dress, and the third hour you had on a black dress. Why?

WALTERS: I'm not sure that that wasn't a mistake—Tom Snyder didn't change. It was a mistake. There's enough going wrong without having to be picked on because you changed a dress. It was a pretty dress. But I'm sorry I did it. It was the first special, night-time special, I had ever, in eleven years, been asked to do. And if you ask me, does it make a difference that I was a woman? Absolutely. Had I been a man, I would have been doing specials years ago.

PROBST: You, of course, did the election night.

WALTERS: That's not a special. I was very pleased that there was that breakthrough, but again, I don't think it should have taken eleven years to use me on election night.

PROBST: On "Today" is there some guideline that is your mark of a good interview?

WALTERS: I think it is important for the person who is being interviewed to say what it is that he has to say. I think that the audience out there should understand it. I think that the interview should have a beginning, a middle, and an end. It's hard, as often happens on the show, for two of us to interview one, and for two to interview two or two to interview three is murder. You really have to have a sense of each other's pace. You have to have compassion and understanding for each other. You have to have almost mind signals. You have to be almost a husband and wife—more so than most husbands and wives—in feeling when the other one wants to say something. That's very difficult. Also, "Today," unlike almost every other program, is live. We—no matter what, we have that clock. If an interview is great it's eight minutes, and if it's lousy it's eight minutes. Walter Cronkite once said, when we were talking about this, that he would find it unbelievably difficult to have to do an interview to the clock, which is why you so often hear us saying, There's only one minute left, please get to the point. While I am sometimes interruptive, it is more important for me to have the person say what he's got to say than for me to come off lovely and charming and relaxed and have that last question left in the control room.

PROBST: How much of you spills over on the tube?

WALTERS: Very much on "Not For Women Only." Very little on "Today." I have strong feelings about Israel, I don't think that shows on the air ... if anything, I'm probably tougher on the Israelis than I am on the Arabs. But it's something that I feel strongly about and somewhat passionately about. It's not only not my place to show it on the air, it would be totally wrong for me to. At that point I am a journalist and a reporter and my views are not important. I think in recent years more of my own personality has come across. I don't think it's important for people to know my opinions. I think it works against it.

PROBST: Are you treated in a special way because you are Barbara Walters?

WALTERS: Do you really think that within NBC that I'm treated . . . don't you think that we're treated the same within our own company?

PROBST: No, you are a celebrity. . . .

WALTERS: In my own company? We're talking about how we're treated every day. At NBC we are not treated specially. In my private life I'm able to go most places totally privately. I'm not recognized. It's lovely when people come up to you. I like it. But when you live in New York you can have as private a life as you want. My personal life, I think, is very private. I don't think anybody really knows about it.

PROBST: What do you think the public perception of you is?

WALTERS: If they watch the show, and if they're secure, then I think they say, She works very hard, she's sometimes tough, she's sometimes intense, she's sometimes funny, and they respect, and I hope, like me. I think if they do not watch the show and they just read the warmed-over newspaper columns, I think their feeling is that I am aggressive, tough, cold, unfeeling. That causes me much more pain than it should at this point in my life.

PROBST: You are very sensitive to criticism, then?

WALTERS: Yes, and I think everybody is. I am less sensitive now. I used to cry over something that was untrue. I don't cry anymore and I don't read everything anymore. But I find it hurts me. I hope I never get to the point where it doesn't. I never want to be that smug. I always want to be vulnerable enough to have things that are really very bad about me or very untrue about me, something that I would want to work on changing or something that I would want to fight. . . . I can't suddenly come on the air and be a totally different person, but I don't want to get to the point where nothing anybody says or does bothers me.

PROBST: Your advice to young women who wanted to become Barbara Walterses was, Don't get pregnant.

WALTERS: I think that in everything there are choices, obviously. The women's movement brought along as a corollary the belief that you could have everything. You could have *the* job and the good marriage and the children and the social life and the Ph.D. And you can't. It doesn't mean that you can't have them one at a time or that you can't have a combination of them. But each of them takes a good deal of work. Whether it's a woman or a man that's getting anywhere, if you are ambitious, you don't give up when the job is grubby and boring. I've had some boring jobs. If you really do want it, you've got to be available to work very long hours—women and men—you have to work longer and harder than anybody else. You have to be available that Saturday. You can't go home at five o'clock, especially in this business. If something comes up and you've got to travel you've got to be able to do it. It is tough with a child, especially in those early days before you've made it, because you don't have the maid to help you and Grandma can't always come. So, I said, If you really do want this and it's important to you, wait. The way life is now, you can have a baby at twenty-eight, or thirty-three or thirty-five. You don't have to have it at twenty. There are very definite choices you can make. You cannot have everything all at once. So I said, very flippantly, Don't get pregnant. Or get pregnant, and somebody else will work until seven o'clock—your husband.

Q *(question from audience)*: Were you subject to adverse criticism on the China trip with Nixon because you worked so hard?

WALTERS: I was not considered a journalist in the sense that the Washington press corps were. I was the only television woman, and television was very resented on that trip, because the newspaper reporters felt we were coming in with all the cameras and all the people. They didn't realize how tough it was for us as well. I think they felt that I was going to walk in and get the first interview with Chou En-lai. I think there was also kind of a feeling, which took me a long time to get over, that I was Nixon's pet because of my interview with Haldeman.

I am by nature very shy. I cannot travel alone. I would sooner die than go downstairs and eat in a restaurant by myself. I can only go places where I have friends. I ate alone. They thought I was very cold. I thought they were ignoring me. They—all the White House reporters—sat together. They were distrustful. I wasn't one of them. I never worked so hard in my life. I never was so unhappy. I remember going in my room one day and closing the door and bursting into tears and saying "Help!" and then realizing nobody was listening, and getting dressed and going. We worked day and night. It was terribly, terribly hard. I thought I was going to come home and be fired. I thought I had done a terrible job. I also felt extremely insecure because I would sit and I could hear Harry Reasoner and Cronkite—who is the most adorable man, Cronkite, lovely man—but there wasn't that much time for amenities. And I could hear them reporting and my style was very different. I came back from that trip to find that I had done more stories than anybody else on the trip. But I think that the impression of this intense, cold girl, who was Henry Kissinger's friend, who knew Bob Haldeman, who the President would say, "Hi ya, Barbara," to—why not, I was the only girl, I was the only one he could spot. . . . It would not happen today. A lot has changed in three years. The people who were the most supportive to me on the trip were the stars. Cronkite, Chancellor, Harry Reasoner. And I am very grateful because they not only defended me, if it needed that, but understood and helped me.

Q: Is there anything about "Today" which displeases you?

WALTERS: Every day. I think the restriction in time. I think we are too stringent about it. I don't think we should automatically say that an interview has to be eight minutes with a two-minute art feature after it. We should have, maybe, more flexibility. However, having said all of that, this is a program which has never talked down to anybody. It amazes me, given the kind of fare that it does, that people are so interested, that they do watch, that it reaches the broad audience it does. I think it speaks to the incredible curiosity and intelligence and sensitivity of the American audience. It is a strange, unique, sometimes very boring, sometimes very exciting show, and I'm intensely proud of it and of the audience who watch it.

PROBST: Do you like interviewing?

WALTERS: Yes. This show has changed my life. I never expected all of this to happen. I meet the most important, interesting, attractive, unattractive people in the world. I can ask them the questions that I think all of you really want to know, rather than the question that is going to make the headline. There is always that terrible choice when you're doing an important interview: Do I want to impress *The New York Times* or am I trying to tell people at home what they should know?

PROBST: You should ask both.

WALTERS: You can't always. But I love it. To be able to ask the most interesting and important people in the world—and even the unimportant ones—everything you're curious about. And then to get paid, and then to get applauded—I have always said, and I mean it, that I would do this job for nothing.

9

EDWIN NEWMAN:

I'm Not the Kind of Guy to Blow a Trumpet and Shout, Charge!

PROBST: People who know you through your work feel that they can trust you, feel that you will not talk down to them, and that if they hear it from you, whether it's funny or not funny, they should pay attention to it. It seems to me that you are in the largest sense a public instructor.

NEWMAN: That may be. If I am a public instructor, it's not the result of any attempt to be so. I hope that we do instruct. On the other hand, setting out to enlighten people in a particular way perhaps would lead you to try to make people think in a particular way or come to particular conclusions. I would accept the term "public instructor" so long as it did not imply that I was trying to impose my views on anybody or so long as it didn't appear that I thought I knew a great deal more than people generally do and that I was in a position to do them a favor by telling them what the facts were. There is to some extent in our business a tendency to think that the public doesn't know very much. I think that's the wrong way to go at news.

PROBST: I think the term "public instructor" means you are saying, This is the way the world looks and let's be adult about it, this is what is important and this is what's funny. I think you're saying, Share this view of this world with me.

NEWMAN: What is implicit in any news program is, This is

what I think matters today. Here it is, as plainly, as clearly, as intelligently as I can put it, with as much appraisal or assessment or weighing as I can give it.

PROBST: You have said that reporting or journalism was an accidental affair?

NEWMAN: It's an accidental affair in the sense that a program should be governed by what the news is rather than by what you want the news to be or by the facilities at your disposal. What makes up news programs should be determined by what has happened and not by where you happen to have your cameras on any given day or by the amount of film that's available to illustrate a particular story. In television production there tends to be a great emphasis on the footage. What have I got? I've got two minutes of this, so I'll use that, and I've got three minutes of that, so I'll use that. You're very often not governed by what the story is.

PROBST: Did you yourself get into news accidentally? You have said that you had a boyhood ambition to be a reporter and that you have in some ways achieved what it is you want to be. You have said you have been extremely fortunate.

NEWMAN: After I began reviewing plays in New York I remember my wife saying to me—and being a play reviewer was an early ambition of mine—"You have to be careful about what you want to be when you grow up because it may come true." That is a quotation from Balzac, I believe. I have been fortunate. During the Depression we were never hungry, never had any real hardship. My father was never unemployed, there was always plenty to eat. I remember seeing a Hooverville along the Hudson River, I certainly remember men selling apples on street corners. But we were lucky, and I think I've always been lucky, for example in having a wife willing to put up with the kind of life this occupation sometimes brings. I have had some thin times, but that would happen to almost anybody.

The ambition to become a reporter came to me when a teacher in my elementary school in New York City told me I wrote well. It made a lasting impression on me. I am not sure how I got from being told that I could write well to wanting to be a newspaperman. It may have had something to do with my older brother, who also became a newspaperman. It may have been a desire to find something very different from what my father was in—at that time, manufacturing men's wear. Maybe we were both trying to get as far as we could from that.

PROBST: You say you were fortunate?

NEWMAN: Luck has a great deal to do with it. During the war I had married and in 1949 I went to London on my own and became a stringer for NBC. I had been working at CBS in Washington, for Eric Severeid, but I decided I would take a chance and go to Europe. I had a Fulbright scholarship to study at the Sorbonne, and I was offered a job by UNESCO in Paris. I had worked for UNESCO for a few hours when a telephone call came saying NBC would take me on as a stringer in London.

PROBST: Is that luck? You had earned the Fulbright scholarship.

NEWMAN: Yes. I suppose one could say that. Luck consists also of taking advantage of the opportunities that present themselves. In our business great opportunities come along in times of difficulty, in times of chaos. That's when you can prove yourself, if indeed you're going to. It's why you welcome what to most people is bad news. You don't go around hoping for disaster, but it's like the understudy who gets a chance when the star breaks a leg.

PROBST: That's the point I'm making. I think the word "luck" is wrong because you can turn a situation into success.

NEWMAN: You can succeed or you can fail. But you have to hope for, it seems to me, the opportunity to try. Sometimes luck is against you. When Robert Kennedy was shot, his body was taken from New York to Washington by train, a scheduled trip of four hours. The trip took eight hours. For a very long time I was in the studio in New York alone. In a situation like that, you prove or disprove yourself. When I say news is an accidental business, I mean I always welcome situations in which things have gone wrong. I've always welcomed emergencies. I've always welcomed the unexpected. That's what you go into the news business for.

PROBST: Have you as a public person had to give up some of your own privacy?

NEWMAN: The privacy I've given up is nominal. You go out in

the street or you go shopping or you go to the theater and people may come up and speak to you, but almost invariably in a kindly and friendly way. Most people in our position would say they're pleased by it, gratified by it. It's quite satisfying, flattering, even. Apart from that, I haven't found I've given up any great amount of privacy. I'm not expected to tell what my holdings are, unlike someone in public office. I'm not expected to make my tax returns public. I'm willing to be interviewed, but I won't be interviewed at home. I've given up very little privacy. I must say that I don't see any reason for any great interest in me as a person. I think I should be judged by what I do.

PROBST: That's a common desire among people I've interviewed.

NEWMAN: I believe this is true also of politicians. They should be judged by their public record. I'm not saying that we can ignore the private lives of public persons, but we have gone very far in the wrong direction. I think that insisting on the revelations of financial holdings of men and women in public life is foolish. I think that requiring them to make income tax returns public is foolish. I think it is thoroughly undignified to take somebody who has been in public life for twenty-five years, like Ford when he was nominated as Vice-President, and send three hundred fifty FBI agents to find out what could be found out about him. Some part of politics, and the larger part the better, has to be left to the people. And if that means that you're risking installing bad people, crazy people, psychotic people, unstable people, unwell people—that seems to me part of the business of politics. It's a risk I would prefer to having, as I say, an inch-by-inch examination of everybody's life before he is accepted for public office. I think the cure is worse than the ailment.

You cannot station reporters in nightclubs in Washington to see what members of Congress are up to. You can't have them parked around the grounds around the Washington Monument to see who's jumping into fountains. You can't conduct a news business or the business of government that way.

PROBST: What's wrong with endless revelations?

NEWMAN: It degrades public life. If purity tests are to become an accepted part of American life before anybody can go into politics, politics is going to be intolerable. It's very nearly intolerable now.

The kind of attention given to men and women in public office is somewhat akin to the idolatrous attention paid to the Kennedys when they were in office. It leads to all kinds of lunatic expectations about what can be accomplished by politicians and so leads to irrational and disproportionate disappointment. It tends to distract us from the real business of politics and the real business of government. Not only does it mislead people about Presidents, it misleads Presidents about Presidents so that they are tempted to do foolish things. And I think the press contributes to this for reasons of its own.

PROBST: What are the reasons?

NEWMAN: There is a tendency on the part of people in my business, and particularly in Washington, to judge a President by his relations with them. Nixon left the presidency, Ford became President—elation in "the Washington press corps," as it likes to call itself. Why elation in the Washington press corps? Because we're going to have an open administration. How are we going to have an open administration? He's going to hold news conferences. In his news conferences, he stands in a part of the room different from the part of the room in which Nixon stood when he held news conferences. Washington correspondents see this as enormously significant.

PROBST: Aren't presidential news conferences useful?

NEWMAN: A President's relations with the press obviously affect the success or failure of a presidency, because they affect the way in which the public looks at a President. But I try not to judge a President by his attitude to me. And I try not to judge a President by the number of news conferences he holds. I try not to judge a President by the number of times he allows his picture to be taken in so-called intimate circumstances, or other circumstances. I try to judge him on what his policy is. I think that's the only sensible way to go at it. The alleged charm of the President, the alleged grace of the President, the alleged dominating political genius of the President—which we heard attributed to Lyndon Johnson—all of this stuff has to be discounted. At some point you have to say, What has he done? What does he want to do? Is it good? Gerald Ford may be the nicest man in the world and have the most delightful family in the world, but at some point you're going to have to say to yourself, Do I want him to be President? I will decide according to the policies he proposes and the chance he has of carrying them out. I will also consider other factors, such as the question of whether a dynasty is being created, whether values that seem to me to be phony are being propagated, as in the case of someone being represented as the prince of Camelot or whatever it is.

PROBST: You speak of revelation of private facts about public figures as degrading, let's talk about another kind of degradation—degrading the language. In your book *Strictly Speaking* you ask what happened to clarity and elegance. Are there speakers you like?

NEWMAN: I could name one. Eugene McCarthy speaks well. He speaks sometimes with a certain impatience toward his audience, I think. But it seems to me that his language is elevated and it's specific and it's funny and it's frequently marvelously sardonic. In fact, very often it gets by you. You don't realize how sardonic it is. Kissinger speaks quite well, I think, but Kissinger is the beneficiary of a generally low level of speech in Washington, so that he stands out. It is not very difficult to stand out in Washington. Senator Gruening of Alaska was a good speaker. Wayne Morse of Oregon was a good speaker, but very long-winded. Hubert Humphrey can speak well if you can limit him. There are persons who speak with passion and clarity and force. But it seems to me that all the tendencies in our lives these days are running against that. There are many, many overpowering forces at work that make the language boneless and lumpy. They come from government, they come from the social sciences, which are twins, and they're adopted by people in my business and by politicians, and they spread. Nobody says "reading" and "writing" anymore. You say, "communications skills." Nobody says, The teacher encouraged the child—you say, The teacher "emitted reinforcers." We are awash in nonsense, I would say. The less you have to say, the lumpier, the more gaseous, the more pretentious the language in which you clothe a tiny idea.

PROBST: You have been called the house grammarian at NBC. Do people sometimes regard you as a crank or a pedant because you are concerned with the standards or values of speech?

NEWMAN: Yes. One man who wrote to me said he agreed with what I had written but that when he spoke to his boss about this—and his boss was half his age—the boss said, "That relic Newman is not with it." Well, I agree that I'm not with it. Not only am I not with it, I don't want to be. That annoys some people or seems foolish to some people or irrelevant. You will be judged to be somebody from the Victorian age. But I don't believe a language can serve a purpose, can serve the purpose for which it was devised, unless some standards are maintained. If the language is changing before your eyes, it ceases to have any value. It's like money. If the value of money is changing from minute to minute, it ceases to have any value as a medium of exchange. The code of courtesy is the same. If that's changing from minute to minute, nobody knows what to do. Language has to have some stability. It has to have some enduring value. It has to have an enduring form if it is to be used as a means of communication.

PROBST: Your view, it seems to me, is one of a perfectionist in a time of great imperfection. Do you feel that you are happily out of step with other people in the news business at times? That you are different from them?

NEWMAN: Yes, I think I am, and in one way I'm happy to be, because there is nothing more comfortable than the feeling that you are alone but correct! On the other hand, you have reason to be depressed because you feel that the fight you're fighting is a losing one. I believe that, generally, the language is going under. I do.

PROBST: Are you working for a concept of purity or truth, or correctness?

NEWMAN: No. What I am doing is trying to convince people that the use of language that is concrete and specific and straightforward is desirable.

PROBST: You don't go to anybody at NBC or CBS or ABC and

ask them whether your use of language is proper. You're not trying to get their approval. In your work as an author, as a writer, as a speaker, as a broadcaster, as a poet, as a humorist, who is it or what is it that you are working for?

NEWMAN: To me, language should, to the maximum extent possible, be a personal expression. It should be the expression of an individual. That's one reason I object strongly to the use of catch phrases and catchwords and whatever the fad expression of the moment happens to be. We ruin, very quickly, many eloquent, vivid phrases by overuse. All I am trying to do is impose . . . accept standards for myself that are acceptable to me.

Q *(question from audience)*: What's your opinion of the younger generation of journalists?

NEWMAN: Many of the younger people go right into radio and television. But unless you have worked for a newspaper or a wire service, you're not very likely to understand how they operate and you run the risk of being taken in by what is nothing more than a rewrite of an earlier lead. Also, in the younger generation there is some espousal of advocacy journalism. I don't believe in that. I believe journalists should be independent, should be detached to the extent that that is possible. Advocacy journalism, so-called, cheats the public, which is entitled to make up its own mind. I believe also that the younger generation has been brought up to believe that words are not very important, that pictures are or that feelings are. I believe that's wrong. I believe it's a mistake. Now whether I believe this simply because I am older than they are, I can't be certain. But I believe it's a mistake. I think that the best way of communicating is language. If we do not protect and preserve our language, we will take the consequences. I believe we already have taken many of the consequences of not insisting on higher standards of expression and on specific and concrete language.

PROBST: But more than language—your standards of your work, of yourself?

NEWMAN: I believe you have an obligation if you're in the news business to report the news as straightforwardly as you can, shedding as much light on it as you can, and that it is not your job simply to emit a stream of sound that sounds vaguely as though it has some connection with news. I take this as an obligation not merely to other people but to myself. I think it's the same sense any writer has. Any writer writes for himself. There are people who believe that if you're on television, you're talking to somebody in a living room in Scotts Bluff, Nebraska, let's say. Well, I don't visualize anybody. I talk to the camera, which is a way of saying I talk to myself. I am trying to write a news program and deliver a news program that I would be interested in, that it seems to me would be worth my listening to. That is what I try to do. I'm trying to meet my own standards, and I think that any writer tries to meet his own standards, or should.

PROBST: George Jessel was on "Today" with you and he equated—attempted to equate—*The New York Times* with *Pravda.* You had tried to get him off the subject, and when you couldn't, you got him off the air. How do you make that decision?

NEWMAN: Jessel had said, "*Pravda*—pardon me, I mean *The Washington Post.*" And then he said, "*Pravda*—pardon me, I mean *The New York Times.*" The interview had made very little sense to that point and this merely climaxed it. There was only about a minute left to go and I might just as well have let him ramble on, I suppose. But I just said, "Thank you very much," and told him I didn't want to hear any more from him and there wasn't a great deal he could do about it. It just seemed to me that this was arrant nonsense. Now, you will say to me, He's surely not the only person in the history of television to have talked arrant nonsense. And I will say, You're absolutely right.

PROBST: What standards or what values do you set?

NEWMAN: I don't know. I had torn a ligament. I was in considerable discomfort. And I suppose in other circumstances I might not have done it. But it seemed to me to be outrageous that this was going out on the air and that I was an accessory to it. I decided more or less on the spur of the moment that was it, I wasn't going to hear any more. What standards can you establish to keep nonsense off the air? You can't.

PROBST: The other day you were asked by a French historian what you see when you look at America and what you foresee.

You've written a book, you're an author who is listened to, and you're on television and you know this country, you travel a lot in it. Are there any values in America?

NEWMAN: Well, that's not the kind of question I'm very good at answering. It isn't the way I go at things. It's tempting to paint the broad picture, it's tempting to be a columnist or a preacher, but I'm not very good at that and I don't have a great deal of interest in it.

I do see in the United States many admirable things that we should preserve, that we should expand if we possibly can. Such civil liberties as we have obviously should be protected at all costs. The rights that were guaranteed under the Constitution must be preserved. I argue that politics has to be left in the hands of the people, that you can't turn it over to psychologists, you can't turn it over to experts, you shouldn't be turning it over to computers, you shouldn't be turning it over to public-opinion pollsters. I can see the values of some specific things. I have a feeling that the United States could have been something like a paradise. It isn't, for a lot of reasons. It is a country with a vast potential to which, luckily for me, in the course of making my own living I could make some contribution. But I try not to be self-conscious about it. I don't believe, for example, that the press should ever think of itself as part of the government. I think we're separate from the government. I think we should be detached, I think we should be independent. I think it should be understood that we're not crusaders and we're not doing what we do for the sake of the public good. Most of us do what we do because we want to make a living and because we find the kind of work we do interesting. And if some good flows from that, fine. That's another reason I regard news as an accidental business. I was once interviewed by *Time,* and I had a reputation as somebody who could do many things in broadcasting, and the interviewer said to me, "Is there anything you're not good at?" I said modestly, "Yes, there's something I'm not good at." "What is that?" "Well, I'm not very good at expressing awe." And I'm *not* very good at saying, This is a momentous occasion. And I'm not very good at looking at something and becoming starry-eyed about it. I'm not the kind of guy who's ever going to blow a trumpet and shout, Charge, and have a great many people follow me. I'm too—well, this sounds self-conscious, but I'm probably too sarcastic in my attitude, too sardonic. I'm too much of a wisecracker ever to go in for inspirational talk.

PROBST: When I have asked a question you said, "Well, that's not how I would go at it." What do you mean? How *do* you go at it?

NEWMAN: Take the example of the impeachment and resignation of Richard Nixon. If you want to, you can describe the story as momentous. You can say, as many members of Congress did, that they had an awesome responsibility in deciding what to do. I didn't think so. I didn't think that they had an awesome responsibility. I thought they had a responsibility under the Constitution which they took on when they were elected to office and when they sought public office. And I don't think that it is an awesome matter to decide whether somebody is guilty or innocent, whether somebody should be impeached and convicted. I think that's part of the job you take on. I would have never gone on the air and said, This is historic, this is momentous, this is awesome. That's not my way of going at it. If I were giving advice on the matter, I would say it's much better if you're faced with a situation of that kind to take it in stride. The country's not going to come to an end because a President resigned. We're not all going to be murdered in our beds because a President resigned. You take it in stride. And if we had been prepared to take it in stride, I think it all would have been over much sooner.

PROBST: My question is too awesome, too broad?

NEWMAN: I don't think in those terms. I'm a reporter. I'm a newspaperman who's gone into television, and I tend to think in terms of stories. This is a story, that's a story, that's a story. And I find it very difficult to say . . . so to speak, to take the temperature of the United States at any given time and know what it is.

I should say at the moment, however, that because of Vietnam and because of Watergate the country is open now, to what seems to me an extraordinary degree, to an attack of common sense, to the acquisition, or perhaps reacquisition, of a sense of proportion about American life, about American politics, and about the American presidency. The country is open to the suggestion that it ought to look very carefully at what it's told, that language matters because ideas are clothed in language and you have to look at words if you want to look at ideas. Also that there's nothing wrong—in fact, there's everything right, in my opinion—with being skeptical about everything you're told, not only by politicians but by people in our business. I think the country is encouragingly open to that kind of reform, if it is a reform. I think that the disillusioning process brought about by Indochina, the disillusioning process brought about by the environmental movement, the disillusioning process brought about by Watergate, all of these things have destroyed a lot of foolish ideas people were led to have. Maybe even wanted to have. If we can now regain some sense of proportion about ourselves, and about our political institutions in particular, we're going to be a great deal better off. If that's a broad enough answer, fine.

Q: You are critical of heroes, yet in a way television figures are themselves the new heroes. Walter Cronkite, according to one poll, is now the most respected man in America. In a time when we don't seem to respect national institutions like politics or the church, television seems to replace them. Is there a danger of our substituting form and face for substance, for ideas, and do you feel a particular burden yourself as a television figure?

NEWMAN: If you're not seeking power, you're not seeking to retain such powers as are given you and you're not directing your conduct to retain that power. You are doing your job. It is possible that what is important is not sufficiently studied and exposed to public view. But I don't see what anybody, let's say in Cronkite's position, is to do about it apart from reporting the news as well as he can. It would be very bad for him to feel a great burden, to become more cautious about what he did or to trim what he did because he feared the consequences of it. I don't think you can be in the news business and work that way.

I think the best thing anybody in my position can do is to be as independent as possible, as detached as possible, as impersonal as possible. Anybody in our business should avoid taking on false importance. We should certainly not pretend to be infallible. We should make it clear that when we present the news this is the news as far as we know it. We should, I think, discourage the idea that we're holding back anything and that we know a great deal more than we're telling. Because of what has happened—the departure of the President, following on Indochina—the press may seem to be very, very powerful. But I must say that I get the sense that people generally are skeptical of us. They are as skeptical of us as they are of anybody else. And indeed they should be.

PROBST: You do not have or believe in heroes and yet you are a hero.

NEWMAN: Well, if I am, which I doubt, but if I am, it's not my doing. It's nothing I've tried to accomplish and it is nothing I would try to continue. I think the best thing anybody in the news business can do is present the news as clearly and as enlighteningly as he can, but try to step aside from it.

PROBST: Do you feel you are a public symbol?

NEWMAN: No. Let's take an example. You're a drama critic. Do you have a responsibility because there's so much money involved in the show? You don't. You can't take account of the consequences when you are reviewing a show. All you can say is, This seemed to me to be a good show—or a bad show, or a mediocre show. When you're reporting, you cannot take account of the consequences. You cannot say—or you should not say—I will report this and then Nixon won't be President any longer, or I will report this and then Nixon will continue as President. If there is one principle in our business, it is you report the news without regard to the consequences. If you stop to think about what the consequences are, then you're getting beyond your depth, you're getting out of your field. If a government stands or falls by what you report, that's not your business. Your business is to report. It's not your business what the consequences are. The consequences are somebody else's business.

PROBST: Why is it that the most trusted person in America is a television person?

NEWMAN: You can ask yourself another question, I suppose, which is, Who would you like it to be? Who would it be? We don't have any national clergymen. Apart from the President, practically speaking, we don't have any national politicians. It's a big country and television is perhaps the only genuinely national institution in it.

10

LYNN REDGRAVE:

You Stand Up with a Famous Name, You'd Better Prove It

PROBST: You said that as a young person you did not want to be an actress.

REDGRAVE: When I was little I didn't.

PROBST: Was that because of the family?

REDGRAVE: It's awfully hard to know. We would go to a party and there would be a lot of actors and they would say, Is this another little actor? I was very shy and I thought that the two were incompatible—I only discovered later it wasn't true. I thought if you were shy you couldn't be an actor. I've since discovered that actors are mostly shy and they stand up *because* they are shy and then they don't have to be. So I would answer, Well, of course not. I'd be very angry. I'd think, Of course I couldn't, I wouldn't want to be an actor. But I loved going to the theater—I went to the theater from the age of five.

PROBST: What does it mean having the name Redgrave?

REDGRAVE: I don't quite know what it means, honestly. People over here sometimes talk about the Royal Family of the Theater or some such highfalutin name. My father is a most distinguished actor, people put a sort of aura about him. And of course he has been a marvelous, marvelous actor. People put the family a little bit more on a pedestal than they should, I think. They make it more special because there's more of us—I don't know that it's that special. But I'm very proud of them.

PROBST: Is it "them"? Aren't you part of them?

REDGRAVE: Yes, I mean I feel proud for all of us. If I do well, they feel proud of me. We all feel proud of each other—but we then have to have a little distance, too.

PROBST: It sounds like a corporation.

REDGRAVE: A little.

PROBST: Has anybody ever compared it to the Fonda family?

REDGRAVE: Yes, sometimes, yes. I think that Jane originally started her political involvement because of my sister and called her daughter after my sister. So, in a way, she was very influenced by Vanessa. I think she's gone further than Vanessa did in being sure about what she's involved with. Vanessa's been more diversified. Vanessa lives her life the way she sees it. I don't necessarily agree or disagree with everything she does and I don't always even think about what she does. Sometimes I do because I can't help my involvement with the person I used to know. I don't know her so well now.

PROBST: Do you think you would have gotten as far as you have as an actress if you hadn't been the daughter of Sir Michael Redgrave?

REDGRAVE: Impossible to tell. It's hard to know how much a leg up it is or not. I know for sure what the disadvantages are. The disadvantages are the instant readiness for the "guns out" that are always there for any celebrity's children. It's very hard to calculate the advantages. The advantages are so obvious that they're not always true. I know that Liza Minnelli and Lorna Luft and the Fondas—any of them have found that the minute you stand up with a famous name you'd better prove it. If you stand up with any sort of a name, you'd better be better than the other people. And you're not necessarily. Maybe you're eighteen and you're not better than anybody. You're just trying. The other thing, of course, is the reluctance of people to give you a job so as not to show they're doing you a favor. Most of your employers in your own country will be family friends—if your family are actors, they're going to know everybody—you're going to find that most directors and producers will know your parents. Very few, contrary to popular belief, will say, I will give her the job because she is so-and-so's daughter. Most of them say, Well, it would look like favoritism, so we don't do it. So you had better be better.

The main disadvantage is that the minute you walk on they're going to watch you. Maybe you're not ready to be watched. You're going to be criticized as if you were a seasoned performer, and you're not. Of course, it opens certain doors to you, and as time goes by, if you continue to work, you get accepted. If somebody who has none of these supposed advantages gets noticed without that name, that's their own achievement. Everybody is prepared to say, Well, of course, it's either born into her or her father coached her, which is always untrue. The last person you go to is your father. I don't think any actors' children I know would ever do an audition piece for their parents. They wouldn't ask them because they don't want to have that connection. They want to do their own thing.

PROBST: Like the doctor operating on his own son.

REDGRAVE: Yes, you can't do that. One advantage is that if one of you is working, nobody's quite sure who it is, so you can take time out to have children without everybody feeling you're out of work. There is the disadvantage of overexposure with everybody thinking, If I hear that name Redgrave again, I'll throw up.

PROBST: You got your training at the National Theatre?

REDGRAVE: The National was an experience I can't imagine anybody having the luck to have again, simply because it was at a time of great creativity. They had a company that you could not reassemble until another generation of wonderful actors comes along. There was Maggie Smith, Robert Stephens, Robert Lang, Laurence Olivier, Edith Evans, Celia Johnson, Derek Jacobi, and the directors, Samuel Beckett, George Devine, and Zeffirelli, and Olivier and Coward and Bill Gaskell and John Dexter. All of them at a peak of energy that was extraordinary. I did some marvelous parts, but they were supporting parts.

PROBST: Were you in *Midsummer Night's Dream* there?

REDGRAVE: No. *Midsummer Night's Dream* I did at the Court. It was my first job. I was at drama school at the time, Central

School at the Embassy Theatre. Jocelyn Herbert, who was the designer, knew me personally and suggested I have an audition. I went to the principal in the drama school and she said, "No, you shouldn't because you're still in the middle of your training. You have another two terms to go." I was then eighteen. I said, "What do you mean, I shouldn't do it?" and she said, "Well, you know, you're not experienced enough," and this and that. That's a bit silly, I thought. I should go even if it's painful, because I should learn how it is to get up and do an audition. I thought, To hell with her, I'll go anyway. I did an audition—and then, horror of horrors, I got it. I didn't know what to do and I went back to the principal and said, "I'm terribly sorry. I did that audition and I don't know whether to take it." First she was incensed, then she said I shouldn't take it, I should finish school. So, I rang up my father, who was in America. I usually used to ask my father about things to see how angry or how pleased I felt at his reception. That was my way of judging his advice. If I felt angry, I knew I disagreed, and if I felt pleased, then I knew that bolstered my own feelings. And so I rang him up and said, "Oh, what should I do?" He said, "Don't do it, don't do it. You're in the middle of your training, and you should finish. You're eighteen. It's crazy." So I felt a burning sense of anger. I said, "All right, Dad, bye-bye." I rang up and I took the job—and it was a disaster. I got a couple of good reviews but mostly was quite well-deservedly slaughtered by the press, and at great length.

PROBST: What do you think when you read good notices about yourself?

REDGRAVE: I don't read them now, mainly because I can't bear to read the bad ones. I don't read any when I'm on the stage until after, when I'm all through with whatever it is, because I have to go and do it again. It's a bit different with a film or television because I've done it, anyway. The last three years I haven't read the reviews until after I finish a play, or well on into the run, because the bad ones depress me so badly and don't help, they just make me feel terrible. And the good ones make me feel that I'm not that good. Maybe it picked out something I did that I wasn't aware of, so now I feel awkward doing it. A good example is something I did in *Mother Courage*. There was a certain scene when the whore Yvette sings a song, and I was hanging out some washing and a reviewer devoted a whole paragraph to me hanging out the washing. I could never hang it out again. It was a wonderful review and I was proud of it—and I could never hang out the washing again in the same way without thinking, This is the bit he said was so good. I never used to do it well before, I just did it. And that, perhaps, was what was good about it. So, there's no pleasing. And there's no helping, either.

PROBST: Have you laid *Georgy Girl* to rest?

REDGRAVE: In my mind I laid it to rest an awful long time ago. It always takes other people a longer time.

PROBST: *My Fat Friend* is something like *Georgy Girl*.

REDGRAVE: To me it wasn't. People hearing about it would say, Oh, that's about a girl who has problems. Georgy Girl to me was a very different person, very ruthless. Most people saw her as a sweet softie. I don't think she was a softie at all. She was manipulating and very shrewd. People loved her, I think, because they recognized their own terrible faults and were glad to see them put up on the screen. I think she was quite ruthless. That's not to say that I disliked her. I liked her for all that.

PROBST: Can you play a role of someone you don't like?

REDGRAVE: I have to find likable things about the bad things they do. If they're cruel people, there has to be something more than that. Some characters are so distasteful I don't think one could play them. I was offered a play a short while ago with three characters, all so unlikable that I couldn't have played any of them—they were so beastly. I saw nothing to identify with or to make-believe in. If you play a murderer or somebody who does terrible things, if you just hate them, you're not going to get anywhere.

PROBST: How did you lose the forty-five or fifty pounds?

REDGRAVE: Bit by bit, eating less and less. I got to a point where it was so easy to be fat, so easy to work as a fat person playing hokey people I hated. I hate doing slapstick comedy and knockabout sort of farcical things. That's not saying I dislike farce—a Feydeau farce or Peter Shaffer's *Black Comedy* is not hokey, it's a technique that is quite extraordinary and very difficult. It was obviously going to be very easy for me to be a funny fat actress, and since inside of me I've never been a funny fat actress—I was a serious actress who happened to be funny, which to me was a big distinction—it suddenly dawned on me that to limit myself physically was to limit myself completely. When you've had five years of being a certain type, you'll never break it because it's too easy, it's just too easy to do, and you can never get out of it. There were so many things I thought I wanted to do. You can always get bigger—there's always padding—but you can't get littler. It seemed to me it was better to somehow face facts. I didn't much like that fat, hokey person, anyway.

PROBST: So there really is a strong person inside there.

REDGRAVE: Well, I think . . . there must have been. It was like a drinker or a smoker or a drug taker. I didn't like food that much, I just had a compulsion. If there had been an Eaters Anonymous then in England I would have gone to them.

I've gained more assurance as an actress than I had. I know more what I do. It doesn't make it easier, that makes it more complicated because there's so many more options now. Before, I used to just get on and get up and say it. Now I have to do it a bit better.

PROBST: Are you happier acting, being somebody who you're not rather than who you are?

REDGRAVE: I think it's more interesting than who one is. Lately I've had a more interesting life, but for many years, somebody else's life, even briefly, was more interesting because it wasn't mine. I think most actors, perhaps, find that. Who is Cary Grant? Or David Niven, say? I call them behavior actors. They're very good at behaving. If you put a camera on them, there'd be no perceptible difference between the way they would behave on screen or off. That takes considerable talent. It's very hard, as amateurs find, to get up and drink a cup of tea as if you're just drinking a cup of tea. I find that if I play a part that's very close to myself, it is not only less interesting but drudgery, absolute drudgery, because it is somebody I know so well and don't like so enormously. I don't have to necessarily like the person to play them, but if it's somebody I know so well, it's really boring for me. I sometimes have to do it, but I don't like to.

PROBST: Do you like the Happy Hooker?

REDGRAVE: I like her, yes. I think she's terrific. She does some terrible things, very ruthless in many ways, but I like her because she's sharp and she's funny and she has a sense of humor about her. I think if she didn't have a good sense of humor, I wouldn't like her as well.

PROBST: What attracted you to the role?

REDGRAVE: I've often played—in fact I've nearly always played—people who are underdogs, who kind of struggle through. I'm always playing strugglers. Either misfits or strugglers or put-upon people who don't win out but survive. This is the first time I've had the chance to play somebody who is a winner right down the line. It requires you to appear to have the most extraordinary ego, to have the sort of confidence I've never had. That's a quality I've never played before. I've played people who've been hurt, who've been betrayed, lost the man, won the man—victims—but I've never played somebody who manipulates everything and everybody around them. Usually you have everybody else to react against or react to—in other words, whoever is the dominating person who is making you the misfit or the loser—they're the power you fight against and that's very much easier to do. But to give out the sort of energy that makes other people move is another thing, and I've never played that, it's hard to do. It was very strange and interesting because it was new to me. Some people play such people all the time. Glenda Jackson does. I never do.

PROBST: How did you learn what a hooker's reactions are?

REDGRAVE: I talked to a number of high-priced ones, posh ones, which is what she was. It's business. And acting. They're all actresses, because otherwise they couldn't look at the watch at the end of the half hour. I talked to one girl. I said, "How do you . . . do you ever get involved?" She said, "No. When I fall in love with somebody . . . I would never fall in love with a customer." She said, "How could I watch the clock? I have to remember to charge them at the end." I suppose some you can guess. I suppose some of it is not so far removed from what we would call our own life. Again, short of becoming one. That, I think, is perhaps like saying, Well, then, I have to kill somebody to play a murderer. I don't think I have to do that to know enough to show it.

PROBST: It's been nine years since *Georgy Girl*. You're a mother, you have a career, and you're a wife and you're an expatriate.

REDGRAVE: It all happened gradually. Just after *Georgy Girl* I met my husband. So, first, I was a wife.

PROBST: How does it feel being a mother?

REDGRAVE: Feels nice. It's good. I can't imagine not being. I don't think with any sort of longing back to the days when I wasn't, with any longing at all. Don't resent it in any way or regret it. Kind of a good extension of everything. . . . When we went back to England because I had a film to do, I was still very connected to my family. The thought of life outside of their circle seemed very odd to me. And John, I think, felt that he would like to go back. But it really didn't suit him at all well, he'd been away so long. Once you've been in America it makes living in England very hard. It's fine for a visit and I think pure Americans love England, or a lot of them do. They find it quaint, and if anything's a bit uncomfortable, that's part of the quaintness. It's like going to the Welsh mountains for a holiday or something. You put up with the quaintness. But then you're not part of that. Some Americans find certain things unbearable here because they are American. I would not because it's not my country. So I can be amused by political situations but I cannot be hurt by them or feel responsible for them in any way. I'm happier living here than in England. England has for a long time not been a very easy place to live in, for English people. You get spoiled for little silly things. You wake up in the morning in England and when the kids go to school you must turn the heat off by nine, otherwise there will not be enough heat in the evening. I was born during the war, when you were rationed, you had the one egg a week. And it is so unbearable to me, having tasted just being warm when it's winter and cold when it's summer—things that Americans very much take for granted. The consistency of just being able to go to a shop that will be open and have what you want—will you be able to get buttermilk on the corner? Not, Will I be able to get caviar?

PROBST: You don't harbor a thought of giving up your blue passport for a green passport?

REDGRAVE: No, not particularly. John did, because he wanted to become a citizen and became one and did not feel any reason to continue to be a British citizen. Our children were born in England and I wish they'd been born in America so that they could have the choice of either.

I don't know whether it's because America's a country of immigrants, but there seem no boundaries to me as an actor there. If I say I wish to presume to be a Hungarian millionairess, or I wish to presume to be a cockney street girl, or I wish to presume to be an East Side matron, I could be anything. Or Xaviera Hollander in *The Happy Hooker.* I would never have played Xaviera Hollander in England. Because in England I'm purely a certain type of English actress.

PROBST: You're a Redgrave.

REDGRAVE: Partly, I'm a Redgrave, which has a certain feel to it. Mainly because of the papers, what they like to build of you, which is not very close to the truth. Partly because the sort of things English people want to see you do are rather different from what Americans would want. I find more freedom here. But I don't know to what extent I can do the quality of work here I can do in England—a play at the Royal Shakespeare or the National.

PROBST: None of the companies here compares in quality with the companies there.

REDGRAVE: That may be true. But on the other hand, I can still go back to do that sort of thing. The world has shrunk, and coming here does not rule that out for me. If somebody says, Can you come next week? if you're free, you can go.

PROBST: Isn't that what you want, not to be typecast?

REDGRAVE: Yes, absolutely. That's what I want. I get offered such a wide variety of things here that I find ... I think it's quite good to be an alien. You see the good things and you can be unmoved by the bad. Your own country can hurt you—you can feel so hurt by things you can't help. They're your problem because you're English, or the same if you're American. I like the distance that that gives me. It may be escapist, I don't know.

PROBST: Isn't there an advantage, in your case, in the distance from your family?

REDGRAVE: Yes, I think now particularly, because my family, my brother and sister are so deeply involved in a political cause which I cannot begin to understand or fathom. And because of their notoriety there I would as well keep my distance. I'm terribly fond of them and love to see them, but it's kind of uncomfortable if I'm not part of it, because it's a small country. But that's not why I left. Neither of them are so important to me that I would skip the country to do it. I've been moving away gradually, I suppose, over the years John and I have been married.

PROBST: Vanessa Redgrave is involved with the Trotskyite party?

REDGRAVE: I believe so. My brother, too.

PROBST: Do they ask you to do anything, to come along?

REDGRAVE: No, no.

PROBST: They've given you up?

REDGRAVE: They've given me up. They relate to me entirely on the old basis, which was that we were fond of each other. I'm about the only person they don't try and convert, I suppose, because they know they can't, or because I don't want to, or they don't want to spoil what they've got. And I don't want to, either.

PROBST: You shared the cover of *Time* magazine with your sister, March 17, 1967. There was that nasty line you "got the break from the crumbs that she had left," the parts that she was offered and did not take.

REDGRAVE: It may well be true.

PROBST: Do you feel you are who you are, in spite of, because of . . . .

REDGRAVE: Certainly not because of, and, I don't think, in spite of.

PROBST: Everyone I've interviewed in effect is working for himself. Everyone seems to have an enormous, insatiable, unquenchable, indestructible ego.

REDGRAVE: Some actors are sure all the time. They're sure

when they would talk to you or to me or to anybody about what they do being right. I'm only sure at the moment I do it. I know I did the best I could at the time because that's all you can do, but afterward I don't know. At the moment I do it, if it's right I know it's right and if it's wrong I know it's wrong, and that I know unquestionably. I didn't used to know. I used to just be in a wave. But now I know when it's right and I know when it's wrong, though I can't always put it right when it's wrong. . . .

11

DICK CAVETT:

I Felt That Fame Would Lift Me Out of All My Problems

PROBST: You say you cried because you realized W. C. Fields was dead and you could never meet him. Do you have a special feeling about celebrities?

CAVETT: Well, there are times when I hope I've grown out of it and times when I wish I hadn't. But I think I had an excessive dose of it as a kid in Lincoln, Nebraska. I must have felt that fame and celebrity would lift me out of all my problems. Bob Hope came there and the Drama Quartet with Charles Laughton, and so on. I used to think, I belong in their world, not the one I'm in. They don't have to worry about getting a date on Saturday night or anything like that. They ride in limousines and everything they do is beautiful and cool. I had some tremendous, almost unnatural craving for fame. I wanted to hear people say, There goes Dick Cavett.

Now, of course, I'm sick of it. No, seriously, I still like it sometimes, it depends on how it's done. Even now, presumably an adult, I still have moments when I think, Gee, there's Sid Caesar, or there's Laurence Olivier, and they're working for me tonight, how can this be? The world is upside down. Bob Hope shouldn't walk on *my* stage. I should be home watching him. Or the Lunts or Noel Coward, the really giant people like that. They, in some sense, still make me the kid in Nebraska with my nose pressed to the window. If I can reach the window.

PROBST: You say, presumably an adult, now.

CAVETT: Doesn't everyone feel like a kid well into his forties? I do at times, and I wonder how I got into an adult's business and why they don't throw me out. Pretty soon they'll ask for my identification and say, What are you doing here, you're only in high school? It's when I come in contact with those people whom I looked up to when I was a kid, who now are in some sense on my level, I'm sorry that the distance between us has narrowed, and I can't quite believe it.

PROBST: It must have turned around. People look to you as the person to be in awe of.

CAVETT: There *are* actors and people who are impressed if I recognize them on the street—an inversion I can't quite get used to. Two nice girls who used to hang out at my stage door even baked me cakes in the shape of my house and my car and my dog and everything. When Chris Porterfield and I were riding in a car, one day the girls pulled around beside us in a cab, and I said, "There are those damn girls again. They drive me nuts." We had agreed that whatever Chris saw he could put in the book (*Cavett*), so he did. And now the girls have stopped. They winsomely wave at me from a respectful distance.

PROBST: You must have Dick Cavett groupies?

CAVETT: There *are* Dick Cavett groupies, I've found to my utter amazement. In fact, there was one who got me on the phone in my hotel room last night in Washington. It was a classic case of her being willing to do literally anything. Fortunately, I was a serious student of my work and was tired. I expected a laugh on that, but not such a *big* one. I've never quite understood groupies. What becomes of old groupies? I don't know.

PROBST: They find old heroes.

CAVETT: I guess so. They find older and older people.

Q *(question from audience)*: Where did you acquire your chutzpah for chasing celebrities?

CAVETT: It seemed to be a genuine compulsion bordering on pathology. When I saw someone famous, I had to have contact with them. Anybody would do, from Olivier to Bert Parks. If I saw them on the street as a kid, if they happened to come through Lincoln, I wanted them to take me along, I wanted to go back with them to their wonderful world. I saw Bob Hope get into a Cadillac, drive off with two beautiful girls from his show, one on each side, and I just thought, Gee, that's wonderful. He's in my sight now, but when he swims out of my sight he will be in a room where there are cameras making movies of him. How does one get from where I am to where he is? Kind of pathetic, isn't it?

PROBST: Let me go a little far afield but with the same concept. . . . Do you see yourself and your wife, Carrie Nye, as Scott and Zelda Fitzgerald?

CAVETT: I think that we could play them, in the sense that we have certain inborn similarities to them—my coming from the Midwest and her coming from the South. She really should play Zelda someday.

PROBST: Your wife is from Mississippi, and Zelda's from Alabama, as I remember.

CAVETT: That's right. I don't see myself as Fitzgerald, not in the deep sense. Except, well, longing for the East. I suppose the siren call of the East, some sense that New York and Connecticut and Long Island were glamour, but not wanting to be possessed by them completely. Still, wanting to retain a distance but feeling seducible by them, I guess. To that extent I feel like Fitzgerald. But I drink so little—and so badly.

PROBST: Were you seduced by the East? Why didn't you go to Hollywood from Nebraska?

CAVETT: It does seem odd, doesn't it? The movies are there and glamour and all of that, but I didn't see myself there. Hollywood just seemed so unreal as to be out of the question. In fiction, I'd read about the East, and I wanted to be here. I had friends who had come back from New York and said how wonderful it was. The pull was entirely in this direction. It was always New York.

PROBST: It would seem to me that to get serious respect one would have to go East.

CAVETT: Maybe that's it. The East is serious, and Hollywood is frivolous. Also, Basil Rathbone had come to Lincoln one time and said, "You people out here are where the action is." Community theater and university theater, and so on. Hollywood and Broadway were dead—but Hollywood was deader than Broadway. I thought, That still leaves the East. I must get to the East.

PROBST: What do you think about New York City?

CAVETT: I love it. I've gone through periods of hating it. I used to do jokes about it to the point where the mayor's office asked me to stop. I just love New York, it's rich, bizarre.

Q: How does a talk-show interviewer appeal to East Coast, West Coast, and Middle America?

CAVETT: I don't think they're that different. I think television has given almost all of us the same references and same vocabulary. People in Nebraska would joke about the Stage Delicatessen, when that was a favorite joke subject on the late-night show, as if they knew it, even though they had never been east of Iowa. I don't even think that the heartland is necessarily the area of yokeldom any more than any other part of the country. Audiences seem to laugh at the same things. Washington, last night, seemed like a small town where the circus had come to town, they were so excited about having a show there. Politicians become sort of flustered around celebrities. I always want to say, But we're supposed to become flustered around you. You're the important ones. Beloved old senators asking for autographs and giggling is not a very reassuring sight.

PROBST: How did you start as a nightclub comedian?

CAVETT: Simply by watching Woody Allen. And becoming a friend of his. I was sent by the old Jack Paar show to scout his act one night at the Blue Angel, and I realized instantly that Woody was doing what I wanted to do, that his life was taking a course that I wanted mine to. I was lucky, to just go around with him and watch him do it and see him go through some of the most awful experiences and some good ones.

PROBST: Has comedy changed since your days at the clubs?

CAVETT: I don't ever see changes in comedy. I just think that brilliant people either come along or they don't.

PROBST: What is the source of your comedy?

CAVETT: Anything I think is funny. That's the best advice I got from Woody, to stick to that standard. When I first sat down and tried to write for myself, it was murder. It was excruciating. Here I'd come from making a lot of money glibly writing for Carson and Paar and Griffin and other comedians. I could turn out monologues with lightning speed. And I thought, This is silly. Why don't I just turn around and turn out monologues at lightning speed for myself? But when I started I couldn't think of a single joke for myself. I realized that what was missing was, I didn't know my style. I knew the other comedians'. I could imitate theirs. All I had to do was turn them on in my head and I could write for Groucho or whoever. But who was I? I didn't know. I wasn't Jewish. I wasn't fat. I wasn't thin enough. I wasn't tall or short enough. For a time I realized I was trying to be Woody. I was trying to write for a Jewish boy from Brooklyn with glasses.

PROBST: When you found out who you were—who was it?

CAVETT: A tall black man. You can go that far wrong in writing for yourself. That may even be a serious answer, because Woody and I were both very affected by Norman Mailer's essay *The White Negro*. Finally I had to ask myself, What's the reality of this situation? I come from Nebraska and I came East, and then I thought, That's an obvious formula right there. A guy from the sticks—what people think of as the sticks—comes East and is either more or less sophisticated than he wants to be. The Yale-Nebraska contrast. The students laughing at me there.

Then I contrived lines that, although they were gags, actually had some basis in that reality. I said, "In my freshman year I wore brown and white shoes." This would get a laugh because people knew you didn't wear those on the Yale campus. But the following line was, "Which wasn't practical because the white one kept getting dirty." This was a gag. My act wasn't as pure as Woody's because he was just funny for funny's sake. I was still writing for other people in a sense, but I had at least a beginning of a character. Groucho helped me a lot. He wrote to me and told me when he thought I was on the right track. He said, "I think you've hit on a mother lode with the yokel-starry-eyed-in-the-big-city act, but don't overdo it." Don't worry so much about your image. You seem to be getting on in the business, and once you've been on a lot, what you are becomes your image.

PROBST: One thing that comes through in your work is a certain dry, highbrow wit.

CAVETT: I always cringe at the word *highbrow*.

PROBST: Well, we won't use it. Are you Dick Cavett or are you somebody else?

CAVETT: Now they know me as whatever I am, not what I have to announce I am. I remember Cosby, when he became rich and famous, saying, "There's just nothing like acceptance. To walk out on that stage, and the minute they see you they laugh." After all those nights in clubs where they looked up and thought, Who is this, when you heard only the MC's hands applauding, and a few surly people slurping coffee would judge you in the harshest terms. And sometimes throw edibles at you.

PROBST: We have an adult Cavett now.

CAVETT: Theoretically, yes. I may spit up at any moment. But I'm verging on adulthood now, I think.

PROBST: Is there anybody you are now in awe of, having grown up?

CAVETT: No, not a soul. Well, I guess some of the same people—Olivier, Welles, the towering geniuses in the business. And certainly a lot of writers. Writing to me is the most awesome talent.

Q: What distinguishes a great comedian from a lesser one?

CAVETT: They're born funny. A great comic or a great artist is born with a great gift. And I can't see anything beyond that. I don't think you have to think about it beyond that.

PROBST: You were the host of Emmy Awards on TV news programs.

CAVETT: That's right, and my Emmy was belatedly presented to me on that show. If you believe in Freudian slips, the man from the Academy said, "We hope you will accept this Enemy."

PROBST: Are there any awards worth winning?

CAVETT: Certainly not the Emmy. No one has any idea why or how you get them. There are these mysterious blue-ribbon panels who get in a room and drink a case of Blue Ribbon beer. I think the Academy Awards are a joke too. I have respect for those Drama Critics Circle Awards and the Tony Awards, yes. But the TV and movie ones seem silly. The idea of a contest in the arts, even the bastard arts like television, is absurd. The only way you can tell a winner is graphically. If one man runs a hundred yards faster than another, *that's* better. But you can never prove that Spencer Tracy's performance was better than Lee J. Cobb's in one year—and that goes for any of the performing arts. If Katharine Hepburn was the best actress last year and she isn't this year, it's up to them to show where she slipped, and to show her, too.

PROBST: Why is TV a bastard art?

CAVETT: To distinguish it from the great arts.

PROBST: Does that make it a bastard—that it's not great?

CAVETT: Well, I would tend to describe television as a bastard art in most senses of the word. It's such a messy medium. Tallulah Bankhead said radio was the mother of television. Someone asked her who was the father, and she said, "Television has no father." That would, in fact, make it a bastard art.

Q: How would Dick Cavett interview Dick Cavett? And is it harder to be a guest or a host?

CAVETT: It varies. It's hard to be a guest on a talk show because you have to score, as they're now set up, in a brief amount of time and be as funny or as interesting as possible in order to get asked back. So there's a lot of pressure on your appearance if you're a beginner. From my point of view, it's much easier to be a guest. I just eat it up. I'm free of responsibility; I don't have to keep track of the show or worry about the time, which is nightmarish when you're the host. But of course, as the host you get to ask the questions, or decide which turn the conversation's going to take. How would I interview myself? I would be foolish to try, but I would avoid all the obvious questions.

Q: What about violence on television?

CAVETT: I don't know if it's bad, but I think it will continue because it makes money. I loved violence and fights on the screen as a kid. I wanted to imitate them. I fell off garages and pretended they were burning buildings and I crashed bicycles and pretended they were horses. I couldn't get enough of it. I looked forward to the time when I could be in a fight and could hit a guy with a chair because I had seen it on the screen.

PROBST: What's good about violence?

CAVETT: I don't know that anything is. But, I also don't know that it's bad to have it on television. I don't know that it incites people to violence. Violence is almost always sanitized on television. There's that famous fight in a John Wayne movie where they fight all the way across one county of Ireland, and no one cuts his face and nobody's teeth are broken. I think I prefer violence where you see the consequences of it. They make it look like fun to shoot at people in films, cowboy films. So I guess I'm suggesting more violence or none at all. A lot of kids think you can do those things. Cartoons, in some cases, lead children to try to hit each other over the head with hammers.

PROBST: Do you mean it's better to see it than to do it?

CAVETT: I just don't want to censor violence. I think it's better to see the real consequences of it than to think that you can hit someone over the head with a chair and that it will just splinter the way it does in the movies and then the victim will get up and be relatively fine.

PROBST: Your interviews are entertaining, but you are part of them. You are not the least intrusive part.

CAVETT: That's good, I think. I like it to be a conversation. I wanted either to get Katharine Hepburn on a conversational level or at least give the appearance of being in conversation with her, and I think I got both. I would like people to write in and say, I really felt like I was eavesdropping listening to you and Orson Welles, or Groucho, or whoever. Of course, I was doing it mostly for myself in a way, too; I wanted to see what it would be like to talk to them. But I also had the idea that I wanted the millions of people who would never get a chance to talk to them—gee, I sound so benevolent and condescending—to hear what it would be like. That's the only goal I think of in interviewing. Once or twice my goal was to make the guests uncomfortable, just because I didn't like them. Or I thought they were liars and I wanted to see if I could prove that. Little specific goals with individuals.

PROBST: What's the best way to seduce a camera or to mislead a camera?

CAVETT: To be a skilled performer of some sort. And almost to have a deep acting ability, like in the movie *Face in the Crowd*. To be able, while you're saying a thing, to convince others and even yourself at the moment that you believe it. A lot of the worst swine in our business, at the moment they're mouthing their sentimentalities, really believe them, I think. They then go out and fly in the face of them, and don't see any contradiction and don't care. They are very good performers. Don't trust the TV camera to tell you the truth.

PROBST: Are you still a talk-show host?

CAVETT: Once you're a talk-show host, you're always a talk-show host. Whether you're working or not is another matter.

PROBST: Where did the pressure come from to change?

CAVETT: There had always been pressure to be more commercial in some way that nobody could ever quite define. I never had any kind of goal in terms of commercialdom, except simply to do what I thought was interesting. A naive idea, I suppose. But it's the only one I had.

PROBST: Could you have gone the Johnny Carson route?

CAVETT: Meaning?

PROBST: The second banana, the girls?

CAVETT: I never saw myself as that different from Carson.

PROBST: You mean, we were all fooled?

CAVETT: It isn't that. It's just that I figure he went out and did the kind of show that was natural to him and I went out and did the kind of show that was natural to me. And we come from a kind of similar background. Not just Nebraska, but wanting to get into the business and deliver an entertaining show.

Q: Are some people in TV particularly difficult to work for?

CAVETT: Almost anybody in television is tough to work for. You just about have to be. Your time is constantly wasted by people who don't do their jobs well. And you're under terrible pressure and you want to get on with it. Your nerves are almost always on edge. No one who isn't a performer understands what it's like to be one. Almost every performer sooner or later gets a reputation of being tough to work with, and it's a well-deserved reputation.

PROBST: If you could do anything you want to at eleven thirty at night, what would you do?

CAVETT: God knows. Some of my so-called serious shows, were full of laughs and had everything that any kind of show could want. If I had eleven thirty to myself, I would do about what I did and maybe be a little more aware that the audience can't concentrate as much as you might have to in a show that, say, matched a philosopher and a logician. I'd really love to get Watergate back for a while, just for a couple of weeks. A certain dullness has set in. Right now a soporific effect seems to have set in. I don't look forward to the news anymore. It's partly post-Watergate depression. I haven't watched Johnny Carson's monologues lately, but his writers always seem to come up with funny things out of the paper. That's murder. I used to do that. You have to go through the papers and try to find someone who swallowed a frog or some silly thing to write about or some new kind of bikini or something to force one more sexist joke out of. I really wouldn't know exactly where to go for comedy now.

12

MARLO THOMAS:

"Run Your Own Race, Baby"

PROBST: Last year you helped turn the play *Thieves,* a comedy about life in New York, from an out-of-town flop into an in-town success. At one point when the play was out of town, the director, the producer, and the star left. Where were you?

THOMAS: In a hotel room in Boston. I was there with Herb Gardner, who I respect as a writer and who also happens to be my "constant companion" as they say in the newspapers, I was there to be with him and support him through the opening of his play and it was somewhat of a disaster. I always thought it was a wonderful play. It's like being at a traffic accident. You either run away or you start taking license plate numbers and try to figure out how to help. So I became the star of the play. The closing notice was up and I had to get into the play in four days. So they called Chuck Groden, who's a friend of ours, and asked him if he would fly in quickly—he had directed me in "Acts of Love and Other Comedies." To do something that quickly you have to be involved with people you know and trust, otherwise you just couldn't do it. I trusted Chuck as a director. We had to do it in four days. The money wouldn't hold out. The audiences wouldn't keep coming to see an understudy, and the closing notice was up. It was the most exciting night of my life going on in that play. I'll never do it again but I'll remember it forever. To go on, especially as a person I'm not an unknown. I was thinking of not having my name up there—how good can you be in four days? You just barely scratch the surface.

After being in television as long as I have been, it was the drama of the living theater. It was like all those Mickey Rooney movies. Somebody was actually saying "You can save the play," and it was irresistible.

PROBST: Did you feel that the character was you? It was a New York woman and you weren't at that time a New York woman.

THOMAS: No, I wasn't. But the character is very much like me. She was the kind of a character who fights hard for what she believes in and doesn't take no for an answer. That's why I think I probably should have played it from the beginning.

PROBST: Why didn't you?

THOMAS: Herb and I had been going together for a couple of years and I'm very much of a perfectionist about my work and I had gotten to realize that he was every bit as crazy as I was about his work and when he first asked me to be in the play, we talked about it a long time and I said, "One of the two things will go, either the relationship or the play. We both won't make it, because I'll fight for what I believe in and you'll fight for what you believe in and either the play will be great and there'll be no us or it'll be an us and there'll be no play." So we made this one mature decision in our lives and it totally backfired. And I didn't do it.

PROBST: What do you think about the experience?

THOMAS: It really was the best experience of my career. I learned so much as an actress. I've been away from the stage for eight years. I'd been rehearsing the same note for a long time on television. I loved playing "That Girl," but it's very much like learning one piece on the piano and then somebody says, Okay, now play that. You just keep playing it. And I just kept playing those notes for five years. I had just gotten a little too smart. I'd learned a lot of shortcuts. Doing the play, I figured out the long, hard way. And the long, hard way is the only way. The shortcuts are okay when you can go to commercial, but when you want to take an audience for two full hours, then you have to really have the character together. I relearned that. Now I feel I'll never stay away from the stage again for more than two years at a time.

PROBST: How did you get your first acting job? Was it on your own?

THOMAS: I just went and auditioned and got little tiny parts, in

California. But my first acting job which really counted for television was "Hawaiian Eye." I walked into this office to read for the part and the man said, "Oh, look at those eyes." I thought, Christ, this is an easy thing. There's Betty Grable with the legs, right? And Marie McDonald with the body. It's going to be Marlo Thomas with the eyes. Anyway, I got the part. It's the part of a nurse in an operating room, and the guy's got a bomb on him, and for the entire thing I'm covered like this—except for my eyes. Looking back and forth at the clock. That was my whole part. I don't think I got another job for three years.

PROBST: How was it to grow up as Danny Thomas' daughter in Beverly Hills?

THOMAS: My father—as a human being, if I had my choice of any father in the world, I would choose him, because he's a really terrific person. He really is a very sincere person. But being the daughter of a person named Danny Thomas is not anything I would recommend for your identity, for your own ego. It's a very rough rap. It's very hard to grow up barely knowing your own name and already knowing that you're the appendage of somebody else. It's a hard thing to knock and it's taken me a long time. I'm finally at the point where if somebody introduces me as Danny Thomas' daughter, I don't get nauseous.

PROBST: Why? Because he was so well known?

THOMAS: It's just that people don't give you a chance to breathe. They don't want to know who you are or what you feel or what you think. The most important thing about you is you're somebody else's something. In the women's liberation movement we're fighting being Mrs. Somebody. Well I was this big and I was already little Mrs. Somebody. It's too much to give to a child.

PROBST: What about daughters or sons of other well-known people in Hollywood?

THOMAS: A lot of them are wackos. No, they really are. I have visited a lot of my friends in sanitariums. A lot of them are alcoholics. A couple of them got totally out of the business, stayed as far away as possible from the public eye, because the comparison is just too much to take. And some of them work on it for a long time, work on it hard with their parents. It really bothered me when I was around eighteen and I was starting to do plays in stock. I was looking for a place to learn. I should have had an opportunity like everybody else to fall on my ass and I wasn't being given that opportunity. They were already reporting how I was doing. It seemed unfair.

Anyway, I asked my father about it. And the thing he was most concerned with was that there not become a void between the two of us. That somehow it not get translated so that I resented him, rather than resent what I should resent, what other people were doing to me, making me feel bad and making me compete with someone who I couldn't possibly compete with at that age. He's very positive and very much a Pollyanna—but it works. It always worked with me. He said, "You're a thoroughbred. You're a thoroughbred race horse and thoroughbred race horses run their own races. They wear blinders and they just run. They don't look at anybody else. And that's what you have to do." He said, "Don't look at any of the other horses in the race, especially me, I have thirty-five years on you. Just look straight ahead." And when I opened in that particular play, this big box came to my dressing room and there were those old horse blinders. And it had a little note on the horse blinders and it said, "Run your own race, baby." It sounds like a sweet, trite story but it's basically the very heart of what I feel about the whole thing.

PROBST: In running your own race have you ever fallen on your ass?

THOMAS: Sure. I haven't fallen on my ass in a real big way yet. I'm sure I will. I did a movie called *Jenny* which sort of laid there, but nobody killed me for it. Mostly I've had pretty good successes but I take a lot of big risks and I'm not scared. The only way I'm going to get any further is to reach.

PROBST: Are you interested in accomplishing something as a women's liberationist or as an actress? Is it symbolic or personal? Or both?

THOMAS: It sounds presumptuous, I guess, but I want to make changes. I want to have affected things. When I did "That Girl," there hadn't been a single girl on television. When I said I wanted to do it, I took *The Feminine Mystique* with me to ABC, this was in

1965. They thought I was out of my mind, and maybe I was, but I said, "Look, there are a lot of women in this country and there isn't anybody on television to identify with." The only person I had ever identified with was "My Little Margie"—it's true—and she'd been off for years. The only single woman ever on television was, I think, "Our Miss Brooks," and you just can't count her. It was a big thing to me. I had this thing I wanted to bring the single girl to television.

When I did *Free To Be,* I never thought it was going to take off like it did. I'm not a writer or a philosopher but I wanted to show parents and children, to give them something to talk about and to laugh with and have a dialogue concerning non-sex-stereotyping stories and the only way I know how is through entertainment. And men should have feelings and we should discuss boys' crying, we should discuss that girls don't have to get married, and all of these kinds of things. When I sold my first special, "Acts of Love," which was about women and how they love, the head of the network called me—and rarely do they make such calls—and said, "Please, when you go on the network, do not refer to this as a Women's Liberation Special." And so I did not refer to it as a Women's Liberation Special, I referred to it as a special about women liberating themselves.

PROBST: Let's get specific. If you were to marry, would you insist on a marriage contract?

THOMAS: Well, first of all, I'm having a real rough time deciding whether I should ever get married. I would have a marriage contract . . . no, not written out. I would hope that I would have a better relationship with the man that I was going to marry than that. I couldn't even like anybody that didn't think the way I do about how men and women fit into the world. As Gloria Steinem says, "If you think passive women are good, wait'll you meet a cooperative one."

PROBST: Have you consciously not gotten married and not had children so that you could pursue a career?

THOMAS: I didn't know that I had done that. I grew up in a generation that made us make choices. And that was unfair and wrong. I'm a victim of that. I thought that a woman had to choose between being a good wife and a good mother and having a career. I realize now, that's ridiculous. But I didn't know that at the time. I knew I very much wanted to be an actress. I had a burning desire to contribute to the world and do these things. And I thought, That means I couldn't be a good mother, good wife, so I guess I can't get married and have children. I'll have to do that later, put it off until I've accomplished these other things, or maybe someday I'll be able to work it all out. That's an attitude society gave me.

There's absolutely no reason for women to make those kinds of terrible choices. Men don't have to. Nobody says to a twenty-three-year-old boy or young man, Do you want to be a doctor or a daddy? Yet young, talented women make those kinds of terrible choices every day. It nearly drove me mad—it's asinine that I had to make such a choice.

PROBST: You were graduated from the University of Southern California in 1960, summa cum laude in English. Before that you'd gone to the Marymount Catholic School. If you had children, would you send your children to a Catholic school?

THOMAS: No, I really wouldn't. Maybe because the sex lore one is given in the Catholic schools could really screw you up for most of your life. We were told in school that if you ever. . . . I went to an all-girls' school called Marymount for twelve years. It's amazing today that I wear underwear. We were told never, ever to sit on a boy's lap, and if you had to, be sure to put down a piece of newspaper first. I'm still trying to figure out all of the symbolism that goes with that. There were little things, too. There's no feeling in the woman's breast, so that if a boy touches you, it's for his enjoyment, not yours. And then little things like don't wear patent-leather shoes because it reflects your underpants. There's more than enough, more than enough. Between Marymount and my father . . . My father told me that virginity is the gift you give to your husband on your wedding night. So of course if you don't have it, you're empty-handed. Enough for Catholic schools.

PROBST: How did *Free To Be You and Me* start?

THOMAS: My sister has a daughter named Dionne. I was reading stories to her and I realized that she was getting the same garbage that my sister and I had gotten about the Prince and the Princess. The Princess falls asleep, the Prince wakes her up. She had one particular book that really made me angry. It was called *I'm Glad I'm a Boy, I'm Glad I'm a Girl.* On each page it has what a boy does and what a girl does. Boys are pilots, girls are stewardesses, boys are doctors, girls are nurses, boys invent things, girls use the things that boys invent. That book was a real motivator. I decided that I was going to put together a group of songs and stories and things. Collect them and put together a book or an album. I got a group of people, Gloria Steinem, Dan Greenburg, and Letty Pogrebin and Mary Rodgers, and we made a list of everything that we felt we could have used in a story in our childhood that would have helped us later. Things like, it would have been nice to know that it's all right to show your feelings and it would have been good to have stories where boys and girls are friends together and it would be good to see mommies not always in aprons and daddies not always with briefcases.

PROBST: I notice you refer to yourself as Miss Thomas. You don't use Ms.?

THOMAS: I lisp. I mean to say Ms. I believe in it philosophically. We don't separate men according to their marital status.

PROBST: Do you go to consciousness-raising sessions?

THOMAS: I have gone to some, yes.

PROBST: What does one learn? How are you raised?

THOMAS: Just talking it out. There's a lot of things that you don't even know you are angry about. People get away with what you let them get away with if you won't stand for certain things, insist on your rights, and demand that you be treated as a human being. Even in my business, which is pretty equal because men can't play women's parts, so we're necessary and nobody can take over our jobs, sometimes I feel patronized by a director who thinks that the best way to get to me is to tell me that I look lovely. It's an extension of "All she needs is a good roll in the hay and she'll be fine." We don't need that, we need to be allowed to grow.

PROBST: Is there a way for a woman to grow old and still be sexy?

THOMAS: Of course, that depends on what one thinks is sexy.

Oedipus liked older women. That's one of the things that the women's movement is trying to fight. Everything has made us feel that we are a salable product. If a woman or a girl wasn't married by twenty-six years old, the family was in total despair. And by thirty, well, forget it, she was obviously a spinster. We don't even hear that word anymore. I think what the women's movement is trying to say is that you stop treating us according to our beauty and the firmness of our skin and the things that are going to go, as they are going to go on men as well, and start treating us for the greatest value that we have, which is our human value, our minds and our souls and our hearts, which will only get better. Everyone has said that the greatest sex organ we have is between our ears.

Q *(question from audience)*: You expound about women's liberation, yet you look very feminine.

THOMAS: I'm a woman. I'm for being a woman. I don't think being a feminist says I don't want to be a woman. I am a woman and I'm happy to be a woman. Do you think my being proud of being a woman and wanting every woman in America to have a chance at absolutely everything means I should come in here in leather? I'm a woman. I'm a female. I have a sex life as a woman. I have female organs and I have long fingernails and I have long black hair. I like to look attractive and I'm glad I'm a woman *and* I want absolutely everything that my abilities and my talents can let me have.

PROBST: What were your relations with your mother?

THOMAS: It's interesting how you feel when you grow up . . . I never thought my mother and I would end up being the ones that are really alike. As far away as we were, my mother was really Supermom in the station wagon, pick the kids up for the ballet lessons, to the dentist. My mother was like furniture, I mean she was really there. She was terrific. Which is why I figured I could never have a career and be a mother, because, my God, there's no time. And now, after all these years, my mother said to me about two years ago, after calling me crazy since I can remember, she said, "I'll be a son of a bitch, you did it right." I don't know if I did it right but I think what she meant by that was I'm doing it my way. It's slow but I'm doing it my way.

Q: How much has your career been helped by being Danny Thomas' daughter?

THOMAS: I don't know. I really don't know. I think it held me back for a long time and I think it was a big pressure when I went on the air. A lot of people wrote that I would never make it. It was a lot of pressure. It's good that I had a strong family around me that made me feel that I'd made it. When they put on the lights and they say "Action," nobody but you goes out there. It's your routine, not Daddy's and you either make it or you don't. And that's what it's all about. The advantage of being his daughter was inheriting and being around a lot of comedy. I think a lot of my comedy timing came directly from the years that I sat around and listened to that flavor. That for me wipes out a lot of the hurt, about getting too much pressure too soon and too much exposure too soon.

Q: How accepting is your father, who is apparently conservative, of your lifestyle, of your position on abortion?

THOMAS: On abortion—we don't get along on that one too well. He's really come a long way, when you realize that a lot of older people don't reevaluate. My father is from a very, very strict family. The fact that he would have a daughter who isn't married and is single and obviously not a virgin—I mean, you would think that he would come at me with an ax. But he's been marvelous. And he's talked to me, sort of strained, about my feelings as a woman. I gather he means sexually. But he's very accepting of me. I once heard and I forget now who it was that said it, but that the definition of love was it is the greatest form of tolerance. Though I haven't committed murder, as far as I've grown, my father has not wanted to be divorced from me. He's wanted to be my friend and I've met him halfway and he's met me halfway.

We don't agree politically at all. He was for Nixon. I was for McGovern. He's very conservative. He had Agnew over for dinner and I left the state. But we have really wanted each other in our lives and so we tolerate the things we don't agree about. We fight about them. In fact, he did a terrific thing. I called him up. I don't know if you know who Mayor Yorty is . . .

PROBST: Sam Yorty.

THOMAS: . . . he's really the worst. My father did a commercial on television for Mayor Yorty. I went to Los Angeles and I saw it on television and almost had a heart attack. So I called my father and said, "Daddy, how could you have done this? My God, it's a mark against the whole family. He's the most terrible man and he doesn't stand for anything and he's this and he's that." There was this long pause and he said, *"Free To Be."*

I was the buffer between my mother and my father. I was an eleven-year-old marriage counselor. One of the reasons I am what my boyfriend calls a "contender" is that my father and I met head-on most of my life and that's why we're good friends and that's why I think . . . they're doing a book now on women and strong fathers. And it's very interesting, the stories that this woman who is doing the book told me about—a lot of very achieving women had very strong fathers who fought them to the death. With my father, everything was not only an order but out of the Bible. Thou shalt go to thy room. It sounded like it was going to be chiseled into granite right after he said it. I was constantly fighting that, standing in the doorway at six years old insisting that I be heard, and I know that's where I got it from. I have a lot of experience in fighting for my rights. A lot of first-born women of strong fathers—I mean, it's almost a pattern.

Q: Don't you think that most men appear to accept women's lib but down deep don't really believe it?

THOMAS: I think for them the old way is easier. That's why I have a very soft spot in my heart for men. I feel very sorry for them in this one way. They were raised to expect a certain utopia. There was going to be this person that they married, who not only would be sexually terrific and with whom they would have a really good time and a couple of kids, but she was going to give up everything to keep the house nice and entertain the boss, just like you saw in "I Love Lucy." It was all going to be wonderful. He expected that. So, you can't expect the male not to be a little disappointed that he didn't get what dear old Dad got. He's got to feel he got short shrift. He's going to have to get over it, but of course for a while there's going to be that resentment.

Why should a marriage exist between one and one-half persons? A marriage has to exist between two whole persons, and when it does, then it has a real chance of existing and growing because both people are growing. This one-and-a-half-persons marriage is bound to be in the kind of trouble that it's in because it's a lie. It's a lie to give up everything you ever wanted and believed in for somebody else's aspirations. I don't believe that. I'm not saying that you don't want to get married and people don't want to raise children, but I cannot believe that there's a human being alive who doesn't want anything. I don't believe that there's somebody alive that doesn't want something because that's what being alive is.

PROBST: Does it bother you at all that you speak so strongly about marriage and children and yet have had neither?

THOMAS: No, it doesn't bother me. I told you before, I regret the fact that society made me believe I had to make a choice. Do you mean, why don't I get off the pot already?

PROBST: One doesn't have to have gone to war in order to be against war, obviously, or lay an egg to know that it tastes good.

THOMAS: I'm saying that I'm a victim of the society of my time. I'm the only girl in my class who didn't get married. My girl friends were terrified to get out of college and not have somebody snagged. They were scared to death and I felt I was making this big choice. The girls that were rushing to get married were wrong because they felt they weren't going to be salable in three more years and I was wrong in thinking that one had to make a choice my way.

When I was ten I wrote a pamphlet called *Women Are People Too* because my father is Lebanese and there are no greater male chauvinists than Lebanese. And my grandfather and grandmother. My grandfather gave my grandmother absolutely no credit for the family. My grandfather had ten children. Nine boys and a daughter. And the nine boys—and I saw this with my own eyes, these were grown people—the nine sons would eat in the dining room with my grandfather, and the daughter would be in the kitchen with Grandmother, her mother, and they would serve. I mean, that's the way they lived all their lives. My father and mother had two daughters, my sister and I first, and my brother came later. And I remember my grandfather insulting my father about the fact that all he could have was daughters. He said to him in Arabic and my father told us later, "In Lebanon we throw the girls back." My grandmother was like a slave her whole life. By the time I was ten I really was militant.

PROBST: What happened to the pamphlet *Women Are People Too?*

THOMAS: My mother has it. It just had a lot of pictures that said things like "What do *you* know?" because my uncles used to say that to their wives all the time: "What do *you* know?" Right. See, they *know.*

13

ZERO MOSTEL:

One Day You Have a Bellyache, You Use It

PROBST: Zero is here . . .

MOSTEL: Not for long.

PROBST: And this is his one day off . . .

MOSTEL: And this nag had to make me come here, on this beautiful day. Where's the exit, in case . . .

PROBST: I've talked to a number of artists—because you are also an actor as well as a painter . . .

MOSTEL: I'll get the laughs here, if you don't mind.

PROBST: . . . they said you have a problem with your painting. That you are so large that you can't get close up to the easel and therefore your detail work is not very good.

MOSTEL: They're fulla' shit. I could have said that nicely, but I din't think these people would understand feces. As a matter of fact I'm a detail man. I am. Really tiny details, that's what's wrong with it. I wish I couldn't get up close to it.

PROBST: I will try to ask direct, well-founded, well-researched intelligent questions and then it will be destroyed because the Zero method is to eat up anything or anybody near him or along side him. Very effective! How did the name Zero come about?

MOSTEL: A nickname. My real name is Sam. I got the nickname in school, because of my marks.

PROBST: How can such a brilliant man get poor marks?

MOSTEL: I was good but I didn't take anything very seriously. And I was a great laugher. So, they used to give me zeros. So I told that to the man who was the press agent for a nightclub I worked in. He sent it out and I was furious—actually, it was all right. He didn't like Sam.

PROBST: Café Society?

MOSTEL: Yes. But I answer to both names like a good dog.

PROBST: Are you legally Zero?

MOSTEL: No.

PROBST: You're legally Sam?

MOSTEL: I'm not legally anything.

PROBST: How did you get into acting?

MOSTEL: Misfortune befell me. I was a Depression fellow. I got out of school in '35 and there was nothing to do. No work anywhere and I used to go around to the liberal clubs and entertain. You know, do chalk talks for good causes which later became thought of as "Red causes." I started to entertain, hoping to make a few dollars for paint. As a matter of fact, they would promise me five dollars for the evening and they'd say, "Well, the liquor cost us . . ." and they gave me two dollars or three dollars and I'd break my neck. Finally, someone asked me to work and I thought I'd work a week and then quit and get some paint, but it didn't turn out that way.

PROBST: Going around working for "Red causes" . . .

MOSTEL: They weren't Red causes. They called them that later.

PROBST: In 1955 you were hauled up before the House Un-American Activities Committee to testify.

MOSTEL: I wasn't exactly hauled.

PROBST: It was a subpoena you couldn't refuse.

MOSTEL: I could have refused it. I would have landed in jail. They were nutty in those days, the people of America. As they are today. They elected that maniac Nixon by the largest plurality in the history of the presidency. Just to get those tapes.

PROBST: What were you charged with?

MOSTEL: I was charged with nothing. I was part of a conspiracy to overthrow the United States government by giving acting secrets to Russian actors. The fact that I didn't know any . . .

PROBST: You were out of work?

MOSTEL: No. I was rather successful financially, I guess, when I began. And I probably would have ended up playing parts in Hollywood—the friend of the guy who gets the girl. Maybe there's some kind of justice or something when you wind up doing things like *Ulysses* and Molière.

PROBST: Wasn't *Ulysses* the first real job you got after the hearings?

MOSTEL: It was not a real job, they paid you very little. I lived on my painting and a few jobs I got on the Borscht Belt, but they kept knocking the salary down all the time. There was one period when I didn't work for a long time. I lived on what I sold from my paintings and drawings.

PROBST: What scars are there?

MOSTEL: I could show them to you. My nature is not to be scarred. Some very well-known artisans in our craft became different kinds of people—one informed, I imagine, just for money, or one's comfort. I mean, what a Communist cell could accomplish in this country, I don't know. What harm? It's all hogwash, all bull.

PROBST: Are the scars healed?

MOSTEL: I don't want to say.

PROBST: In the book, *Zero by Mostel,* you were asked, Of all the parts you've played, which would you like to play again? You replied, "I would like to do Bloom in *Ulysses* again." Now that you've done Bloom in *Ulysses* again, did it come up to your expectations?

MOSTEL: It came up to my expectations, but . . . oh, now we're getting very serious. At the time it was done, 1958 I believe, probably the start of the Off-Broadway theater and modern plays, we could not do Joyce the way it was originally written because of censorship. Everybody involved hoped to do it someday exactly the way Joyce wrote it. The fathead critics, even when they say good things about it, don't receive it as well as they should. They're dealing with a work of art and a critic doesn't know how to deal with one. They can deal with cheap TV shows which become Broadway hits, but they cannot deal with something written by a genius, a literary genius. William Blake said a wonderful thing once. He said, "They praised Michelangelo for everything for which he had contempt." Even those who liked it don't know what to say about it.

When you do a work of art they don't know what to do with it. We have to suffer the double standard critics use when they see a play. Once you present a work of art, like all works of art, they don't know what to think of it or how to accept it or how to relax.

PROBST: I thought that the '58 production was a better evocation of Joyce than this one.

MOSTEL: The usual thing is that something that has been done is always better than what one is doing now. Of course, now we could use things we could not say in those days. When we played in London they wouldn't allow us to do that version in the public theater. We had to play it in a club, where you pay a fee to go and see it. What we have in the play is the exact thing that happens in the book. Also, one must judge what one sees on the stage and not the book. I'm tired of the pedant who says, Why didn't they put so-and-so in that Joyce work? It's impossible to put everything in it. We constructed a play from what we thought would make a new kind of theater, a different kind of theater, not as boring as the theater we have, or as rotten. The theater doesn't deserve to live if they don't support something like that.

PROBST: Are you more disciplined in this Leopold Bloom?

MOSTEL: I don't know what that word means.

PROBST: You're not as outrageous. You're always in character.

MOSTEL: It all depends on what one does. And also I'm not a stamp actor. The typical producer on Broadway would like to have a replica of what one did the first night—if it was a hit. They say that the actor is a machine that can reproduce exactly what one does every day. Absolutely hogwash. You cannot repeat. One day you have a bellyache, you use it. Someday you feel good, you use that. It always should have a feeling of spontaneity.

PROBST: You *were* more disciplined—there was less Zero and more of Leopold Bloom.

MOSTEL: Well, I'm always going to be Zero. But I'm also going to be Leopold Bloom. I can't be Eli Wallach doing Bloom. I can only be myself. One should appear as if he's not disciplined. The discipline shows up in doing it, that's all. The *other* kind of discipline . . . directors who go on long sabbaticals and come back tanned and say, You've altered my piece, give me a pain in the ass, frankly.

PROBST: Let's get to the nudity in *Ulysses.*

MOSTEL: Oh, please . . .

PROBST: Was that the way it was originally or was it added in rehearsal?

MOSTEL: No. That's exactly what we couldn't do in the first production. He's in the brothel looking for Stephen, he thinks of Blazes Boylan and his wife, at home. And he's thinking of them having sex. So, then we did it the way it is exactly in the book.

PROBST: Was *Ulysses* made nude to make the play more interesting? I remember the last time Siobhan McKenna did it.

MOSTEL: Well, I think one couldn't take Siobhan McKenna nude. This lady who does it, does it with great dignity and beauty. It's exactly the way it is in the book. The stage directions are in the book. The description of what the character is to do is in the book. Joyce was a stickler for accuracy. When he was in Zurich, he wrote a famous letter to find out whether the fence in Seven Eccles Street in Dublin was tall enough for Bloom to jump over it.

PROBST: I remember the tricky answer I got in Dublin from one Irish official, "Ah, all of Dublin is a monument to Jimmy." And, of course, they'd done nothing for him.

MOSTEL: Also, the theologians hate him to this day. He hasn't been allowed to be done there.

PROBST: A guy who wrote dirty books.

MOSTEL: But the net effect is not dirt at all.

PROBST: You worked in Hollywood, and later you said, "I hated Hollywood." Why?

MOSTEL: Because I'm a New Yorker. First of all, I don't look good in tennis shorts, with a Toulouse-Lautrec under my arm and a pitcher of Bloody Marys. All you hear is the sound of the car door closing and opening and the roar of the engine. You can't take a walk anywhere, unless you go to a mountain. There are no streets or social life that has any interest for me or anybody who's normal. Which is what I am.

PROBST: There's a Zero sense of humor. Where does the humor come from?

MOSTEL: From my *tukhas.* My mother was a very witty person, although she was very bigoted. She never said a straight line in her life. I guess you're near your mother's pocketbook when you're born. And you wind up that way.

PROBST: In one of the things that you wrote for *The New Yorker,* you said your father never came to see you onstage because it was against the Orthodox religion to make fun of another human being and what you were doing was belittling.

MOSTEL: It was an interview with somebody with a tape recorder—and they still made mistakes. I think all the inventions we make are going to ruin theater. There was some kind of lovely unfolding in the old days when they knocked on your door and said, Half hour. Now it comes over a sound system that scares you to death. And the stage manager doesn't watch the stage but a television set for when to give the cues, and there are too many lights and too many other things. It doesn't need as much as one gives it. Why am I saying that about the tape machine?

PROBST: About your father not coming to see you onstage . . .

MOSTEL: He was a very Orthodox Jew, with a beard. . . . It was because of the miracle plays, which were all anti-Semitic in the old days, and then Prohibition came and they would not go to the theater. Yet I think he sneaked in once in a while to see something without telling anybody, which is a curiosity every human being has, I suppose.

PROBST: Humor, it seems to me, is in a sense subversive. It may be undermining. It may question a situation or hold it up to ridicule. For that reason probably your father didn't want to go to the theater, because it made fun of things.

MOSTEL: But I'm not my father. Neither is my father me.

PROBST: Is the person who paints the pictures the same person who acts? Is there a unity in that person?

MOSTEL: Yes. This question scares me.

PROBST: You avoid thought by action?

MOSTEL: No, no. I don't know if I'm interested in dissecting thought so much. I like to look and have the patience to understand it. I also have a feeling about things. I think your definition of humor is not quite accurate.

PROBST: All right, let's have the definition of humor.

MOSTEL: I think it's part of the life force. In some people it's excised completely. And in some people it's there. Humor is a certain look at the world. What's the opposite of humor, seriousness?

PROBST: Tragedy. Strength. Humor is bent.

MOSTEL: There is humor in tragedy. And there is tragedy in humor. You would say that there is no humor at a funeral, yet there is.

PROBST: Plenty in that funeral in *Ulysses.*

MOSTEL: You say, By God, what if he were alive, they ought to put a telephone in the coffin. That's a very instinctual thing. You mask tragedy.

PROBST: Do you like being called a subtle clown?

MOSTEL: Say that to my face.

PROBST: Has comedy changed for you in America since you started working at Café Society Downtown?

MOSTEL: Changed in a sense that the times change. There was a time you weren't allowed to work.

PROBST: What do you mean by that?

MOSTEL: Because of what they thought were my politics, I wasn't allowed to do comic stuff. I did probably the first political things in this country, yet the show-offs nowadays never mention my name. But the first political stuff that was done I did on the radio show called "Chamber Society of Lower Basin Street." Goebbels called me "a third-rate Jewish vaudevillian" and said I was on "the list"—on international radio—they called me the "fat Jew Mostel" and said I would be eliminated once they captured America. That was a political thing, also, when they blacklisted you. And then they started gentle little jibes at governmental things. I did it all in terms of character. It was a different thing. Nowadays you can say anything you want.

PROBST: Is there anything you cannot make fun of now? Or wouldn't want to?

MOSTEL: That has to do with your inner thing. I don't like to make fun of people. I like to make fun of things, institutions. I like to make fun of pomposity. I hate pompous things.

PROBST: What do you think of television?

MOSTEL: VD. I don't like television at all. I think it's kind of moronic. Television enters your living room, which is a private place, yet they put a set of rules on that you can only do a thing a twelve-year-old mentality can accept.

PROBST: Nudity?

MOSTEL: I never felt the necessity of getting dressed.

PROBST: New York City?

MOSTEL: New York City is an example of a city that may disappear someday because of the realtors and the architects. I think some of the greatest villains in the history of civilization are the statesmen and the architects. They build up places so that life can't exist. They take Sixth Avenue, which had little shops and places where people could go and have a drink, a bite, read a book, and turn it into a jungle with no life. The buildings are some kind of a distortion of the Bauhaus principles, and they rise and there's nothing there. They're dangerous.

PROBST: In your scale of priorities, painting is first?

MOSTEL: I think your breath is first and then the look is second, where you are and your ability to enjoy life. I love painting and I go out of my way to see painting and I don't have huge rules. I just enjoy it very much. I love it.

PROBST: Painting for you has a higher creative quality than acting?

MOSTEL: When you do a thing like *Ulysses* you're doing the work of a great genius. I'm honored to do it. I love to do it, just as I love to see a great Matisse or a Cézanne or Rembrandt.

PROBST: Are you puzzled that acting is what you've become celebrated for?

MOSTEL: I don't live by being celebrated. I got letters about the "disgraceful play *Ulysses.*" One said, "A man who played Tevye, how can you do this thing?" And that's also the great American dream—if you do one lousy thing over and over again, that's your image and that's what one becomes. It's inherent in the understanding of an artist that he does things which are always different.

You can count on one hand, perhaps, the artists who look at everything they do differently—in acting or in painting or in writing. Very few work that way. They get that one formula and they do it over and over again until it becomes successful. It's the mass production of the mind.

PROBST: Is your painting related to your acting?

MOSTEL: I don't know. I go to act at seven thirty and I go to paint at twelve thirty. And sometimes at night I'm too tired to paint, so I look at painting and sometimes I sleep.

PROBST: What do audiences like?

MOSTEL: They don't like good things, the people. They like teddy bears and Tevye, sugar candy—all that stuff. Not that I sneer at those things. The musical comedies can be rather wonderful, too. There's a place for that, but for theater there's no place in this country at all. It would probably belong to some government or subsidized thing. I have a theory that if something is rotten on the top, it seeps all the way down to the bottom. I also have a theory that there's one artist who always has anguish out of the thing, and that's me. They fool you unless you have complete control. The only artists that were in film were ones like Chaplin who had complete control of what they did. I know Chaplin very well and I said to him once, "That's marvelous, the fight scene in *City Lights.* He said, "It's very interesting that I did it and I put it together and I didn't like it." I said, "What did you do?" He said, "I reshot it." Twenty-six weeks more. He could do it. We can't. They work for time and clocks and what time you get in and lunch breaks and overtime and all that junk.

PROBST: Besides Chaplin who else?

MOSTEL: All of Pinter, Beckett, Ionesco, comes from James Joyce. And Tennessee Williams comes from James Joyce and nobody else. But one was a genius and the others are merely talented. And therefore a work of art is not easily understood. That's almost a sign of art. You can look at a Cézanne and say, It's a mountain, but that mountain is a different kind of mountain than anyone has ever painted. It is not something you understand quickly. If it's an artist's work, you can be sure you won't understand it. A nonartist you'll understand anytime.

PROBST: I would quarrel with that definition, that because it is not understandable, therefore it is art.

MOSTEL: An element of it is. I just said you could recognize a mountain, but the way it's done is the mystery of it. There's the fantastic thing that nobody's explained a work of art. Do you know of anybody who has? Sir Herbert Read hasn't. E. M. Gombrich hasn't. Everybody who's ever written on it has never successfully, somehow, described what a work of art is. Except that it will last longer, *Ulysses,* than Jacqueline Susann's books.

PROBST: Because it is more complex, therefore it is better?

MOSTEL: I'm saying a work of art by its own definition is something you must live in in order to get something out of it. This is not Neil Simon. We don't tell jokes. When Joyce tells a joke it's on five levels. One, two, three, sometimes seven levels. For instance, you say you don't understand when Stephen hits with his ash plant, hits the lamp to shatter the image of his dead mother coming back in his eyes, he said, "Nothung, nothung," which in Irish means "nothing." "Nothung" is also the sword that Siegfried forged when he killed the dragon, and *nothung* also means "not hung." He was castrated by his mother. You're not dealing with a joke: Did you take a bath? Why? Is there one missing? You're not dealing with that. You're dealing with something where you have to use your noodle.

Q *(question from audience):* Are there actors other than yourself who would be considered the best actor today?

MOSTEL: I'd have to give you a huge list. The best actor I ever saw in America was Marlon Brando in *Streetcar.* And the best American actress I ever saw was—I don't believe that best thing, anyway—was Laurette Taylor in *Glass Menagerie.* I never saw anything like it.

PROBST: Why do you say Brando was the best actor?

MOSTEL: Oh, he was fantastic on the stage. He was an animal. He was everything an actor should be. It had a distortion of a piece of art. It was much more than acting, really reproductive acting.

PROBST: Is it true you've taken no acting lessons?

MOSTEL: None.

PROBST: But you went to The Actors Studio. What did you do there?

MOSTEL: Got out of there.

PROBST: Doesn't that count as taking lessons?

MOSTEL: Well, I was invited to go and so I went. But I thought it was very cruel of the students to criticize the other actors. I found it kind of a cruel system of doing acting. Robert Morley, the great English actor, watched one session and he said, "What are you doing here. Why aren't you out working somewhere? This is child's play. Bunkum. My God, go out and find a job somewhere. You're doing this for nothing?" And I agreed with him.

14

SHIRLEY MacLAINE:

I've Come Out the Other End of My Tunnel

PROBST: Two years ago you went to China and you took a delegation of twelve women. You came back from China with great passion and, I think, a deep, deep feeling of carrying out the message of what you have seen. Do you feel that there's a sense of acceptance? Is there resentment?

MACLAINE: I think it's probably the most volatile subject around today. This business of belief in oneself is the most controversial thing you can say to an American. Americans will tell you, very complicatedly and very elaborately, how it doesn't help to believe in yourself. The vested interest in cynicism is so profound that when you really get under the core and under the skin and say, Hey, wait a minute, no matter who you are, or what your capacities are, what your IQ is, what your talent may or may not be, you are somebody.

PROBST: Do you feel that the Chinese have instilled within their own people a sense of being worthwhile?

MACLAINE: Yes. High self-image. High self-esteem. The belief that you can light a match and it will start a prairie fire. *Here* it is the opposite—they'll grind you down, the system not only doesn't work but it's inoperable. And people are powerless to do anything about it.

PROBST: Before, you wrote that your series on television was a cesspool and the studio system in Hollywood was barren. After, you went back to Las Vegas, made a movie, and, I assume, will make television shows. Have television and Hollywood changed?

MacLaine: No. I think *me* in it has changed. If I were attempting to do another series again now, I would have the guts either to walk or to question more or to demand at least to meet the writers. Things that I didn't have the courage to do four or five years ago I've got the courage to do now.

I used to suffer from an overrespect for the other person's point of view. A lot of that was the problem of being a woman and getting out of that bag of being in a man's world, where they *must* know better, and the whole middle-class psychology that the authority figure must know better or they wouldn't be an authority. In my series they told me that if a free, independent woman did not experience things of guilt as she went out around the world practicing her profession, having a love affair here or there, enjoying herself and the people she met, then the product-buying audience would have nothing to identify with. They really sold me. I did walk, you know. I did say, I'm quitting. I called my agent. He said, Go if you've got twenty million dollars, groovy. And they put that bag on me and so I couldn't leave. Today, if I had that again, I would proceed with much more knowledge, courage, self-esteem.

Probst: You're a stronger person.

MacLaine: Yes.

MacLaine: I wasn't sure . . . what the audience would think about my television show, "Shirley's World," am I a writer now or a political activist? She's got a big mouth—okay—but can she make us laugh again? I think they were confused. I think they are confused. They see me do four talk shows a week talking about my writing and China, then show up as the MC looking like Loretta Young at the Academy Awards. I feel I've come out the other end of my own tunnel, somehow. I'm dying to get into the exercise of doing Amelia Earhart. That is the kind of woman I can really understand now.

Probst: Who decided you would do Amelia Earhart?

MacLaine: I did. In 1966 I got interested in her and have been doing research and stuff ever since. She was a woman you don't have to associate with the men in her life. All you really care about is where her plane is, not where her man is. She loved the adventure and the challenge of nature. She was a very committed anti-Fascist, by the way, and worked extremely hard for Roosevelt. Would do anything she could to protect what she called democracy, was an early feminist, made speeches in front of the DAR—mostly to silent faces—about the inclusion of women, that said war wouldn't be so attractive to men if women were in it, met usually with, as I said, a stony silence. But she was a very intelligent, idealistic, committed challenger. Her relationship with the men in her life, and the relationship with herself, is what I find interesting. It's the first time I've seen a role of a woman on the screen, even since the days of Joan Crawford and Barbara Stanwyck—I mean, they might have been playing ballsy women, but they always ended up in the lap of some guy in the third act. This one doesn't. I'm not opposed to that, but are you ever really interested in who John Wayne sleeps with? You're interested in what he's there for.

PROBST: Then Hollywood can be used to good purposes, as in Amelia Earhart?

MACLAINE: Well, I'm an actress, I think. I love to communicate and I love to emulate human life, I really love that. That's why I got involved with politics. And I have a social conscience. I've had it since I was very little.

PROBST: When did that start? Going back to Caryl Chessman is the first time I remember. . . . Marlon Brando, Steve Allen, and you went up to prevent Governor Pat Brown from executing Caryl Chessman—and you failed. Did Pat Brown ever explain why he . . .

MACLAINE: Oh, sure. It was part of the system. He was an institutionalized politician. He apologizes for it, by the way, every time I see him. He's a very sweet man, with a real conscience, and he's never forgotten it.

PROBST: What were your first recollectons of becoming politically aware?

MACLAINE: I think when I was about two and I heard my father call someone a nigger. It really bothered me because he was my best friend. My own father didn't like the fact that he was using that word—and yet, he was using it. Everyone on the block used it, therefore he used it. I'm sure everyone in the privacy of their own home felt ashamed, but nevertheless, if they were ever overheard, they had to use it. I was going to dancing class across the river, with black people, Jewish people, all these people my family was making fun of at home. We're a Wasp family, we're a real tub of vanilla. When Dad read my book and people asked him what he thought of it, he said it was true. He's a fantastic person.

PROBST: He voted for McGovern just to please you and your brother, although he knew he would lose?

MACLAINE: He said, "I voted for McGovern overwhelmed with security that the son of a bitch was going to lose."

PROBST: A couple of weeks ago Marlon Brando was in town and he told me he did not want to speak about acting, in a sense the way you don't want to speak about acting. . . .

MACLAINE: Oh, I love to talk about acting. I think he makes a mistake to get on and only talk about the Indians. I want to know where Marlon Brando is coming from, then I'll understand what he's saying about the Indians.

PROBST: But he feels the way you do, he wants to talk about the serious subjects. China is his Indians.

MACLAINE: It's like me going on the Johnny Carson show with my velvet skirt split up to here, right? I've got to get their attention first and then I'll hit them over the head.

PROBST: For some people, being an actress, is a life. In your case it is not enough.

MACLAINE: I would really rather be a fly on the wall. I just love to look at other people. That's why I ended up being an actress, because after you look at them long enough, you want to *be* them. But I am more comfortable just sitting around on a street corner watching the people go by. I just can't think of anything more fun. But maybe there's no difference. Maybe we're all both expressers and observers, but we're so damned pigeonholed that we get the feeling we have to do one or the other, but we can't get away with doing both.

PROBST: When you go to Las Vegas and do a show, how much technique is involved in that?

MacLAINE: That's professional, theatrical technique. I'm there to entertain the people. The technique I have to observe is to be good and not to talk about politics on the stage, and I don't.

PROBST: What is your feeling now of Shirley MacLaine as an actress?

MacLAINE: I think now I could really be a good actress. I don't think I've been a good one. I have the natural talent, and frankly, I walk on a sound stage, they turn all those lights on and I feel so relaxed I want to go right to sleep. Everybody's looking at me and they love me and they're there to make sure I do a good job and that I'll look pretty and if I spill anything in the course of a scene, they'll clean it up.

Now, I can really act and I think I will. I'm taking it seriously because I'm taking the business of being alive more seriously. I'm taking the business of my contribution more seriously. I took my writing much more seriously than my acting, because it was harder for me. For instance, I can tell you all my idiosyncratic demands before I write. I need the right kind of paper. I used to use those yellow pads until I heard Richard Nixon used them, then I had to find some other color that worked and I needed just the right kind of pen and just the right kind of window to look out of. I couldn't tell you what I required in my acting environment. I could get on my head and do it. I wasn't in touch with my needs as being an actress Now I'm taking my real talent more seriously because I think probably my real talent is to communicate and use whatever facility I have, whether it's my body or my voice or my intellectual-emotional coordination, to convey human beings to other human beings. Also, I was just so infinitely more interested in what went on on the opposite side of the camera than I was on my side of the camera, that I didn't spend enough time being self-centered. Even today, my propensity is to walk into a place and forget that I'm who I am. You can take the girl out of the chorus but you can't take the chorus out of the girl. I've gotten all of those other things in sync with the business of being a star. I would have a hard time playing *Irma La Douce* with any real conviction today. It is so surface and it's too unimportant.

PROBST: Did you ever have an acting coach?

MACLAINE: No. The best way to learn how to act is to get out there and act. There's nothing like being in front of people and trying it and falling on your face, seeing what happens and learning from the experience.

PROBST: Ginger Rogers led you into dance?

MACLAINE: And Eleanor Powell, all those women in spotlights. . . . I was born with deformed ankles, I didn't have the strength to stand up, so Mother sent me to a ballet class therapeutically. But I loved the discipline, the self-discipline required, and I loved the music and I loved the feeling of the physical strain. As soon as my ankles got strong, I realized I was hooked on the whole coordination of mental and physical stuff, called dancing. The first thing I want to know when I play a character is, How does she move? How does she walk? How does she sit? Because I'm a dancer, I work from the outside in, where that's concerned. And then all the other stuff begins to bubble up and make connection. But I have to know those external things first.

PROBST: Do you have a greater respect for writing because it's something that you came to much later in life?

MACLAINE: No. I have a greater respect for writing because it's lonelier. I have great respect for loneliness, because the correlation between freedom and loneliness is very fragile. You're not lonely when you're acting. If you can trust the people around you—and you're usually acting with someone else and it's essentially a group experience—if you can trust that, you have real support. You have no support as a writer. There's nothing more deadly than that piece of paper that's just flat blank.

PROBST: Do you like to write?

MACLAINE: Well, it's more painful *not* to.

PROBST: That's not an answer.

MACLAINE: I don't know that I like to write. I like to act. I love to act, if I can stay awake long enough on the set. The first time I did it in *The Trouble with Harry* and all those lights came on and Hitchcock and the others walked over and they said, You know, you really have a very sensual way with your eyes, what they didn't realize was I couldn't keep them open because I was too comfortable.

PROBST: A long time ago you were making a movie on a sound stage, called *Can-Can,* and Nikita Khrushchev came by. Later he registered a moral protest at the sensual activities. And you had some snappy reply.

MACLAINE: I thought his was pretty snappy. He said, "The face of humanity is prettier than its backside," talking about the can-can. But what my snappy reply was, was that he was upset because we wore panties. He knew that the legitimate can-can was done with masses and masses of velvet, under which there was nothing. You couldn't do that at 20th in those days. He was a very interesting, kind of . . . a cuddly kind of dictator. He had a real warm way with people. He really did. He was very mischievous and humorous.

PROBST: And Mao?

MACLAINE: Well, I wouldn't call Mao a dictator. I would call him an educator.

PROBST: You wouldn't call him a dictator?

MACLAINE: No, I wouldn't. I'd call him a teacher. I would really say that for the first time I saw what is described as the dictatorship of the proletariat. I'd say the peasants are the dictators in China. They make most of their own decisions. My goodness, it takes a long time. To get one bicycle pump took a commune three months to decide because of the debate, the pros and cons, who would blow it up, what about the bicycle to get the pump. The dictatorial decision would have been made by the one person who runs the bicycles. But that's not the way it's done in China. Everybody has some input to the decision-making process. That's the dictatorship of the proletariat.

PROBST: You went to China two years ago. Yet you've waited for your book and your movie to come out.

MACLAINE: I did go on the Jack Paar show. He knew that I would be talking about China. So I got on the air and there was Peggy Cass sitting next to me. Jack began to go on about where did you have your shirts done, did they have starch on the collars, then when he got through with that nonsense, someone in the audience yelled, Jack, why don't you let her talk? And I began to talk and I began to try to describe what I had seen. He listened for a minute or two and then interrupted me again. He got hysterical. Whereupon Peggy Cass leaped in. I was stunned. Well, this subject is too combustible to discuss. I'm going to have to sit down and take stock of how to handle it before I go on the air again. The audience came backstage and said, Now, will you tell us? and in the privacy and the sort of low profile of the backstage area, we sat in the hallway and talked for hours. After that, I thought I'd better wait and get my own thoughts together. I didn't realize it was as volatile as it was. I sat down and finished the book which took me most of the next year. I got my own responses more succinctly together before I decided to go talk in public—hence, the delay.

PROBST: There's a line in your book in which you say that your sex drive diminished while you were in China. Was it because of China or was it because of something else?

MACLAINE: China makes you think about things much more important than sex. Somehow you start thinking about sex like you think about food, it's a utilitarian necessity every now and then.

PROBST: Which the state doesn't provide.

MACLAINE: I would say, on a scale of one to ten, sex is somewhere as low as seven. It's not a priority that they really ... remember, they have no erotic stimulation to speak of. The dress—the men and the women don't play these sex-game, role-playing things we do here. They all dress the same. Very utilitarian, unwasteful kind of attire, and they don't have ads for bust pads and bras and feminine hygeine spray and perfume and how to smell good and then you go to do the thing and afterwards you've committed this sin. They don't have that kind of hypocrisy. They don't have the stimulation or the sin. Once a week, I figure, they do it.

MACLAINE: They're very amused by all our sexual questions. They think we're absolutely compulsive about it, which we are. We would sit down for our women's liberation meetings and they would be talking about organization and we would be talking about sex, like who was on top and stuff. And at one point, one of the women in our delegation was saying that we had made such strides in the United States with the lesbian wing of the movement. And the Chinese said, The what? And she went on to explain it. Well, you never saw . . . they didn't know what it meant. They had to go to the dictionary and look it up because they wouldn't believe our description, what the meaning was. They have no idea what those sort of complicated, rather affluent experiments are that go on in a society that hasn't got enough to do. They don't know what all that means. They're out there organizing themselves to get the fields plowed. You've got time to do that with your girl friend in the bunk? One boy I met—he was thirty —didn't know what *prostitute* meant. That's the truth.

I asked about a hundred and fifty people, What do you look for in a mate? Is it humor? Is it sexual attraction? I just felt so dumb after a while because they were all my Western connotations, what I would look for. They all said, without exception, political consciousness. So that led me to the next question, Does that mean you can marry *any*body if they have high political consciousness? And then they said, Well, naturally, human selectivity takes over, but the highest quality in a human being is whether he is involved and committed to the revolution.

PROBST: How did China affect you?

MACLAINE: It's going to sound awfully naive, but when you see masses and masses of people believing that they can make a difference, it's very moving. What it did to me was to make me want to make a difference to myself. There's no way I can move this society, to speak of, except by being a better person, using whatever talent I've got, whatever capacity I've got, whatever potential I've got. They probably weren't as talented as me, but they sure as hell are moving faster than I am. How do you repair the system? How do we make more contact with each other? How do you start believing in hope again? That's the irony of what's happened in the West—a participatory democracy no longer participates.

Q *(question from audience)*: Do you have the same curiosity about how the Russian system works?

MacLaine: I did when I was in the Soviet Union, but frankly, I was depressed. It's a paranoid place; people are frightened in Russia. They're all looking over their shoulders. It's like a nation of barracudas wondering who's coming down the pike. I was followed everywhere. I wasn't allowed to go anywhere freely. The corruption is incredible; people trying to rip us off to get dollars or catch us in compromising positions. It was just total. And the feeling of paralysis in the people, this feeling that they have no hope. You could hear shuffling feet and no laughter.

Probst: What is your third book about?

MacLaine: It's a novel. I don't have to be limited to the truth now. It's really something. I go through periods when I write twenty pages a night and then I don't write for three months. It's like some of the experiences I had acting with an improvisational technique once. When the director said, Go ahead, if you feel like taking off emotionally from the scene, do it. And it scared me. A lot of freedom can be frightening. It's an exercise in facing many selections. But it will be about me, I'm sure it will, and all the things that either I wished I had done . . . be really juicy, won't it? People think I have this great life, what will they think of what I *wanted* to have!

15

ANGELA LANSBURY:

If I Think It's Honest,
I Can Sell You Anything

PROBST: I am intrigued by a comment you made once that, "When I'm onstage I often think, What the hell am I doing here? I realize that I want to go home."

LANSBURY: I've thought about that statement. It was instinctive. Somebody had asked me how I felt onstage, and I tried to crystallize my feelings. I was appearing in *A Taste of Honey,* an extraordinary part—as in *Gypsy,* another dreadful mother. I was terribly unhappy playing this ridiculous person, and when I said, "I think I want to go home," I meant that I wanted to go back to being myself. Being onstage and working continuously can be extremely exhausting business if you leave yourself at home, as I try to, and if you emerge from the wings as somebody else. I miss myself and I want to go home.

PROBST: In *The Last Interview* by Lillian and Helen Ross, John Gielgud said, "When I get into the theater, then I'm home." You don't feel that way?

LANSBURY: I do in a sense, yes. The theater is a tremendous retreat—when I want to get away from that person who's at home, I can go to the theater and be in another world, a different emotional milieu from my own.

PROBST: Woody Allen has said, "My one regret in my life is that I'm not someone else." Do you feel that?

LANSBURY: No, I'm very happy to be both people. I'm never satisfied with myself, but I guess no one is. I really like being somebody else very much, but when the curtain comes down, I want to turn off. People always expect me to walk out the stage door as the lady they've just seen onstage. There have been periods in my life when I had acted my way right into the car and right down Broadway. That was acting and not myself. Some people live their entire lives as other characters and they are never themselves. I have a running battle trying to say, You've got to sit still for me because I am Angela Shaw and I have another life. I have to have another life. Does that confuse you?

PROBST: Yet you speak of leaving yourself at home and playing someone else. Have you ever played *yourself*–Angela Lansbury?

LANSBURY: No, I think she's dull as ditch water and that's one of the reasons I don't ever want to show where she lives. But it's silly to say that. I have a lot of other interests besides acting and I always have a continuous tussle whether I'm going to be acting or whether I'm going to be home. I can honestly tell you, though, if I could, I'd spend three months doing nothing and then nine months acting. In the theater you get into these long runs and you're in for two years and then you go out on the road and the money's great but it's very time-consuming. If only there were some way that you could have a little more time.

PROBST: You have to have another life besides the stage, though the other life is sometimes dull. Is the stage more of a home?

LANSBURY: I live a divided existence, I am very much at home onstage. I love being an actress and an artist in the theater, I really do. It's a very powerful situation to be in. Very, very powerful, indeed. And if I'm crazy, I've got a lot of company.

PROBST: You've talked elsewhere about being a mother offstage. Is that a divided existence, too?

LANSBURY: I know some professional mothers who are fantastic mothers, they manage to do both extraordinarily well. My ability to be a good mother or a bad mother had to do with me as an individual, not whether I am an actress or not. I thought I should keep my children out of my professional life, and I did that assiduously, though I think they suffered from it. If I had let them be around me in the dressing room, part of my life, they wouldn't have seen me as this rather overblown person who is stared at on the street. If they had known that people always did say, Oh, look, there's Angela Lansbury, they would have understood there was nothing peculiar about it.

PROBST: Is there something embarrassing about the stage world that you were trying to protect them from?

LANSBURY: Yes. You are embarrassed when you're with your children and people behave as they do around stars. They lose their dignity. You don't lose yours, they lose theirs and they become driveling idiots sometimes. This is highly embarrassing to you, it's also embarrassing to young children, who don't know what's going on.

PROBST: What specifically does a driveling idiot do?

LANSBURY: They say, AAHH!, you're not—? Oh, my God! They carry on. Or they say to the children, What does it feel like to have a big movie star for a mother? It sounds so asinine and childlike, but that is exactly what happens. You have to stand there like an idiot saying, Yes, I am. Yes, I am Angela Lansbury, and these are my children, and how do you do. People just absolutely "go bonkers," as Lynn Redgrave would say—she's my neighbor, that's why I can say it.

PROBST: You have a different feeling toward it now?

LANSBURY: Yes, I do. I just make my children muck in. And I think people are far more adult about actors and actresses now.

PROBST: Your son is going to the same drama school in London you went to, Webber Douglas.

LANSBURY: I'm rather pleased, naturally. It's a very good school. I haven't seen his work, however—I'm not allowed to see it for two years. I don't know how he's going to come out of it, whether he's going to be a good actor, or a terrible actor, whether I shall have to say, Honey, you stink, or, I don't like your work, or, Quick, shift into something else. Which I won't say. None of those things will I say to him, incidentally. He'll find that out for himself. But if he asks me, Do you think I have a chance? that's a big question. I guess he really shouldn't ask me.

PROBST: It does not disturb you that he wants the same work. . . .

LANSBURY: No, it took him a long time to realize that's what he wanted. My own opinion is that he'll be a good director. I think he has a critical facility. He's a good selector and I think he'd be a good director.

PROBST: Do you like to act, yourself?

LANSBURY: Enormously. I love the craft of acting, of creating somebody else, simulating emotions and physical characteristics that are not natural to me.

PROBST: How do you become another person? How do you become Auntie Mame?

LANSBURY: I've never really tried to nail down exactly how I do it. I've collected an incredible memory of trivia, of people, attitudes, expressions, movements. I am terribly interested in everything that's going on around me—economics, politics, but in a sort of apolitical way. All of this information seems to have been packed away within myself. I draw on all this. Although I left school when I was twelve, educated myself, in a sense, read a lot when I was young. My grandfather was certainly not an intellectual, but my father was close to being one, and my mother adored the arts and culture. All of this was channeled to me as a child. Not scholastic learning, but simply living learning. All of that has remained with me. People say, How can you take on the attitudes of somebody you weren't even alive to know? I learned from books, from old movies, from the theater, from knowing people—a strange, curious procession of people. A lot of my acting ability goes back to my grandfather, who was a fantastic public speaker.

PROBST: George Lansbury, leader of the British Labour Party, 1931 to 1935.

LANSBURY: That's right. My whole family are terribly Labour, I have to tell you. But I'm not—as I say, I'm apolitical. But my grandfather was a man of tremendous conviction, an idealist, a humanist, an extraordinary human being. I admired him so much. I saw what he could do to a crowd, in places like the Royal Albert Hall in Britain, maybe that's . . . part of a seed I think was planted at a very early, tender age. People fell about with excitement at his presence.

PROBST: You had left England during the war for Hollywood.

LANSBURY: It was incredible, a dream come true, in a way. In my early youth in England, I was a complete movie maniac, I went to the movies every afternoon. I never dreamed that I would ever end up in Hollywood myself. A childhood friend and I carried on a fantasy life about Hollywood and the movies and we drank orange-juice cocktails. When I actually did go to Hollywood it was a wonder of wonders. I did not relate one to the other, the real to the unreal—only years later I realized I was living what I had dreamed years earlier.

PROBST: You worked as a wrapper in Bullock's Wilshire?

LANSBURY: I came to New York first and went to drama school for two years, then went to Hollywood as an aspiring actress. We needed the money at that time, still do, so I took a job in a shop—I couldn't get a part—and became a wrapper, and then a saleslady at Bullock's Wilshire.

PROBST: There was a time when studios controlled your life.

LANSBURY: Yes, they did. Now I look back on that whole movie experience, it's a wonder I ever got out of it. It was just sheer luck. I stayed in the studios for twelve years at MGM. If I hadn't got out and gone to the stage in *Hotel Paradiso,* I think my whole career would have fizzled out.

PROBST: You did more than seventy films?

LANSBURY: No, I made about forty-eight—not many, actually.

PROBST: You played terrible roles and you were hissed at publicly. Did it affect you to play people who were ugly or unliked?

LANSBURY: Yes, it was bound to because I was really very young, only nineteen or twenty. I wanted to be like the other girls at the studio—Gloria DeHaven, and June Allyson, Ann Miller, and all those other glamorous girls.

PROBST: Why were you picked for the hateful person?

LANSBURY: Because I had a viperish air about me, I suppose. I really don't know. I suppose I was a very mature young actress.

PROBST: What was your low point?

LANSBURY: The fifties, really. I wasn't moving forward. It was the era when the studios started to collapse, television suddenly was the big noise and everybody rushed there. We all made our living on live television—"Studio One," "Playhouse 90," plus all the half-hour television shows we did in Hollywood. I was forced to do an incredible show called "The Pantomime Quiz." For nine weeks over a summer we did charades—and I can't do charades at all!

PROBST: But then you had a second career and you broke out of all that. Was it accident?

LANSBURY: Yes, it was. It was a kind of luck and destiny, fate, or whatever you want to call it. I think inside myself I was very ambitious, although far too timid to do anything about it.

PROBST: Are you more confident today in *Mame* than you were in *Gaslight?* Or were you more confident then?

LANSBURY: I was very confident then. I had my tuppenny worth of training and my own instinct and a feeling for characterization—that's been my big card as an actress—my ability to characterize and be somebody not myself. Nancy, the cockney maid, was a wonderful way for me to start. It really was. It embodied everything I would know, coming from England. Cockney accent, easy. Victorian England, I understood that. It still existed around London when I was a child—maids, caps, all of that shtick. It was a good thing to start off with, I was very fortunate. I did have an innate ambition to do good work, to do something better. It had to do with music, and, in the end, with the theater. Musicals finally put me across and made me a "star."

PROBST: Do British actresses have an advantage in living and working here?

LANSBURY: Most British actresses, unless they come from the cinema, are trained to be professional. They're really very good at their jobs, so they come over here and they get a lot of work. That doesn't mean they're better, but they're better trained. I don't think that's going to be true necessarily much longer. Also, they can make more money here. That's a very important reason. You can't make any money in Britain in the theater.

PROBST: Are you happy you no longer live in California?

LANSBURY: Yes.

PROBST: Why?

LANSBURY: Because I lived in California all through the forties and the fifties and I had it up to here and I don't want to live there anymore. I find it stultifying and enervating. I tend to sit around waiting for a movie and get bored stiff. As I get more mature I find that I really love to work. The more mature you get, the more necessary it is to work. When I work, I get very well paid for it. The problem if you don't work a year—and it's very easy for us to go a year and not work—is to keep up the standard of work that we want to do. When I say I go where the work is, that means not that I'm money grubbing, it's because I want to work and I want to do interesting things, so I go where the interesting things are.

PROBST: You've done forty-eight movies and you've done a number of stage plays and musicals. Is there any one thread that goes through all those performances?

LANSBURY: If there's one thread, it is that I want to approach every character I play with an innate honesty. That's one very overworked word! It has to be truthful. I have to feel I'm being honest on the stage, even though I'm pulling the wool over your eyes. If I think it's truthful and honest, I sense that I can sell you anything. I can sell you that I'm the most evil woman in the world or that butter wouldn't melt in my mouth and I'm the sweetest person you ever met. As long as I believe it, you will believe it.

PROBST: You say you bring something to the character. Do you keep working on it?

LANSBURY: It takes me about two months to arrive at a character with an audience. And then, once I get there, I stay there, I've refined everything and technique takes over. I don't get it in rehearsal necessarily and I probably haven't got it on the first night. But then the grooves start to deepen and suddenly everything becomes easy and no problem and it works. You refine it to the point where you know that on a certain line the audience will respond in such a way and on another line in another. The whole thing put together adds up to a total experience.

PROBST: Is it more difficult to do somebody who is evil or a harridan than someone who is likable?

LANSBURY: I suppose it is. It's much more fun to play a real bitch on wheels. Mrs. Iselin, in *The Manchurian Candidate,* I've always felt was the absolute embodiment of evil. A woman like that, of course, is fascinating. She doesn't have a crooked nose . . . she doesn't have any overt signs of being evil, she just is. The core of her is rotten.

PROBST: Do you see yourself as having any responsibility as a star? Does it make any difference in the way you live?

LANSBURY: I think I really am a rather conventional person, an unconventional conventional person. I am concerned about appearances. When you're an actor or an actress who is very well known, you are a kind of example—that sounds middle-class, corny, and lowbrow, but in a curious way I am self-conscious about how I conduct myself with people.

PROBST: There is a burden that goes with the applause.

LANSBURY: I think there is. I expend a tremendous amount of energy with people, trying to be easygoing and nice. I can't work in an atmosphere with underlying tensions, unhappiness, misunderstandings. I always go out of my way to try and create an atmosphere which is conducive for me to work in. I'm being very selfish, in fact. I suffer from wanting to be liked. I cannot stand for people to dislike me. For that reason I won't be late, I won't keep people waiting. I go through the most incredible hoops because I'm terrified they'll think badly of me.

PROBST: How do you feel about the audience?

LANSBURY: I care about them very much. I want to hit them all very hard. My trouble is, I'm always trying to get everybody, instead of just trying to hit a small portion of the audience.

PROBST: Can you feel the audience when you're onstage?

LANSBURY: I said earlier that there's a tremendous power to being an artist. There are times when you can hold the audience spellbound, and then drop them like a hot potato, just by what you're doing up there. And you know you're doing it. You know you've got them. Like a net, like a fish on the end of a hook. And that's a terrific feeling, especially when you know that they're loving to be treated in that manner. I'm fulfilling my function, which is to entertain. I'm taking people out of themselves into another sphere, which is the theater. Make-believe or forgetting, transporting themselves out of themselves, for a moment. Even that tiny little moment is worth it.

PROBST: Is there ever truth in films or theater?

LANSBURY: I think there is, if the actor understands what it is he is trying to sell to the audience and if they understand. You have a fusion of two truths, a universality. You share a truth.

PROBST: What's Angela Lansbury selling?

LANSBURY: I'm recreating reality out of unreality. I'm trying to let you into a moment or a scene. I'm trying to make you believe it's happening.

PROBST: Who do you work for? You work to make a living, yes. But do you work to make the audience laugh, to hold the audience?

LANSBURY: You're working to win and to entertain the audience.

PROBST: To win what?

LANSBURY: To make them buy your truthfulness and to allow themselves to be taken by the hand and carried along in thought for two hours or whatever it is. It's what they paid for. If you sit in your seat all night long and you're aware that your ass hurts or the man behind you is kicking the seat, those are obviously things you are aware of in the theater, but nevertheless there must come a moment when there's nothing between you and what is happening onstage, when you are transported out of yourself. And I think if you can provide that for the audience in the theater, you are winning and your work is worthwhile.

PROBST: How do you know when you're winning?

LANSBURY: Simply by the attention, the quiet, this crackling something that passes between what's going on onstage and what's happening in the audience. It's the moment when you demand that they listen. It's the something which forces them to pay attention and to allow themselves to come with you for that moment and to cry or to laugh or whatever it is that you want them to experience along with you. You want them to understand. What you are trying to do is to crystallize an experience.

16

GWEN VERDON:

Your Head Will Forget and Your Body Will Remember

PROBST: You were born in Culver City, and Culver City is another word for Hollywood.

VERDON: My father worked at MGM studios, he did the lighting for Garbo's movies. People have always said, Oh, you were so lucky, you must have grown up knowing Garbo! But he also did the Tarzan films. So I grew up knowing all the animals in the Tarzan films.

PROBST: You were born knock-kneed and wore corrective boots.

VERDON: Knock-kneed sounds like nothing. They wanted to break my legs and reset them. I was in a double-hinge cage from the hip down to the foot, my spine was like a figure S and my head was over on one side. But my mother, who was a dancer herself, said, That girl is going to dance. When she heard them say, Break this, and Operate on that, she said, No. The doctors had explained that the muscles are splints for the bones while they're growing, so she decided to fix the splints which were the muscle and *not* let them break the bones. I had to wear corrective shoes, and she filled my bedroom full of sand so that I would never walk barefoot. I learned to write by holding a pencil between my toes, I could play marbles with my toes. Everyone sat on chairs, I sat on a barrel. In addition to all that, I was also cross-eyed. My mother got two silver dollars, which were very hard to come by in those days, she would roll them around and I would have to follow them with my eyes—and my eyes straightened out! This was all a game with my mother. I began to dance when I was two, I don't even remember beginning—I just danced.

PROBST: When you were six, you were "the fastest tapper in the world" at the Million Dollar and at Loews' in Los Angeles.

VERDON: When I was three, I ran away from home. Just recently I went back and I looked at the spot where I was sitting at three years old and it was a half block from where I lived. I was convinced I had run away from home! At least it satisfied the need that I had. I remember looking at the bubbles in the tar. I can still remember thinking, Gee, is this all there is? I couldn't wait to get out of there.

PROBST: At sixteen, as you've said, you hated dancing, and you stopped dancing and got married.

VERDON: I didn't hate dancing. I had to lie. There was a time when it was not chic to have a child when you were sixteen and not married.

PROBST: But you said you hated dancing because you had too much of it.

VERDON: There really *was* a time when I didn't like it. There was so much discipline imposed.

PROBST: Are there limitations on your body now?

VERDON: I still do exercises. One knee was operated on. . . . Did you know that most of the great dancers have limitations caused by injuries—Fred Astaire, Gene Kelly, Ulanova in the ballet, Margot Fonteyn—all of them? Doris Humphrey had an arthritic hip, she could not move. Even twenty years ago, Martha Graham sometimes had to be lifted in and out of a hot bathtub before she could dance—once you get moving, you can do it. If you've got anything wrong with you, don't think it's a problem, it could be a blessing. It could be something that makes you absolutely unique. Ricardo Montalban has one leg that is shorter than the other—he did *Jamaica* barefoot, and you would never know he limps. Gene Kelly cannot turn his legs forward, it's almost a displaced hip. Have you noticed he always dances with his legs turned out? It's become a style of dancing. Fred Astaire can hardly bend his knees. And that's why he has that marvelous style. For almost any actor or dancer you can mention—but primarily dancers—a style has evolved out of an old injury or something you were born with and can do nothing about.

PROBST: What is dancing, then?

VERDON: Dancing, I think, has to do with being mute. I don't think dancers like to communicate with words. You go to any country and you don't have to have language—through the arts you can communicate. Dancers just *dance* together. And dancing is pure—you don't have to bother with semantics, there's no way of slanting it. With dance, either you do it or you don't. There is just no way to fake it. Chita Rivera and I were in *Can-Can* together twenty-three years ago, and we have waited all these years to work together again in *Chicago.* When people are really good you don't envy them, you're not jealous of them, you admire them, especially dancers because there's no easy way to dance. You can't fake it. Even if you're not very good, it's still hard. There is no easy way.

Even if actors say, I'm going to walk through it, they don't, their ego won't allow it. They want to be good. You work as well as you can by your own standards. But once the public gets out of that theater, I don't do anything for them. I don't want to stand and sign programs. I say, Walk with me. I always have someplace to go and something to do and a life to live. I've done what I'm supposed to do as well as I can do it.

PROBST: When you are dancing in *Chicago,* who are you dancing for?

VERDON: Me. That's the way it should be for everybody, not only dancers. You can't depend on somebody else to know if you are good, they may say you were good on a night when you know you were bad. And then you feel like a fraud.

PROBST: A number of performers have said that they felt fraudulent. Where does that come from?

VERDON: There are times when you do not do things as well as you want to by your own set of standards, and you feel guilty. One night you hit a few clinkers along the way, or you miss a scene. In twenty-two months in *Redhead* I sang and danced and acted well in only six shows.

PROBST: You kept track, you kept a log? Why was that?

VERDON: To find out what the average is. How often can you even expect to be good? It is so undermining, I never did it again.

Q *(question from audience)*: What do you do if you draw a blank with a line or a dance routine when you're onstage?

·VERDON: You always know what the scene is about. If you've studied acting, you can improvise a line so it doesn't scare you. If you're dancing, your head will forget and your body will remember. I hadn't done *Damn Yankees* in twenty years, and last summer I thought, Well, I'll never remember it. But when I turned on the record my head couldn't remember but my body was doing it.

Q: What do you think about after you've got the routine set? Does your mind wander?

VERDON: No, it doesn't. There's always a slight difference—microscopic, but it's never exactly the same.

Discipline is essential to a dancer. I really work at dancing very hard. As a dancer you train, you are an athlete. And I do research on the people I'm playing. For *Damn Yankees,* I must have spent at least six to seven months living on Columbus and on Eighth and Ninth avenues only to learn the accent. And for *Sweet Charity,* I went up to those dance halls.

PROBST: Are you still scared on opening night?

VERDON: I spent five years in analysis because all that time I thought I was scared. But I've discovered that excitement and fear are close in physical feeling. Horses in the starting gate are so excited that their skin is quivering and everything's going. But those horses aren't scared, they just want to get going. It's the same with me. I decided I never was scared.

PROBST: Not even on the opening night of *Chicago?*

VERDON: No. You want to do it right—not for the critics, strangely enough, but for the author and the director and the others who put in all that time, you really want to do it for them.

PROBST: How does it feel to be famous again?

VERDON: I didn't know what it felt like to be famous in the first place. I know I'm more in the public eye now, but I can still get through life without seeing anybody, if I want to. I'm like those horses at Aqueduct or Belmont who wear blinkers. I only see what I want to see.

PROBST: At the end of the show *Chicago,* you get a terrific ovation. What do you see when the lights are in your face?

VERDON: You can see people adoring you. You can see women—this always disturbs me—who look at Chita and me with the tears running down their faces. They never look happy to me. The men stand up like Tarzan and flex their biceps. I said to Chita, "Is that a new power sign?" It's some kind of joy for the men. The men had been college athletes, beautiful with muscles, and they got out and became salesmen, and the muscles went, and now they've all had heart attacks. If they'd kept both things going and worked out with the kids . . . it is so much better to have a full life. Your head becomes scrambled otherwise. But the women bother me the most. I always feel that they're very unhappy because they made some kind of compromise. Most of them are about forty years old, maybe had some interest in theater or dance and had been convinced that to get married and have kids is a better life. There is nothing wrong with that, but you can do *both,* no one ever told them that. I think that's sad.

PROBST: How difficult is it for you to do both, to be a mother and a star on Broadway?

VERDON: Time, that's all. To me the most valuable thing is time. Having a full life independent of being a mother makes me a better mother, I think. If your child grows up knowing that you are a human being, it's easy. You must be allowed to explore your own interests just as the child does. A nine-month-old gets in a dirty sand pit and explores everything. The mother has the same right, and the child grows up knowing that. It doesn't mean you neglect your child. Nicole comes here with me. She takes notes. She tells Bob Fosse what she thinks is good in the show. She's very much a part of our life. But she has her own life. She paints, I can't paint. . . .

PROBST: How old is she?

VERDON: Just twelve . . . When Bob Fosse, her father, had open-heart surgery, we went to the hospital every day. The family were the only ones allowed in. So we dressed our daughter—you have to be fifteen or sixteen—in my shoes with rubber bands to keep them on and false eyelashes and big hats. And she'd go to the hospital and visit him. He kept saying, "It looks like a Fellini movie."

I don't work at having a career. I work two years and then take five years off, then I work two years and take five years off. I'll do this show for two years. And then I take my daughter with me, we snorkel and live on islands. I have many things going. We grow our own vegetables in an organic garden right in the middle of New York City. We have the good bugs who eat the bad bugs. I want her to know that everything that is usable today has to be made by somebody. She knows that somebody had to take the time to make that garden. There are many things I like to do I can't do when I'm in the theater. I love to go to football and baseball games and I like to teach, I'm very involved with the Churchill School for brain-dysfunctional children, and I work at the Postgraduate Center for Mental Health. I'm involved in dance therapy—I hate the name, I always imagine people with fake flowers straightening their head out, as Ruth St. Denis used to say, "going to heaven in a pink light." But it's not that at all. To me it's movement therapy and it's very much like Rilke—if you've got an emotional block, there's also a physical block, and if you can't reach it one way, get it the other way. I don't do analysis—I'm not equipped—I can only say what is not moving. After all, the first thing the human body does, even before it's born, is move. If you have a bad day, get down on your hands and knees and crawl or rock, it's the most reassuring feeling.

PROBST: What do you do when you have a bad day?

VERDON: I crawl. My daughter crawls. She's very poor at math, and so am I. So I say, Let's crawl around the room and have another go at it, because neither one of us can do it. So we do, and it's amazing.

PROBST: Are you a Rilkean?

VERDON: Well, yes, in a way. I think he contributed a great deal which they're really beginning to recognize now. You sometimes wonder why some people are uncoordinated and they don't have to be.

PROBST: How do you learn new steps?

VERDON: I try to learn it to the left. I'm a dominant right, and if I can learn it to the left, then I can always do it on the right—my left has no preconceived idea on how to do it. And once one side learns it, that side can teach the other.

PROBST: Is a dancer respected today?

VERDON: More than they used to be. "Dancer" on your passport used to mean "prostitute." Jean Coyn, who was married to Gene Kelly, had "dancer" on her passport, and they arrested her in Iran as a prostitute. Now they understand that dancing is a profession—it takes as long to learn to be proficient at dancing as to become a doctor.

PROBST: What does your résumé say?

VERDON: I always say, Dancer, actress, singer.

PROBST: In *Chicago* you play a character named Roxie Hart, based on Beulah Annan, who murdered her lover. You've been nagging people to do the role for about twenty years. Why is that?

VERDON: Actually, it's been twenty-three.

PROBST: Why are you attracted to her?

VERDON: Well, I saw a rerun of the movie when I was in *Can-Can,* and I thought the movie was terrible but there was something about it. She was a killer, it was based on an actual murder trial, and it was the first case of plea bargaining.

PROBST: The Roxie Hart character is similar, as you must feel, to many of the other characters you've played—the sad dregs, the almost prostitute, the person society runs over. Is that a theme in your life onstage? You especially like to play the down-and-out?

VERDON: *Chicago* is mostly based on a study of society and of people who were trapped in a certain life because everything was so corrupt. The only rules were that if you did not get caught, that made it right. Or if you had a price and they would pay it, that was okay, too. I think it's terribly contemporary.

PROBST: *Chicago* seems something like the Brecht play, *Resistible Rise of Arturo Ui,* about Hitler and a corrupt city. Is that just a feeling of mine?

VERDON: Oh, it was determined to do it that way. Maureen Watkins, who wrote the play, in a letter said she had seen *Arturo*

Ui—she was very familiar with Brecht and Kurt Weill. And she said it is very much like that in the city of Chicago. She said it just does not appear to be that decadent because they fly the American flag, everyone is so busy standing up applauding that they do not realize just how corrupt and decadent it is. The real Roxie Hart, Beulah Annan, had worked in a laundry. Many women were in jail and she was one of them. They had no way to seek any kind of help, there was no place they could go. They would sometimes spend four and five years in jail before they were brought to trial for the crime of which they were accused. It sometimes happens now.

PROBST: But she was brought to trial within a month.

VERDON: Because she said she was pregnant, which she was not. But she has a child. Someplace in the world there is a child by this woman. By the way, she did not shoot the man. He died in a totally different way. And apparently it was so horrendous a crime that they said, Never mention how you killed him and you will be acquitted.

PROBST: What was so horrendous?

VERDON: He was castrated, but not with a knife, according to a reporter at the time.

PROBST: What with, then?

VERDON: Well, there's a film called *Jaws*. . . .

But what interested me most was the jail and the women in jail. An attorney and the matron, they ran Chicago despite the politicians who were always going to start a rehabilitation program. The matron ran the jail as a house of prostitution. She was also a bootlegger. And all this is in the original transcript.

PROBST: You've played prostitutes so much, does it ever embarrass you for your daughter?

VERDON: No. She's seen everything I've done.

PROBST: How do you feel about playing a prostitute yourself?

VERDON: I don't think they choose to be a prostitute the way little girls say, I'm going to be a bareback rider, or a ballerina. There have always been prostitutes, so there must be a need for them. Some people have to find someone who is less than they are, they can feel better than that person. I've known a lot of prostitutes who raise kids and their kids are terrific. They are more understanding. They're more liberal. They're much more honest. They won't pretend they know something if they don't. They're willing to say, I don't know. With a little bit of luck they would have been terrific schoolteachers.

PROBST: What do you think your function is onstage? Is it to teach?

VERDON: No, to entertain, that's all.

PROBST: You've said about love and prostitution that "When it comes to love, these girls I've played in *Damn Yankees, Sweet Charity,* and *Chicago* are naive and pure. They are looking for someone to love."

VERDON: I don't think most people really know what love is. I sure don't think it's what you see in ninety percent of American homes, which is cannibalism if you ask me. Dog-eat-dog. They are not giving. They don't allow the other person to have a different point of view, which is the only thing that is going to make it interesting. They try to prevent someone's growth, they're so afraid they're going to lose something. They don't know that if the other person grows, they, too, can grow. Prostitutes understand that feeling. In *Sweet Charity* I played the girl as though she was childlike, because I think she was innocent. I don't care how many people she slept with, she's innocent.

PROBST: The victims are the innocent? I want to go back to the characters you've played. You feel that women have not been dealt with properly. Do you have a strong feeling about the whole position of women in the theater?

VERDON: In the theater? No. Women have always had it very lucky in the theater. They've never had a problem there.

PROBST: In society?

VERDON: Oh, yes, in society, I think so. I don't know what good it does going around without a bra if you need one, but I do know there is inequality. I tried to buy a house in the name of Gwen Fosse, which is my legal name—Bob and I are legally separated. The bank wanted to know my marital status. They then said they would give me a loan *if* I would turn in the first page of Bob Fosse's income tax. Well, I wouldn't ask him for that. I didn't ask to look at that when we were married.

PROBST: The theater hasn't been wholly free in presenting sex in the past. Was there anything you couldn't do on film or onstage because of that?

VERDON: Yes, they cut me out of the movie *David and Bathsheba.* I was supposed to dance for Uriah, so Uriah would go home and impregnate Bathsheba to keep David from being accused. The dance is in the Bible but it was not permissible in the film. They cut me out because it was an erotic dance. Babies came out of cabbage patches in the movies in those days. Those were the days when two people could not be in the same bed, until finally they allowed two people to be in the same bed as long as the man had one foot on the floor! I don't know what that one foot does. . . .

PROBST: It seems to me that your playing these roles is part of your relationship with the real world. You're concerned about problems like mental health or the war in Vietnam. In the roles you play, you are concerned about people who are uncared for by society. It all seems to be part of you as a person. What you do in pretense on the stage is also what you do in your own life—you are concerned about people who may not have had a fair shake.

VERDON: I don't think parents know how to give their own kids a fair shake. If they would just give them time and not treat them as though they are stupid when they're only two years old—they're not stupid, they just don't have any information yet. If they would only answer their questions and not be afraid of not knowing. They have proven at the Institute of Human Potential that the enthusiastic mother is the mother whose child recovers very quickly. The one who does everything but swing from the drapes when he walks the first time, their kids progress ninety percent faster than the others. The mother of the child who says, That's fine dear, do that again, her kid doesn't respond nearly as quickly. I have seen people hitting their kids in the street. I don't know why someone that big is hitting someone that little.

PROBST: You have a sense of social responsibility. You've stood on corners protesting against the war in Vietnam.

VERDON: That's what I mean about having my own life to live.

PROBST: You worked for George McGovern, you worked for McCarthy. . . .

VERDON: And Stevenson.

PROBST: How much of your life do you owe to what is called the public?

VERDON: I don't do it for the public. I do it so my children will have a better understanding, and therefore, a better life.

17

WOODY ALLEN:

I'm Not Subverting,
I'm Complaining

PROBST: Did the reviews of *Love and Death* surprise you?

ALLEN: I always think, always think I got away with another one. Critics have had a tendency to encourage the things I am able to do well and not to abuse me for the things I obviously can't do well.

PROBST: Do you find you're working too much? Do you try to figure out a pacing or rhythm?

ALLEN: I like to be working all the time if I can, it's relaxing for me and I always like to begin my next project before I finish my last one. I don't need the time off. And I don't work as hard as people think. People that do street construction and drive taxicabs—that's work—or they go into an office and put in eight hours in hot and cold weather. But to perform in a nightclub or on a Broadway stage, what is that? You sit all day, and at eight o'clock at night you go into the theater and talk for two hours and go home. It's a loafer's life.

PROBST: You are really working for yourself, there's no intermediary. It's Woody Allen writing for Woody Allen, directing for Woody Allen, starring Woody Allen. You have a vertical monopoly of your energies.

ALLEN: It's like a hobby. People pay me to do what I would do anyhow. If they're going to pay me, it's wonderful.

PROBST: How much of your career is accidental?

ALLEN: Well, I'm not sure accidental is the right word. People have a tendency to think you are more in control and you know more than you do. When you undertake to make a movie, you don't control it as much as you think you do. You're dependent on a lot of contingent elements. More than you realize is luck.

PROBST: Everybody I've talked to has said they've had luck, and yet, when pressed, they say the luck has been an opportunity. It seems to me it is more than luck.

ALLEN: It was luck for me that I became a comedian when nightclubs were around—the Blue Angel, the hungry i, Crystal Palace, Mr. Kelly's. I got to play them in the last wave, when they were meaningful. Shortly after I stopped performing in clubs, they went under. That era's over. A young comedian doesn't have the same opportunity I had. When I wanted to switch to films, who was going to give me a chance to direct? To this day I can't splice two pieces of film together or thread a Movieola, but Palomar pictures was forming. They happened to like me and they had faith in me and they couldn't attract more significant filmmakers because they were a young, new company. They gave me a break.

PROBST: You indicate you got away with something. Do you feel you're a fraud?

ALLEN: That may be a heavy word. It's conceivable that more people have more regard for my work than I feel it deserves. I don't think I'm fraudulent in the sense that my films are exploitive. I think they're honest. I'm trying to do original films. But I think there's such a difference between what I set out to do and what I accomplish that I can never get a good feeling about them. When I try and write something for *The New Yorker,* I have a concept and very often I bring it off, but it's only three pages. With a film I start out in January, and twelve months later I come out with a film. In January it looked wonderful, I had a million great ideas. I saw great comic scenes and great characterization. By the time the film comes out, it's sixty percent of what I had hoped it would be. The execution is quite difficult and never lives up to your expectation. I always get a feeling that I wrote a funny script and blew it in the making.

PROBST: Many persons who are creative seem to feel that

inspiration comes from the outside, that it isn't always there and may vanish. There's a certain uncertainty.

ALLEN: I don't ever have that feeling; that has never afflicted me. I'm not saying it couldn't happen. I have a million fears, but that just doesn't happen to be one of them. I never think that I'm going to run out of jokes or comic ideas. It's all I can do to work fast enough to keep up with them. If I could just press a button and have a script written, I could be six scripts ahead now. I don't have the time to write the ideas that I have.

PROBST: Is it always there to be called on?

ALLEN: I can call on it often. My original training was as a television writer—you wrote a show to be seen at the end of the week and there was no room for pussyfooting. You had to write something. And writing something is three-quarters of the battle. Most people strike out by never writing anything. I can go into a room at nine o'clock in the morning with no ideas and come up with something. I can dredge it up. It may not be as good as when a terrific idea hits me, but I don't think you can spend your life waiting for that to happen.

PROBST: You've been writing gags for other people and yourself for a lot of years. Is it easier to feed your own monster than somebody else's monster?

ALLEN: No, because your standards are much higher for yourself. I used to fob jokes off on comics that I would never in a million years do myself. I always felt, Ah, well, it's good enough, they can do it. And they'd do it and they'd get a laugh. But for myself I write twenty-five jokes and throw out twenty-three of them because I'm so fussy. It's much easier when you're doing it for someone else.

PROBST: Why are the standards so high? Are you thinking of the audience? Are you thinking of something inside yourself?

ALLEN: You're thinking of both. In comedy it's impossible to please just yourself. In drama you can, and hope that even if an audience doesn't respond they may think about it, it stays with them and they mull it over. With a comedy, if they don't give you the immediate big laugh on the spot, the boat has sailed and you're dead. They can't go home and think, That was kind of funny. I want big laughs from the audience but I don't want them at any cost. I want them on jokes that I don't have to be ashamed of in front of my friends. So that makes it tough.

The first problem is writing terrific jokes. Then I tell them to an audience. I throw out the ones they don't laugh at and I'm left with very little.

PROBST: How did you know they would laugh at *Love and Death?*

ALLEN: I didn't. That's why it's a harrowing business. You guess. My guess is better than the average guy on the street, so I'm a professional, but my guess is by no means foolproof. I'll write a hundred funny bits and then they laugh at sixty of them. I wind up throwing out tons and tons of material that I thought was uproariously funny when I wrote it and when I shot it. I show it to an audience and it's not. I never know why. I can cut it in different ways, shorten it, tighten it, rejuxtapose the shots, but they never laugh. Charlie Chaplin used to shoot some enormous ratios. I don't know what it was, but for every foot he used, there were many, many that he didn't use.

PROBST: What do you do if you're shooting a movie and something just won't work? Do you go to the next thing?

ALLEN: I table it and give myself time to think about it and shoot it later. We go on to something else. I think about it on the weekend and try to rewrite it.

PROBST: When you made *Love and Death,* you shot the wrong kid for three days.

ALLEN: Things go wrong when you're involved in a massive undertaking. There were supposed to be two kids playing me at different ages and I shot the wrong kid. I had to reshoot. It caused me to lose two days' work.

PROBST: Didn't you use some of the incorrect shots in the picture and then make a crack, We'll see what the UCLA film school thinks about this?

ALLEN: No, this is totally apocryphal. Although frequently the most trivial and the most inane mistakes that find their way into a picture are seized upon by critics or students of film. They muse on it and wonder what you meant by it. They concoct elaborate theories. People are hungry to overanalyze films, even ones like mine that are offered up for laughs. I'm sure Chaplin or Keaton or the Marx brothers just tried to think of a funny idea. But there's a tendency in this day and age to be very heavy about film and superanalytic.

PROBST: Was it easier to be a nonverbal comic? Did Buster Keaton or Chaplin have an easier time of it?

ALLEN: In my opinion, much easier. I'm not disparaging them, because they were geniuses, but it was a simpler problem for them. With sound it's like three-dimensional chess—you're adding another element. Things that are hilarious without sound are very complicated when the people start talking. They suddenly cease being abstractions and become real people. If you had heard Chaplin speak, he would not have spoken like the dumb little tramp. He was an intelligent man and he would have either had to put on a foolish voice or speak as he spoke and assume a much more sophisticated character. It would have led to enormous complications. When he finally did speak in pictures, he spoke like an intelligent man and it wasn't too funny.

PROBST: What do you think about your own five films?

ALLEN: I think I've failed in every one of them and I feel that unequivocally. I don't think that they're bad films, they're enjoyable to people, but for what I set out to do, I failed, undeniably. I did gain some technique in filmmaking. I've gotten more aggressive as a performer—in my first two movies I was desperately afraid people were going to say, Oh, he writes and directs and he leaves his own close-ups on the screen, all the time the camera is always on him, so I was very, very shy about it. But I found that people did laugh at me, so I've gotten more aggressive. On the plus side, there's that. I think I've been trying to get more complicated and deeper. I think *Sleeper* was a little more satirical and also *Love and Death.*

PROBST: *Sleeper* and *Love and Death* are very strong social commentaries, it seems to me.

ALLEN: Perhaps stronger than I've made before, but I want to do it on a deeper, more sophisticated level.

PROBST: In the movie *Love and Death* you imply that God doesn't exist, and if he does, he really can't be trusted.

ALLEN: I have only the most hostile and paranoid feelings about nature, life, the universe. In the movie the guy being me is promised a reprieve at the end and then he is shafted, which is what I think the universe or God or whatever does to you. I think in the end you're led up the garden path.

PROBST: You've gone after God, you've gone after this society. . . .

ALLEN: When you say go after it—I was just kidding around. I would like to attack a problem in a really significant way. I might strike out completely—I may make a film that attacks the problem but is a disaster. I'd rather it was hilarious and missed the problem. I'd like to try and attack a serious problem, but in a comic way.

PROBST: You've said you've gotten more aggressive in your performances. Have you gotten more aggressive as a person?

ALLEN: No, I'm not more aggressive as a person at all. I wish I were. I am more aggressive on the screen, I'm willing to step out more and give myself more verbal jokes and physical jokes and spend more time on myself and take responsibility. A good example of that was *Sleeper*. In *Bananas* and *Take the Money and Run* the scripts are hilariously funny to read. They're kind of actor-proof. The jokes are there. If the guy takes a serum in his arm and turns into a rabbi, you could have fifty actors do that and people are going to laugh if they like that joke—it's self-contained. But in *Sleeper* the script is not very funny and I relied on myself to make it funny. I went in with a lot more trepidation with the flying packs and the big vegetables and the robot suits. There were no jokes there. It was what I was going to do with it. I was willing to take that chance. I would never have done that two years ago.

PROBST: I remember Woody Allen slouching, if he was going to be before a crowd, hyperventilating, hiding, sneaking around —and here you are, in effect the surrogate President—Woody Allen and Betty Ford at the Martha Graham ballet.

ALLEN: No, I am going to be slouching, sneaking around. I'm going to do all those things. I went to a screening of *Jaws* and

Rollerball and went with my hat jammed down and my collar up, and slouching, and parking my car a block away so I could hide. The Martha Graham evening was a pure accident and strictly promotion. I adore Martha's work, but the people making the evening tried to get as much ballyhoo as they could because they were trying to raise money for a very good cause. I tried to cooperate as much as I could—it's like asking me to do it for the Heart Fund. I would never say no to a good cause like that. But it's not my idea of a casual evening. I never go anyplace and I never do anything. I never ever promote my pictures.

PROBST: Why?

ALLEN: I have a tendency to shun that kind of public personality. I find it hard to handle.

PROBST: If you have any respect for your own work, it is cheapening.

ALLEN: I find it that way and yet many people disagree with me. Many firstrate people feel that when they do a picture, millions of dollars have been spent on it and it's a big undertaking and if they go on television and around the country it reflects in the box office. My pictures make less money—one of the reasons is because I don't promote them. If I went around the United States and went on the Carson show and the "Today" show . . . people told me if I just would go on the "Today" show and talk about my book it would really sell. And I didn't do that. I'd rather the book sold less. The same even with film clips. We didn't give any film clips to TV . . . my own instinct is to low-key that stuff. Mel Brooks promotes his film and they make a fortune and he loves it and the audiences love him and they laugh at him. He's emotionally equipped to do that. It builds his public and creates a general sense of good spirit. Many, many stars and directors do it. Big stars, bigger than I am, classy stars. They do those things and they do them gracefully. I just can't get into that myself and I think I suffer because of it. I sometimes wish I had a more outgoing personality.

PROBST: But you wouldn't be Woody Allen.

ALLEN: I wouldn't be as I am now, but I might make more money.

PROBST: How much does the public have a right to know you?

ALLEN: I would say that they don't. Certain people feel a work of art must exist on its own and other people feel that it is perfectly right and proper that you can know everything about the artist, that with an artist like Yeats, for instance, it would be impossible to understand his poetry without knowing a lot about him. I don't happen to agree with that. When you create something, either the things works or—if you've got to know stuff about the person—forget it.

PROBST: Do you see yourself as a small star, little star, Orion-size star?

ALLEN: I am definitely a small star, there's no question about that.

PROBST: You don't like being a big star?

ALLEN: I don't like it and I would have no choice if I did. I just don't think I could ever do it. I'm a small star. I don't say that with any fake modesty, just an accurate appraisal. I'm not and never will be that kind of star like Paul Newman or Dustin Hoffman or Jerry Lewis or Chaplin or Jack Nicholson. I'm just not. I have a special audience. I don't know who they are. There's enough of them to support me and my pictures. They do nicely but not incredibly well. They hit a certain level and stay at that level. I'm just happy to work, that would be fine.

PROBST: How does Mel Brooks's work compare with yours?

ALLEN: I think he gets more fun out of it than I do. Mel loves to perform. He's joyful and I'm depressive. His films are quite funny, in an affirmative, kidding-around, joyful sense. I'm funny in a more anxious sense. This is how I would see it.

PROBST: Dick Cavett said that you were his point man. You had told him at one time to decide who he was. It seems to me that you've made it clear who you are. You have played the game of failure successfully.

ALLEN: No more than any comic. Hope or Chaplin or Groucho or all of them, they're all scuffling to make money or scuffling to get the girl or escaping from some danger. I'm a standard comic that way, absolutely standard. I do one-line jokes like Hope or Henny Youngman, the same kind of jokes every American comedian has always done—womanizing, girl chasing, braggart, frightened, no different from what Charlie Chaplin was doing or Keaton going after the girl or scared of being lost at sea in the boat. We're all out of the same mold.

PROBST: In Phil Berger's book, *The Last Laugh,* he said you were the last man in the batting order, you were at the end of everything—at the wrong end, I suppose.

ALLEN: Berger's wrong about that. I was always the first man in the batting order. I was always the lead-off hitter. I was always a good hitter and I was not the last man. I was one of the first people picked.

PROBST: You're the weakling who wins.

ALLEN: No more than Hope or Chaplin.

PROBST: Hope wasn't weak.

ALLEN: The girls always took Crosby over him.

PROBST: It seems to me you have earned each step of the way.

ALLEN: I think I'm a hard worker. When I was a nightclub comic, I played every night in every joint all over the country and slept in hotel rooms by myself for months and months and did three shows a night. I have worked hard at it. One of the problems is that I've had to do all my learning in public. I learned all my craft while people watched me doing it. I was learning in *Take the Money and Run* and *Bananas.* I was experimenting and learning how to make a film. I didn't know the first thing about it. Even up to now, I'm still playing around and people see it . . . people see learning. It's a tough position to be in. It would be nice to learn someplace else like school or television—and then go and do it.

PROBST: I believe you flunked or tried to get into film-editing school and you couldn't make it?

ALLEN: I studied at NYU and flunked out in my freshman year and then went to City College for a few months and flunked out there. I was a film major in both places and didn't like either film course, although I preferred NYU.

PROBST: A painter paints, but you don't see him with the work. Peculiar to your work is the fact that we see you with your work, and if we don't like it, we also don't like you. That's very tough on a person.

ALLEN: It's gambling for big stakes. I'm willing to write the picture and star in it and direct it and gamble for it. When someone doesn't like one of my pictures and they give it a real good full rap, they rap it and me right down the line. Sometimes I agree with them, sometimes I don't. Sometimes I think some of what they're saying might be right and I'm overlooking something. Sometimes I think they have taken a hatred to me—but it's always *me*.

PROBST: How sensitive are you to criticism?

ALLEN: If I think I've done a bad job and someone says so, I feel they're right and I screwed it up. If I've done a good job and someone doesn't like it, I feel they've made a mistake. I've never really had to deal with venomous criticism, I've never felt that it's ever been personal.

PROBST: Are you still as nervous about going out before an audience as you were, let's say, ten, fifteen years ago?

ALLEN: I was really, really frightened then. I've gotten so much more acceptance now that it's easier for me, but I still am nervous.

PROBST: Why?

ALLEN: I don't know. It's either because I'm afraid they won't like me or I won't like them, I'm not sure which.

PROBST: Have you ever not liked an audience?

ALLEN: Sure. If I've gone out onstage and I'm doing my best stuff and they don't laugh, you think, My God, what's the matter with them? And then they start talking or not paying attention and you feel terrible. There's nothing you can do. When I first started, I used to throw the show then. I figured, Ah, the hell with it, they don't like me. I would do my act mechanically and go. But then I found that the responsibility was mine. I had to use the time out there to see that when I got off the stage, they loved me. I never throw a show anymore. I'm fully committed.

PROBST: Do you learn from yourself? Are you in awe of anybody in the business? How do you learn to do what you're doing?

ALLEN: You learn from watching good directors' pictures. But the stuff that really counts, you're born with, you don't learn. I'm sure I had an instinct to film a joke before I ever filmed one. Directors like, say Bergman and Antonioni, might not be able to film jokes very well. It's got nothing to do with their abilities as filmmakers because they're the greatest in the world. It's got to do with an inborn instinct. Mel Brooks can film a joke for you.

PROBST: What makes things funny?

ALLEN: It's something that's unexplainable. People say, Well, it's the timing or the intonation or the way they look. You can never really figure out what it is. When a great clarinetist blows into the clarinet, he just blows the tune and it sounds beautiful. I blow into it and it doesn't. He's not improvising, but there's a feeling. It's the same thing in jokes. Hope tells them or Groucho says a line to some woman and it's hilarious. A thousand other people say the same line and it's insulting or unfunny.

PROBST: You play the clarinet every day?

ALLEN: Yes.

PROBST: What else do you do to keep yourself alive?

ALLEN: I play tennis and I play the clarinet and chase girls.

PROBST: Is it easier to catch them now?

ALLEN: Not a lot easier . . . I guess it's easier than when I was sixteen. But it's not quite as easy as I would like it to be.

PROBST: Is it an ever-normal granary? On both sides it gets more complicated?

ALLEN: It's like insects—they develop a greater immunity and resistance to me.

PROBST: Sometime ago you told a story about telephoning your analyst from San Francisco. What was all that about?

ALLEN: When I was making *Take the Money and Run,* I was away from home for about six months or more, so I used to do analytic sessions on the phone. If you're in your apartment it's fine, but at times I would be filming and we'd break for lunch and I would go into a phone booth on some hot San Francisco street and I'd make a long-distance call, feed a lot of change in. I'd be talking for fifty minutes in a phone booth with traffic in the background.

PROBST: It sounds like a very funny scene in a Woody Allen movie.

ALLEN: It is funny but it's real. It's absolutely real. It's ridiculous.

PROBST: Are you still in analysis? How many years have you been going?

ALLEN: It's been about twenty now.

PROBST: Does analysis shut off, caution, block, reduce whatever it is that's you as far as work goes?

ALLEN: No, no. My own opinion is that it enlarges it. You don't suffer quite as acutely and consequently can work more. You don't obsess as much. It tends to make your work less weird. The more you can relate to human beings and integrate your personality, the more you can do your humor on a humanly meaningful scale. If you're nonintegrated, your comedy will have a very limited point of view. To the degree that I can mature, I can make my comedy relate to adults in a better way. I'm for it. Analysis is someone to discuss things with, to try and get some perspective with. I wish it was more helpful to me. I wish it made me wonderful.

PROBST: What do you think about Transcendental Meditation?

ALLEN: I'm always very suspicious of everything. When I hear the testimony of people involved in various self-help plans and then see what their life is, it doesn't seem to be working at all. But I wouldn't rule out the possibility that some bizarre forms of therapy might help certain people.

PROBST: Are you an existentialist?

ALLEN: Philosophically, I am a survivor. I'm eclectic. Politically, I've voted for Republicans, I've voted for Democrats, and wouldn't hesitate to vote for Communists. Whatever reconciles itself with my commonsense observation of things, I latch onto. At the moment some of the more anxiety-ridden philosophers interest me because they mirror a lot of what I feel.

PROBST: Who are the writers that you've read or like to read?

ALLEN: I like reading philosophy.

PROBST: Which philosophers?

ALLEN: Sartre and Camus, Kierkegaard, Berdyaev, Buber. Contemporary philosophy interests me more, I guess because it's more relevant to me. But I've enjoyed reading philosophy in historical perspective—Renaissance philosophy, Greek philosophy. As a general rule, I don't enjoy fiction as much, although I do like Jane Austen—if I enjoy reading too much, I feel that I'm wasting time. If I hack through Hegel, I really feel that I'm reading, but if I'm reading Balzac or Flaubert, it's so enjoyable that I don't trust it.

PROBST: We enjoy ourselves at the movies, but do we ever see truth?

ALLEN: I do think we see truth, but I'm a firm believer that art is not a useful thing regarding social change. It's a pure entertainment, and that goes for opera, drama, classical music, painting. The fine arts are entertainment on a very high level for people with refined sensibilities and higher intellects. Beethoven's string quartets or paintings of Picasso are the refined sensibilities' version of the "Beverly Hillbillies." They're purely for fun. People ask me sometimes, Shouldn't movies say something? Yes, they should, they should have content, but the content never changes anything. You see problems examined in a drama and it's more pleasurable to one's intellect because it has content. But it doesn't change society. If your entertainment sensibilities are on a high level, you listen to more complex and sophisticated artists. Comedy the least of all. People always think the way to attack a social problem is to laugh at it and satirize it. I say that's pure entertainment. You show how pompous and ridiculous the Nazis are and they still come and kill you. Humor is entertaining but ineffective. Revolution is a socially viable mode but comedy is not. Comedy is entertainment.

PROBST: Including Woody Allen examining why human relations are unsatisfactory?

ALLEN: It's a way of creating a better entertainment. If I'm successful, a person with decently refined sensibilities can go in and have a good evening's entertainment. But it won't advance human progress at all. Aeschylus or Tennessee Williams or Arthur Miller are entertainment for intellectuals.

PROBST: What *does* advance people?

ALLEN: They might obtain advancement in certain pragmatic things, social programs, science, all the things that are dull, all the things that are rational and dull and that you tend to think are unromantic, these are the things that are socially useful. There's a tendency to undersell rational and scientific thinking because it doesn't happen to answer everything. But it's more valuable than art in a certain sense.

PROBST: But comedy is much more acceptable to everybody, it seems to me, except perhaps for pornography.

ALLEN: Pornography is not acceptable or fun to most people. I think people enjoy laughing, but in the end drama is more enjoyable. What sticks to the ribs is *On the Waterfront, Grand Illusion*—that kind of picture stays with you. Of course, I'm always down on comedy because I'm so immersed in it.

PROBST: What do you think about America?

ALLEN: When I was in high school, every kid in school knew Nixon was dishonest, and I can't believe the mass of sophisticated adults years later didn't see that. I think they did see it. So I was disappointed in them. I'm skeptical of people. I have a misanthropic view they have never failed to corroborate. The United States is an enormously hypocritical country, full of pretension. If it didn't claim to be so much, you could appreciate it for what it is. It claims to be wonderful and democratic and nonracist, when it's not. But I do think it has as much more going for it than anyplace in the world.

PROBST: Is this an age when we expect more truth?

ALLEN: Truth and candor is becoming a politically manipulatable commodity. The people don't change—they manipulate the externals differently. Right now it's fashionable, but I think years ago Mort Sahl summed it up perfectly—the issue is always fascism. There are people who are basically humane and liberal and pro-freedom and pro-life. And those who are pro-exploitation and thought control, basically fascistically inclined. It has nothing to do with whether you're American, Chinese, Russian. The boundaries are not geographical. Some people feel insecure unless life is controlled, and some people can cope with life's unpredictability. I'm for the second. I guess everyone would say so. But the issue is always fascism.

PROBST: What is the role of the artist, then?

ALLEN: To try and experiment in their work.

PROBST: Can't you be a Fascist experimenter?

ALLEN: I think you probably could. It's individual choice. But because of the demands of expression made on an artist by himself, artists have a tendency to be liberal. It's hard for an artist to function in the service of social ideas rather than in the service of his artistic muse. An artist needs freedom. Some can function in the service of the state, but very few. Socialist art is usually pretty bad.

PROBST: Isn't art subversive? Aren't you, in *Love and Death,* subverting organized religion's respect for God?

ALLEN: I'm not subverting, I'm complaining.

PROBST: You're humiliating those theories, it seems to me.

ALLEN: Not in a way that's going to do anything about it. I'm complaining about it and being angry about it, but in the end nothing will happen until groups get together and decide that they want to change and it manifests itself in social organization.

PROBST: Aren't you putting down your own work? Doesn't making fun of something lessen its importance and change the climate? Have you had any complaints from religious groups about your movies?

ALLEN: No. I'm sure I will. I've had complaints from groups on other movies I've done.

PROBST: Who's complained?

ALLEN: The B'nai B'rith complained about whipping the rabbi in *Everything You Always Wanted to Know About Sex.* I've never considered rabbis sacred as I've never considered any organized religion sacred. I find them all silly. Costumed and bearded just like popes, to me it's all absolutely absurd.

PROBST: Have you ever been prevented from doing anything you wanted to do in film because of taste or censorship?

ALLEN: On television I have, but never, never in movies, I've always had one hundred percent freedom. Final cut, no script approval, no casting approval—I've had complete freedom in all my movies.

PROBST: Are your movies getting less sexy?

ALLEN: I've never been sexy. This is a myth about me. Even *Everything You Always Wanted to Know About Sex,* I kept very clean. There's practically no sex in *Take the Money and Run*. It's a PG picture. *Bananas* is a PG picture for kids. *Sleeper* is for kids, PG.

PROBST: Why are you regarded as a sexy fellow?

ALLEN: I'm not. I'm regarded as someone who does a lot of sex jokes. It's like Tabasco sauce—you add two drops and you think that's all you taste. If you do two sex jokes or two God jokes or two Jewish references, they think that's what it's all about. But it's just like adding a spice. They're such strong references that they have a disproportionate feel to audiences.

PROBST: On a public and private level, what's it like to be Woody Allen?

ALLEN: For me, personally, rough. Some people enjoy being recognized, I don't. I consider myself lucky that whatever I do gets made or produced. I feel good about that. If I write a book or a short story or a film script, I get it produced, and that's a wonderful, wonderful thing. But the life-style is a little rough if you don't cotton to being recognized and having to deal with strangers and people in crowds, which I don't. It's hard for me.

PROBST: It seems to me that there's a problem in success—wanting to enjoy it and yet being in fear of being immobilized or limited by causing a stir wherever you go.

ALLEN: I don't like that. That is tough on me. That's why I wear my hat practically all the time jammed down low, and try and avoid being recognized as much as I can.

PROBST: You look as though you're hiding.

ALLEN: I decided for a week or so to go out without my hat on. And without my hat I was recognized constantly. With my hat I was able to cut down with my recognition by eighty percent.

PROBST: What happens when you're recognized?

ALLEN: It depends. People come up and they ask for an autograph or they come up and talk or they yell your name from a car as they pass or they look at you. They're generally very nice about it. But it's difficult for me.

PROBST: What are the good things about success?

ALLEN: I get my stuff produced and it pays well.

PROBST: You should be fabulously rich, but you're not?

ALLEN: I'm not. I don't work for much money. I sacrifice the money for creative freedom. Show business is so overpaid it's absurd. I just like to make a reasonable amount. I am willing to take a very, very low salary to do my work in return for total freedom on the picture. If I demanded a big, big salary, that would jack up the price of the picture enormously and you would have guys hovering over you, saying, Listen, this picture's costing us four million dollars to make and it's got to make ten million to break even. But if I can make the picture for two million—and that's the whole picture and everything—for two and a half million, then I've only got to make five million to break even and I can make a picture more for my friends and for a more select audience and not have to worry that I'm losing a guy's money for him.

PROBST: Who do you make the picture for?

ALLEN: I'd love to please a large audience but the first thing is that I have to be happy with it, which, of course, I never am. If I feel that audiences and critics love it but I'm ashamed of it, that would be death for me. The important thing is that I get some good feeling of it myself. I want an audience to like it but not at any cost. I wouldn't do anything that would violate my sense of taste to get an audience laughing. I won't make it easy on them. *Love and Death,* for instance, for broad slapstick comedy is also fairly literate. Someone said to me that people probably couldn't even pronounce the names in the reviews, much less enjoy the picture. And that may be true. They say I am doing jokes from Kierkegaard and Dostoevsky and Tolstoy and Turgenev. I know it's going to limit my audience. It's not going to have the same size audience as a picture like *Young Frankenstein*—every human being in the world has grown up with Frankenstein. But few have read Dostoevsky or Kierkegaard or Turgenev or Chekhov. I know I'm limited—that's why I have to work for less money.

PROBST: It's a good exchange.

ALLEN: It's good for me. When you say less money in show business, you're still making more than a public school teacher.

PROBST: Do you see yourself in the old Greek sense as a public instructor?

ALLEN: No. I see myself strictly as court jester, as entertainer. When people are finished working at the end of the day, they can go out to the movies or to a club if I'm at it and have a good time and go home.

Index

About the Author

LEONARD PROBST, termed "the dean of TV drama critics," by Jack Gould at *The New York Times*, originated the reviewing of plays on television in 1964, appearing regularly for WNBC-TV on the eleven p.m. news. He met his first celebrities at the age of six when he sold newspapers outside 20th-Century Fox studios in Hollywood, was a movie extra while at UCLA, and Hollywood correspondent for United Press in 1948 after a stint in the Navy in World War II. In Europe from 1949 to 1957, he worked for CARE and was press officer for the United Nations High Commissioner for Refugees in Geneva. He worked for UP in Geneva, Paris, Dublin and London.

Probst has appeared on "Today" as byline reporter on the arts, has been arts editor for WNBC-TV, and is now NBC radio drama critic and producer of NBC News commentary programs. He teaches critical writing at the New School in New York City and has written for a number of magazines, including *The Sunday New York Times, TV Guide*, and *The Village Voice*. He lives in Brooklyn Heights with his wife Bethami and their children Kenneth and Kate.